Fighter Aces of the
RAF
in the
Battle of Britain

Fighter Aces of the
RAF
in the
Battle of Britain

940
544

PHILIP KAPLAN

Pen & Sword
AVIATION

First published in Great Britain in 2007 by
PEN & SWORD AVIATION
an imprint of
Pen & Sword Books Ltd
47 Church Street
Barnsley
South Yorkshire
S70 2AS

ISBN 978-1-84415-587-3

A CIP catalogue record for this book is
available from the British Library.

Typeset by Concept, Huddersfield, West Yorkshire
Printed and bound in Great Britain by Biddles Ltd, King's Lynn

Pen & Sword Books Ltd incorporates the Imprints of
Pen & Sword Aviation, Pen & Sword Maritime, Pen & Sword Military,
Wharncliffe Local History, Pen & Sword Select,
Pen & Sword Military Classics and Leo Cooper.

For a complete list of Pen & Sword titles please contact
PEN & SWORD BOOKS LIMITED
47 Church Street, Barnsley, South Yorkshire, S70 2AS, England.
E-mail: enquiries@pen-and-sword.co.uk
Website: www.pen-and-sword.co.uk

Contents

Acknowledgement

The author is grateful to the following people for their generous assistance and contributions made in the development of this book: David Masters, Roald Dahl, Neville Duke, Peter Coles, Adolf Galland, Horst Petzschler, James H. Doolittle, Mark and Ray Hanna, Gunther Rall, Neal Kaplan, Virginia Bader and Duke Warren. My special thanks to my wife, novelist Margaret Mayhew, whose unflagging support, keen eye and constant help and encouragement contributed so much to this effort. My thanks to the late Al Deere, Brian Kingcome, Geoffrey Page and Peter Townsend for permission to use both the content of my interviews with them and their previous writings on their military careers.

Foreword

On 1 August 1940, Adolf Hitler issued his order of the day No. 17: 'I have decided that war against Great Britain will be pursued and intensified by sea and by air with [the] object of bringing about the country's final defeat ... The *Luftwaffe* must deploy its full strength in order to destroy the British air force as soon as possible.' Days later the officers and men of the RAF were told: 'The Battle of Britain is about to begin. Members of the Royal Air Force, the fate of generations lies in your hands.'

Sixty-seven years ago, in the blue skies of a late English summer, history's first great air battle was fought. Those whom the new Prime Minister, Winston Churchill, called 'The Few', thwarted Hitler's plans for an invasion of Britain. While it was happening, not many people thought of it as 'The Battle of Britain'. Churchill had used the phrase but once publicly, in his reference to the Fall of France.

The average fighter pilot defending Britain in the summer of 1940 was a bit more than twenty years of age. He was unmarried, had not quite completed his formal education and had an exceptionally keen interest in fast cars and aeroplanes. He had joined the RAF less than ten months prior to being posted to his operational squadron, and had fewer than twenty flying hours on the Hurricane or Spitfire types he would fly in that dramatic fifteen-week series of aerial combats later to be known as The Battle of Britain.

All the great struggles of history have been won by superior will-power wresting victory in the teeth of odds or upon the narrowest of margins.

– Winston Churchill

I saw my reserves slipping away like sand in an hour glass.
– Air Chief Marshal Sir Hugh C.T. Dowding,
C-in-C, Fighter Command

This book looks at the experiences of a handful of Royal Air Force Fighter Command pilots, all exceptionally high-achievers in the Battle of Britain period and after. Included are Adolf 'Sailor' Malan, Al Deere, Geoffrey Page, Brian Kingcome and Peter Townsend. In this series, the accounts of the experiences of actual fighter pilots throughout the entire history of air warfare are based on archival research, letters, diaries, published and unpublished memoirs and personal interviews with the pilots themselves, veterans and present-day aircrew.

The writer and historian David Masters put it so well in *So Few*:

> ... the airmen who are risking their lives against the much-vaunted German air force in order to save our civilization, a civilization which has been built up slowly and laboriously over the centuries, to a large extent on British inventions and ideals.

> These young men who fly unafraid through darkness and storm, who mount at dawn through lowering clouds until they emerge miles above the earth out in the clear sunshine, are modern knights of chivalry, carrying on a greater crusade than mankind has ever known; they spring from all classes of the population in Britain and the Empire, bus conductors, shop assistants, clerks, aristocrats, insurance agents, farmers, electricians, engineers, men of all creeds, but they are the same breed, running true to type in the face of danger.

*   *   *

Malan, Deere, Page, Kingcome and Townsend were all national heroes, highly regarded, highly decorated for their accomplishments, credited with the destruction of many enemy aircraft, they all survived the war to become legendary in the history of Royal Air Force Fighter Command.

From Group Captain Peter Townsend's introduction to *The Few* by Philip Kaplan and Richard Collier:

> When in 1933, aged eighteen, I entered the RAF as a flight cadet it was not, frankly, through sheer patriotism nor in the hope of winning glory in some future conflict. No; I was driven only by a longing to fly. *Luftwaffe* pilots, long after the war was over, told me it was the same with them – the sound, the sight, the touch and the smell of an aeroplane had an irresistible appeal to all senses. More is the pity that it led us to kill each other.

> After two years at the RAF College learning to be an officer and a gentleman and, of course, a pilot, my first posting in 1935 was to No. 1 Fighter Squadron at Tangmere, in Sussex. The airfield was in truth a huge hayfield where, after the crop, sheep did softly graze – except when our biplane Hawker Furies took off and landed. The hangars were built by German prisoners in the

First World War; the next generation of Germans, in their bombers, would demolish them in the Second World War. Not far away, near the coast, tall lattice masts were being erected. Occasionally someone might indiscreetly mention RDF (radio direction finding, later Radar) but the inventor, Dr Watson-Watt, was unknown to us, the subject taboo and the masts themselves in a no-go area. We fighter pilots enjoyed our pastoral life, conscious of belonging to the best flying club in the world.

At the time Fighting Area (as it was called) was but thirteen fighter squadrons strong. In 1936, faced with the menace of Hitler's Germany, the tiny RAF began to muscle up. Yet at the Munich crisis of September 1938, Fighter Command (as it was now called) was utterly incapable of repulsing the threatening *Luftwaffe* bombers. At Tangmere our station commander was Group Captain Keith Park, tall, lean, good-looking, but severe. We called him 'The Saint.' I was now with 43 squadron; our Furies, with their twin Vickers guns mounted in the cockpit, were slower than the enemy bombers. We all, pilots included, spent a night daubing our silver aircraft with drab camouflage warpaint. Supposedly, Britain's first line of defence, yet conscious of our shortcomings, I must admit we felt rather silly.

Then came the Prime Minister, Neville Chamberlain, back from Munich waving a little white paper, signed by Hitler and guaranteeing 'Peace in Our Time.' Not everybody was taken in: RAF expansion and re-equipment continued apace. By December our first Hurricanes arrived – swift, sturdy fighters with a terrible firepower. Spitfires were coming too, though more slowly. Anti-aircraft, radar and civil defence were being organised; workmen were digging trenches in the London parks and children, their baby faces made grotesque by hideous-looking gas-masks, were being told what to do – in case. As for us, the fighter boys, once we had mastered our new aircraft, our morale soared until we felt 'let them come, we will bust them.'

Soon after 3 September 1939, when Britain and France declared war, our commander-in-chief, Sir Hugh Dowding, paid us a visit. Solemn and unsmiling, 'Stuffy' Dowding's genius lay in faultless generalship and his concern for us so-called 'chicks'. Shortly afterwards No. 1 Squadron flew to France and we ourselves steered north to protect the coast-bound convoys and the naval base at Scapa Flow. There, above the tumultuous winter seas, we fought our first combats. In May 1940, shortly after the German offensive in Europe began, I travelled south by train to take over command of 85 (Hurricane) Squadron just back from France. During the journey I fell in with some *Luftwaffe* prisoners. One of them jibed 'Your navy OK, but where is your air force?' Another assured me with a smile that he expected to be back home in Hamburg for Christmas. Both were in for a surprise.

We of Fighter Command were joined by pilots who came from near and far – volunteer pilots from other RAF commands and from the Royal Navy; pilots from Canada, South Africa, Australia and New Zealand, from European countries whence they had escaped the Nazis and, notably, from Poland and Czechoslovakia; as well as illegally, from the neutral United States. Living – and dying – in that exuberant, varied company, that band of brothers, has marked me for life.

*   *   *

The drama, adventure and excitement experienced by 'Sailor' Malan, Al Deere, Geoffrey Page, Brian Kingcome and Peter Townsend are chronicled here, partly in their own frank and candid words. An American fleet admiral, while watching pilots being launched from the deck of his aircraft carrier in the western Pacific, asked 'Where do we get such men?' Where indeed.

CHAPTER ONE

Al Deere

There was something special about the airmen of New Zealand who flew and fought in the Royal Air Force during the Second World War. They seemed to have a special spirit, a special level of dedication and commitment to the cause at hand, a special kind of toughness, and a special set of standards they applied to their work – the elimination of the enemy air force's ability to make war against the Allies. And of these New Zealanders, Air Commodore Alan C. Deere was extra-special.

Deere was one of many young men on the Pacific Rim who saw the world war coming before most people did and followed the dictates of his adventurous nature and his sense of responsibility half way around the world to England in 1937. There he enlisted and began flight training in the RAF and, by the start of the Battle of Britain in July of 1940, was an experienced flight commander in No. 54 Squadron stationed at Hornchurch in Essex, east of London.

* * *

Al Deere was born in Auckland in December 1917. His childhood was spent in rural Westport at the foot of New Zealand's Southern Alps. It was there that he and two of his five brothers saw their first aeroplane, a tiny silver biplane that flew over one day and landed on a wide stretch of beach four miles from their home. The boys ran the four miles to where the plane sat surrounded by curious locals, most of whom, like themselves, had never seen an aeroplane up close before. They pressed forward to stare into the cockpit, fascinated by the simple instrument panel and the control stick. Eight-year-old Alan made up his mind that day that he would become a pilot.

He grew up there in the wild, rugged bush country of New Zealand's west coast, enjoying the area's marvellous opportunities for fishing, boating and swimming. When he was twelve his family moved to Wanganui, a city on the west coast of the North Island. There he turned from the boyhood pleasures of his rural upbringing, which had shaped and toughened his character and developed his sense of

1

independence and adventure, to focus on academics. During this time Wanganui was visited by the pioneering aviator Sir Charles Kingsford-Smith in his tri-plane, the *Southern Cross*. Kingsford-Smith had inspired people everywhere with his record-breaking flights across the Tasman Sea and was then touring New Zealand and giving brief passenger flights at 10 shillings per person. For this thrill young Alan eagerly paid his money: 'The great day arrived, and it is impossible to describe my thoughts as the aircraft became airborne. My dreams had come true. Suffice it to say that the seed sown in that summer nine years earlier had been fertilized, and was to grow through the ensuing years until it finally came to bloom in far-away England in the winter of 1937.'

He was encouraged in his ambition by Kendrick Christie, the Deere family doctor. Christie, a qualified pilot, told Alan about the opportunities then developing in the Royal Air Force for interested young men and when it was announced in the local newspapers that the RAF was about to enter a large expansion programme, Alan was among the first New Zealanders to apply. But knowing that his father would oppose his joining and would almost certainly refuse to add his required signature to the application, Alan persuaded his mother to sign it. She reluctantly agreed and his father didn't learn of the application until Alan received official notification that he was to attend an RAF selection board. The board consisted of three air force officers, one being Wing Commander the Hon. R.A. Cochrane (later Air Chief Marshal), as chairman. Alan was well qualified academically, was a star athlete in rugby, cricket, and boxing, and was very keen to fly. His interview went well and within weeks he was on his way to England for pilot training with eleven other eager Kiwis, all aged between eighteen and twenty-one and all, like himself, leaving their country for the first time.

Several weeks later the S.S. *Rangitane* (later to be sunk by a German raider), anchored in the mouth of the Thames, and the sight of the heavily-laden barges riding low in the water, the passenger vessels and the grimy coasters, brought to Alan's mind the John Masefield lines:

> Dirty British coaster with a salt-caked smoke stack
> Butting through the Channel in the mad March days,
> With a cargo of Tyne coal,
> Road-rail, pig-lead,
> Firewood, iron-ware and cheap tin trays.

* * *

Among the many firm and lasting friendships Deere was to make in England was that of W.J. Jordan, the New Zealand High Commissioner, who greeted him and the others on their arrival in London and their visit to New Zealand House. Jordan wished them every success and assured them of the advice and assistance always available to them from the staff of New Zealand House during their stay in England. Alan was to remember him as 'Old Bill,' a wonderful ambassador for his country.

The next stop for the little group of Kiwis was the De Havilland Civil School of Flying located at White Waltham airfield near Maidenhead, west of London. There they underwent a three-month period of preliminary training prior to acceptance in the Royal Air Force for pilot training. Of the Englishmen with whom they trained and would later serve, only a few would survive the war.

While the rest of his mates began flying training, Deere's start was delayed for two weeks. His pre-flying medical examination turned up a blood pressure irregularity which caused his doctor to send him to RAF Halton for observation. He was eventually released and returned to White Waltham where he set out to catch up with his fellow trainees. His sympathetic flying instructor cooperated, giving him extra flying hours and he was soon ready to solo in a de Havilland Tiger Moth biplane trainer. 'Remember your height and turning points on the circuit and make sure you are nicely settled down on the final glide-in before choosing your spot to land. If you are in doubt don't be afraid to go around again and have no hesitation in doing so if you bounce badly on touch down. I only want you to do ten minutes and in that time you should be able to get in two landings,' the instructor told the pupil. 'I was really straining at the leash by the time he had delivered these homilies and thinking he had finished, banged the throttle open, and so into the air, solo at last. One, two, three landings, around again and again I went, the ten minute limit completely forgotten in the thrill and excitement of this momentous occasion. Finally, having convinced myself I was just about the best pupil that had ever flown a Tiger Moth, I taxied back to the airfield boundary, purring with pleasure. "I thought I told you to make only two landings and not to take longer than ten minutes," said an infuriated instructor, greeting me on my return, his rather large moustache waxed solid with the cold. Somewhat deflated, I answered "Sorry, sir, I thought I was to go on until I was satisfied that the landing was perfect." "If that was the case, you would be up there for a week," was the sarcastic reply. "Not only did you disobey my instructions, you didn't even have the decency to wait until I had finished speaking, before opening the throttle and bloody nearly blowing me out of the field with the slipstream."'

Deere had his ups and downs with his instructors. The second phase of his flight course took place at No. 6 Flying Training School,

Netheravon, in the Wiltshire downs, where he flew the obsolete but pleasant Hawker Hart biplane. After one particularly difficult session, a heated exchange occurred between Deere and his instructor, resulting in a subsequent dressing down of the pupil, an apology to the instructor, a second chance granted to the pupil, and a thoroughly chastened Acting Pilot Officer A.C. Deere resolving never to repeat such behaviour and keeping to that resolve.

Following that incident, Deere was asked by the Secretary of the The Royal Air Force Boxing Association to box for an officers' team against London University. In New Zealand Deere had boxed in the National Amateur Championships and this invitation led to his fighting and winning on several occasions for the RAF during his first year of service. Before giving up boxing upon joining his squadron, he won the middleweight division of the RAF Individual Championships and successfully defended that title in the following year. He was chosen to be a member of the Royal Air Force team to tour South Africa in the summer of 1938. Just before the team was to leave on the tour, he was withdrawn by his superiors to allow him to complete his flying training course expeditiously. The decision proved a vital one for Deere, as the aircraft carrying most of the boxing team crashed near Bulawayo killing all on board.

With graduation came the presentation of the coveted RAF pilot's wings to the new airmen who were speculating about their impending postings. It was common knowledge that a surplus of fighter pilots existed to fill current squadron requirements and a large number of pilots were being held in a fighter pilot pool in the North of England. The new graduates who had chosen to fly fighters and been trained to do so sweated out their coming assignments. The day came when the list of postings appeared and Alan was relieved to find himself assigned to No. 54 fighter squadron at RAF Hornchurch in Essex.

He travelled to Hornchurch with another Pilot Officer, a Canadian named Arthur Charrett. It was Charrett who christened him 'Al', the half-name that stuck with him throughout his service career.

Hornchurch was a small First World War grass airfield with three large hangars. It lay among a crowd of houses in a heavily built-up area east of the capital. In its early days it had been known as Sutton's Farm. When Deere and Charrett arrived at the nearby Elm Park railway station, they were disappointed to learn that all of No. 54 Squadron was away on leave and would not return for another two weeks. The pair were temporarily attached to No. 74 Squadron, one of the other two units then operating from the Essex station. Al was assigned to 'A' Flight which was commanded by Adolf 'Sailor' Malan, a former Merchant Navy man, who was married and older than most in the squadron. Malan would go on to become one of the greatest fighter pilots and tacticians of the war.

In his two and a half years at Hornchurch, Deere was served by a batman named Fox who looked after him with the greatest care and saw to it that he was aware of and adhered to the many rules and regulations of the station, which the new pilot officer was otherwise inclined to disregard.

These were pre-war days and the pilots of No. 54 Squadron wore bright white overalls with the badge of the squadron proudly emblazoned on the breast pocket. A pilot had to serve a three-month qualification period on the squadron. His flying ability was then tested by the squadron commander and only then was he entitled to wear the badge on his flight suit. One of Al's proudest moments came when he submitted his Flying Log Book for endorsement: '... Certified that Pilot Officer A.C. Deere has qualified as first pilot on fighter landplanes w.e.f. 1-1-39.'

*   *   *

The unimaginative mindset of the British Air Ministry in the 1930s dictated that its fighter squadrons spend the bulk of their time and resources in the pursuit of perfect formation flying, believing that their attack methods would be guaranteed success through this practice. In Al Deere's view, and in reality, this approach was utterly hopeless in relation to effective shooting as it was simply impossible to sight on a target in the time available when a pilot's primary duty was to keep station in his formation. He felt that the time, training and resources devoted to gunnery was wholly insufficient to the needs of the fighter squadrons and that it was mainly the pilots' morale that brought many of them through the early fighter combat of the war and certainly not their ability to shoot straight.

On 6 March 1939, Deere made the transition from the relatively sedate and mannerly fabric-covered biplane fighters of the 1930s to the sophisticated, high-performance, streamlined all-metal low-winged monoplane fighters of the next decade. On that day he flew his first Spitfire.

*   *   *

Al Deere said of the Spitfire, 'The versatility and the deceptive toughness of this fighter made it, I think without question, the outstanding fighter aircraft of the Second World War.' Paddy Barthropp: 'The aircraft was part of you and, when frightened, either in testing or in combat, I think one used to talk to one's Spitfire, and you may be equally sure that it used to answer.'

In the late 1920s a small 1,300-employee firm called The Supermarine Aviation Works was a subsidiary of the 80,000-employee shipbuilding, engineering and armament company, Vickers Limited. Both organizations were headquartered at Southampton and Supermarine had, from the end of the First World War, built its reputation on the design and construction of flying boats and the series of racing seaplanes that established world speed records and a winning record in the Schneider Trophy races of that era. The renowned English motor car maker Rolls-Royce had served the Allied war effort by expanding into the design and manufacture of military aero engines which it continued to supply to the Royal Air Force through the ensuing years. That effort declined in the post-war years, however, as budgets waned and the executives at Rolls felt compelled to return the company's direction to that of luxury automobile production. Then, in the mid-1920s, Sir Henry Royce became interested in the American design of the Curtiss D.12 liquid-cooled engine and designed the engine that was to become the Kestrel, a liquid-cooled V-12 powerplant that sparked the aero engine future of Rolls.

Slowly reacting to the threat it perceived from the Nazi regime in Germany, the British government in the early 1930s began the development of aircraft programmes to prepare for a new European war that was seeming increasingly inevitable. The well-equipped and powerful Royal Air Force at the end of the First World War had been reduced to an obsolete and virtually impotent force by the mid-1930s when the Vickers Supermarine Spitfire fighter first took to the air. Britain was a long way from being ready for that coming war, but in the Spitfire, and the new Hawker Hurricane, it had the potential for combatting the German enemy with a new and fearsome capability, if it could somehow bring the new fighters into mass production and wide availability in time.

A young aircraft designer from Stoke-on-Trent in the English midlands, Reginald J. Mitchell, who had grown up building and flying model aeroplanes, was the brain behind the highly successful Supermarine flying boats and racers. Mitchell's relationship with Rolls-Royce began in 1927 when he persuaded them to develop a more powerful engine for the next Supermarine Schneider cup racer, the R-type, which would power the new S.6 racing plane. Over the next few years, Rolls-Royce refined the engine, leading to Schneider victories for Britain in 1929 and 1931 and its retirement of the famous trophy.

In the Aeronautical Engineering Supplement to the *Aeroplane* edition of 25 December 1929, Mitchell wrote:

During the last ten years there has been an almost constant increase in the speed of our racing types. To maintain this steady increase very definite progress has been essential year by year. It has been necessary to increase the aerodynamic efficiency and the power-to-weight ratios of our machines, to reduce the consumption, and the frontal areas of our engines; to devise new methods of construction; and to develop the use of new materials. The results obtained in the form of speed have been a direct and absolute indication of our progress in aeronautical development ... Speed in the air must always be a measure of aerodynamic efficiency which in turn must always be the most important consideration in all aircraft design.

It is quite safe to say that the engine in this year's winning S.6 machine in the Schneider Trophy contest would have taken at least three times as long to produce under normal processes of development had it not been for the spur of international competition. There is little doubt that this intensive engine development will have a very profound effect on our aircraft during the next few years.

Three years later Adolf Hitler and the Nazis came to power in Germany and clandestinely began the rebuilding of the German Air Force.

The development of the Rolls-Royce Merlin V-12 engine followed. It was planned for an output of 1,000 horsepower. Under the leadership of Ernest Hives who became the General Works Manager for Rolls after the death of Sir Henry Royce, the Merlin II was produced. The engine completed 100 hours of flight testing in June 1937, becoming the definitive production engine of the type.

Work on the prototype Spitfire, K5054, was proceeding at the Woolston works of Supermarine. On March 6, 1936, Joseph 'Mutt' Summers, Chief Test Pilot of Vickers Aviation Limited, climbed aboard that prototype aeroplane and took it up for the first time in a flight lasting just fifteen minutes. Despite the historical interpretation by many writers of Summers' remark after that first flight, 'I don't want anything touched,' the aeroplane was still wholly untested and certainly required the usual weeks and months of changes, adjustments, and general debugging needed with all new aircraft types. But he knew from that historic first flight that the Spitfire was extraordinarily well designed, light and well-balanced to the touch, a pilot-friendly machine. He probably had some inkling too of the potential for development afforded by the little fighter which would evolve through many marks, from the 1,030 hp Mk.1 to the 2,350 hp Griffon-engined Mk.F and Mk.FR47.

Two days after that first Spitfire flight, German troops marched to reoccupy the demilitarized zone of the Rhineland in defiance of the

Treaty of Versailles. Being committed to the doomed policy of appease-
ment, the governments of both France and Britain seemed paralysed.
Fortunately for the British, however, the mid-1930s development of
what would later be called radar, and of the Spitfire and Hurricane
fighters, gave at least some people in the corridors of power reason to
be hopeful about their nation's safety in the coming conflict.

* * *

The Spitfire is a low-wing, stressed-skin, all-metal, single-seat fighter
plane. It posed a complex and demanding construction challenge for
the many skilled and unskilled workers around Britain who would
build it in great numbers over the war years. It was a far greater
challenge than that of building the less complex Hawker Hurricane,
which had been designed largely with ease of production in mind. The
Hurricane was about half fabric-covered and was not as lovely to look
at as the Spitfire, nor quite as fast, but would prove its worth in many
ways from the Battle of Britain onward through the war. It was the
charismatic Spitfire, though, that captured the imagination of the
British public and the hearts of nearly all who have flown her during
the war and since.

* * *

Only two days after soloing in a Spitfire, Al Deere was sent from
Hornchurch down to Eastleigh airfield near Southampton to collect a
brand new Spitfire from the factory there. He was to bring the new
plane back to the squadron in Essex, but the weather that day was
terrible and he had considerable difficulty locating the Hornchurch
airfield. His relief, when he finally did find the field, was such that he
could not help but do a short 'beat-up' of the base, a practice frowned
upon in the extreme. He then landed and taxied in to the squadron
hangar where several of his fellow pilots waited for him as well as his
flight commander. The FC tore a strip off the embarrassed Deere, not
merely for beating up the field, but for neglecting to change the pitch of
his propeller after his take-off, which caused excessive noise during his
beat-up and covered the new Spitfire in oil from the over-revving new
engine. Deere felt lucky to get off with only a severe tongue-lashing by
his commander.

Another incident that Deere would always remember occurred in
May 1939. An immense cloud layer covered much of south-east
England and he found himself entering it at about 2,000 feet. The
oxygen system then employed in the Spitfire required the pilot to
adjust the oxygen flow regulator with increasing height at 5,000 feet
intervals. He climbed steadily through the heavy cloud to 27,000 feet.
He was still in cloud at that altitude and was so intent on his instru-

ments that he had forgotten to increase his oxygen flow after the first 5,000 feet of climb and oxygen starvation took effect. As the Spitfire finally broke out of the cloud layer, the last thing he recalled was the dazzling sunshine and the intensity of the blue sky. And then he lost consciousness.

Some time later, he had no way of determining how much time had passed, he came to and thought at first that the nose of the plane was still pointing at the blue sky above. He soon realized though that the blue was that of the sea and he was hurtling toward it at a very great speed. As his head cleared he had the presence to pull hard on the control column, just managing to bring the plane out of the near-vertical dive he had been in. His recovery ended very near the sea surface and he was greatly shaken by the experience. Worse, he had suffered a burst eardrum in the extreme dive, which left him in con-siderable pain. The resulting injury caused him to be taken off flying for the next three months and attracted the interest of several RAF doctors who subjected him to various medical examinations. In fact, Deere suffered no significant hearing loss from the incident, but did thereafter always have difficulty clearing his sinuses when descending rapidly from high altitude.

As 1939 wore on, to the last weeks before the German attacks on Poland, activity in preparation for war increased dramatically at Hornchurch where the squadron aircraft were dispersed far from the hangars on the opposite side of the airfield. Out there in the remote reaches of the field ground personnel were hard at the task of putting up tent accommodation for the pilots, the riggers and fitters who serviced and maintained the planes. From that point the pilots were required to spend many hours of the day at readiness, a condition in which they had to be on hand near their aircraft, fully dressed in flying gear and ready to take off on very short notice. The squadron would essentially remain 'at readiness' until the point in 1943 when it was judged that the German Air Force no longer posed a significant day-light threat to Britain. In late 1939 blast protection bays, known as fighter pens, were constructed around the field to shelter the many operational Spitfires there. The pilots spent most of their time filling sandbags used in the building of the dispersal pens. They sweated alongside well-paid civilian workers who were doing the same job. It kept the pilots occupied in a period when their flying time was greatly restricted in order to save wear and tear on the aircraft.

It was on a Sunday, the first day of the war. One of the Hornchurch squadrons was sent up to check on an aircraft plotted as being a 'hostile' over the Channel. The intercepting squadron then became split up and ground plotters then plotted some of those aircraft as hostiles. More fighters were sent up to investigate the situation and soon chaos reigned in the operations plotting rooms around southern England as most of the RAF fighter squadrons based in that part of the country were scrambled to become part of the now enormous interception effort. The many aircraft were being given more vectors, most of them erroneous, than they could possibly follow. Al Deere's Spitfire had been reluctant to start that day and, when he finally got airborne, it took him nearly an hour to locate his squadron and join with them. It was the beginning of the air war. The entire operation was a shambles, but worse was to come.

Another of the Hornchurch squadrons scrambled in the chaos was No. 74 led by Sailor Malan. It would be some time before aircraft recognition was mastered by the fighter pilots and that failing, along with the problems in the British air control and reporting system at the time, proved disastrous on this day. The three Spitfires of the rear section soon encountered two Hurricanes from a squadron based at nearby North Weald. The Spitfire pilots mistook the Hurricanes for enemy aircraft and in their zeal and excitement for battle, attacked and shot down the British fighters, killing one of the pilots. The tragic incident was subsequently referred to as the 'Battle of Barking Creek.' As Al Deere recalled,

> ... it was just what was needed to iron out some of the many snags in our control and reporting system and to convince those responsible that a great deal of training of controllers, plotters and radar operators, all of whom had been hastily drafted in on the first emergency call-up, was still required before the system could be considered in any way reliable. It is significant to note that on five out of my next six training flights I was engaged on tactical exercises in co-operation with the control and reporting organization.

* * *

In those early days of the war the pilots of No. 54 Squadron were frequently assigned to the role of 'night readiness,' an experience which Deere remembered as the most hated and feared job he ever had. Up to that point his night flying time on Spitfires had amounted to only a handful of circuits and landings and a few short trips from the airfield, always in good weather. He was, therefore, less than comfortable when sent off into the pitch-black nights in the time before adequate radios and homing aids were standard equipment in the fighters of No. 54 Squadron. On one such flight, Deere's No. 2 was a Canadian pilot named Don Ross. The pair were flying a late day Channel convoy patrol off Harwich, which meant that they would be returning to base in darkness. At the far end of the patrol they were well out of radio transmission range as they turned for the leg back to Hornchurch. After about five minutes of flying Deere picked up the voice of the Hornchurch controller and asked for an accurate heading for the base. He was given a series of vectors which he followed doggedly. He was flying mainly on instruments with his wingman close by his side when suddenly the area immediately ahead was starkly illuminated by searchlights and they knew that they were crossing the coast into England. At the same instant, Ross yelled over the R/T, 'Look out, Red Leader, there's a balloon straight ahead of us.' Al looked up from his instruments in time to see the balloons of the Harwich barrage and yanked back on the control column. The two Spitfires barely cleared the deadly balloons whose anchoring cables were intended to snare low-flying German aircraft. In his anger at the controller who had stupidly vectored them directly into the middle of the Harwich balloons, Deere forgot that his R/T was switched to the automatic transmit mode as he unrestrainedly cursed the controller. Unfortunately for him, the Hornchurch station commander was present in the base operations room, as well as the staff of blushing WAAF plotters. The commander was not amused.

As the two Spitfires approached Hornchurch to land, the field was gripped in fog that was worsening by the minute. Their fuel state was such that diversion to another airfield was out of the question. They had to land and soon. Al ordered Ross to land first and, in the time it took the wingman to complete his approach and touch down, the fog had become a classic pea-souper. The goose-neck flare pots used to light the runway and approach were invisible below about 800 feet and Al was forced to make his landing on instruments. A low light tower known as a Chance Light was positioned at the landing end of the flare path to illuminate the touchdown area, but the light was not functioning. A few witnesses to his landing said that he touched down hard and bounced well over the Chance Light, careering down the field and ending up in a fence at the far extremity, relatively undamaged. Deere was uninjured but was soon fuming on his return to the dispersal area where he was severely reprimanded for his use of foul language over the R/T. The rotten weather of the final months of 1939 and early 1940 found No. 54 Squadron temporarily moved to the forward field at Rochford where their flying was minimal and their boredom substantial until, in the early spring, the dismal period finally passed. Improved weather brought an end to the tedious waiting for action and the downtime had provided one advantage – an opportunity for the essential improvement of the fighter control and reporting system in time for the coming battles of the summer and fall.

* * *

The situation of the British Army in France had deteriorated considerably by the evening of 15 May when the pilots of No. 54 Squadron were gathered in the billiards room of their officers' mess to hear a briefing by the station commander. It was before the introduction of briefing rooms on RAF fighter stations. All British fighter operations at the time were defensive in nature, launching at a moment's notice, with practically no information about their mission. The station commander, Wing Commander 'Daddy' Bouchier, told the pilots that the situation in France was very serious and that British withdrawals were planned for Calais and Dunkirk. He said that Fighter Command would be providing as much air cover as possible for the withdrawals utilizing Spitfire squadrons from bases around southern England. The operation was not referred to as a full-scale withdrawal, and No. 54 Squadron was to take off just after first light the next morning and patrol to ten miles inland from Calais-Dunkirk where they were to engage any enemy aircraft they found operating in the area. He concluded with, 'Good luck, good shooting and show 'em what 54 can do.'

Al Deere was among the most experienced pilots at Hornchurch on 16 May and was one of the twelve pilots of 54 Squadron who took off at 0800 hours that morning and headed for the French coast. He was flying the Spitfire he had named *Kiwi 1*. The squadron climbed to 15,000 feet and levelled out to continue at an economical cruising speed. In minutes they were crossing in over Calais. The leader called over the R/T for the fighters to spread into battle formation. The peaceful French countryside below gave no hint of it being a war zone. They flew the patrol route for the next thirty minutes and became increasingly frustrated with the lack of enemy contact until their fuel state required them to turn back for their base. At Hornchurch the ground crews were equally disappointed by the lack of action of their pilots, but went about the business of refuelling the Spitfires.

That initial foray into the continental combat zone, without result, had left the pilots of No. 54 Squadron with a range of emotions, nearly all of them negative. They itched for contact with the *Luftwaffe*, but the more mature among them realized that they would very soon have all the action they could handle. Now their task was once again to be at readiness, day and night, for the next seven days and the continuing patrols of the Calais-Dunkirk area. On each of these patrol missions the pilots were allowed to venture farther inland into France, and to do so at lower altitudes, in an effort to draw the German Air Force up for battle, without effect. They did spot an occasional lone enemy aircraft, but never near enough to attack.

A radar plot in the morning of 21 May caused No. 54 Squadron pilot Johnny Allen and his wingman to be sent out over the Channel to investigate the source which turned out to be twenty Junkers Ju 88 bombers in tight formation. On the way out Allen's No. 2 developed engine trouble and had to return to base. Allen chose to attack on his own and waded into the swarm of bombers. He somehow evaded the heavy crossfire from the German gunners and shot down one of the Ju 88s to achieve the first recorded aerial victory of the squadron in the war.

The shooting war began for Al Deere on 23 May. The squadron returned that morning from yet another dawn patrol in which no enemy aircraft were encountered. Al went off to a late breakfast and just as he sat down to eat he was called to the phone. Squadron Leader J.A. Leathart, the flight commander, was on the line asking Al to meet him and Johnny Allen out at the dispersal immediately for a flight over to Calais-Marck airfield to pick up the commanding officer of No. 74 Squadron who had just been forced to land there with another case of engine problems. Leathart said that he would fly the two-seat Miles Master trainer to collect the man and Al and Johnny would escort him in Spitfires. He said that there was quite a lot of enemy activity in that area at the moment and that their best chance of successfully picking up the CO was to cross the Channel at sea level and hopefully avoid being spotted by German fighters. He would land the Master at Calais-Marck and keep the engine running while the two Spitfires would orbit low over the field to protect the Master. The trip across the Channel went off without incident and Al watched Leathart land and taxi towards a hangar. There were broken clouds over the airfield when they arrived in the area and Al told Johnny to climb above them and orbit the field at 8,000 feet to guard against their being bounced by enemy fighters. As soon as Johnny reached that altitude he shouted over the R/T, 'Al, they're here. Huns! About a dozen of them below me and making towards the airfield. I'm going in to have a go at them.' Al concurred and said that he would somehow try to warn Leathart not to take off.

The Miles Master was not equipped with an R/T and the only thing Al could think to do was to dive towards it and waggle his wings on the chance that Leathart would realize there was danger above. As he began to dive, Al saw the Master taxiing out to take off. Within seconds he spotted a Messerschmitt Bf 109 fighter boring down through the broken cloud, aiming for the unarmed Master which was then just becoming airborne. The 109 passed within range of Al's guns and, knowing there was little chance of hitting the German plane, he fired hoping to distract the enemy pilot from the Master. The German was already firing on the British training plane. With his throttle wide open, Al chased the Bf 109 into a turn.

'Red One, I'm surrounded. Can you help me?' yelled Johnny. Al replied that he would be right up as soon as he had '... killed this bastard in front of me.' The German pilot then made the fatal error of pulling out of the turn and up into a vertical climb, offering Al a nearly perfect shot from below. Al fired and smoke and flame erupted from the engine of the Bf 109. The German fighter reached the zenith of its climb at 3,000 feet, fully engulfed in flame, and fell off vertically until it struck the beach near the water's edge. Al turned back to Calais-Marck airfield and was relieved to see the Master parked by the perimeter fence, evidently undamaged in the attack by the Bf 109.

He climbed through the scattered cloud and called Johnny to say that he was coming up to help now. On the way up he encountered two more Bf 109s, diving apparently for their base. The leader spotted Al and wracked his fighter into a steep turn. Al followed and easily managed to stay inside the German pilots' turning radius. He closed to firing range and sent a long burst into the Bf 109 of the wingman, which began shedding bits of metal and then fell to earth. The other Bf 109 pilot entered a diving turn inland. Al fired at him and the German jinked and twisted in an attempt to evade the chasing Spitfire. Al closed to firing distance but found that his ammunition was exhausted. He then played for time, thinking that if he suddenly broke off and turned for England, the German pilot would realize he was out of ammunition and he would be a sitting duck, possibly a dead one. But the German merely continued inland making for his base.

Al contacted Johnny again and received the reply, 'I'm just crossing north of Calais but am rather worried about my aircraft. I can't see any holes but felt hits and she doesn't seem to be flying quite right. I'll make for the North Foreland at my present height of 8,000 feet. See if you can join up.' The two pilots did join up over the Channel and Al inspected Johnny's Spitfire, noted several holes and decided that Johnny should be able to make it back to Hornchurch. The pair continued on to that base and both managed safe landings. The other squadron pilots and ground personnel gathered around the two Spitfires to hear Al and Johnny relate their experiences of the day. Johnny allowed that next time he would prefer better odds than the 20–1 and 12–1 he had experienced in the two engagements over France. While they were talking, Leathart and his passenger arrived in the Master. He explained that they had watched the air battle overhead from a ditch near the airfield boundary.

> The moment I left the ground I saw from the activities of Red One that something was amiss. Almost at once an Me 109 appeared ahead of me and commenced firing. I pulled around in a tight turn observing as I did so, the Messerschmitt shoot past me. I literally banged the aircraft on to the ground and evacuated the cockpit with all possible speed, diving into the safety of a ditch which

ran along the airfield perimeter. Just then I saw an Me 109 come hurtling out of the clouds to crash with a tremendous explosion a few hundred yards away. Almost simultaneously another Me 109 exploded as it hit the sea to my left. From the comparative safety of the ditch my passenger and I caught momentary glimpses of the dog-fight as first Me 109 and then Spitfire came hurtling through the cloud banks only to scream upwards again. It was all over in a matter of about ten minutes after the fight ended, and when it seemed safe I made a hasty take-off and a rather frightened trip back to England and safety.

* * *

So began the war for Al Deere. The afternoon brought a message to the squadron from Air Vice Marshal Keith Park, Air Officer Commanding, No. 11 Group: 'Air Officer Commanding sends congratulations to No. 54 Squadron on the magnificent fight put up by Flying Officers Deere and Allen who so severely punished superior numbers this morning.' With the afternoon patrols came the realization that the so-called Fighting Area Attacks the pilots of RAF Fighter Command had been trained to perform in battle were utterly useless in the new reality of air combat. The squadron's attempt to put them into practice that day convinced Leathart of the futility of such tactics and he informed the pilots to their obvious relief that the FA attacks would no longer be employed while he was their leader. Their first day in the war had been eventful, and especially so for Deere who had flown four patrols with a total flying time of seven and a half hours, been involved in two air actions with the German Air Force and had been credited with three enemy aircraft downed. In all, the four squadrons then based at Hornchurch had accounted for thirty-seven enemy planes destroyed. Not a bad start.

From that first day of war the demands on the pilots of 54 Squadron grew until, by 26 May, their operational strength had been reduced to just eight serviceable Spitfires and twelve pilots. It was during his first patrol of the day. He had already downed two enemy fighters and was heavily engaged in a fight with a large formation of Messerschmitt Me 110s and Bf 109s when, for the first time in his life he heard, felt and saw his Spitfire being hem-stitched by a series of cannon shells. The pilot of the Bf 109 that had bounced him from above had scored a hit on his starboard wing, flipping the Spitfire onto its back. The German then cut off the attack in the apparent belief that his victim had been shot down. Al fought to regain control of the Spitfire through a descent of 2,000 feet. He headed for Hornchurch but the crippled fighter proved difficult to handle. He finally reached base and landed safely despite one punctured tyre. On his return to the squadron dispersal he learned that he was the newly appointed commander of 'A' Flight.

The next day the pilots of the eight serviceable Spitfires witnessed the massive pillars of black smoke rising from the blazing oil storage tanks near Dunkirk on the French coast. They crossed the beach where hundreds of thousands of British, French and Belgian soldiers would soon gather awaiting evacuation to England. On his return from the sortie Al was told that the remains of 54 Squadron were to be moved north and rested from operations following a dawn patrol on the 29 May.

Awakened by his batman at 0330 hours to face the bitterly cold, wet and black Essex pre-dawn, Al and seven other pilots of 54 Squadron were soon off for their last patrol of the Dunkirk area. They were not alone. Three of the Hornchurch squadrons had taken off and formed into a wing to cope with the large enemy formations they expected to meet in France. They cruised towards the French coast at 1,000 feet in the poor weather, the rain and mist preventing their keeping tight station on the other Hornchurch aircraft. Leathart had remained at Hornchurch to arrange for the squadron's move north and had put Al in charge of the squadron in the air.

Entering France at Gravelines, Al brought his pilots onto a north-east heading to begin their patrol. Almost immediately a Dornier Do 17 dropped from the cloud cover about 1,000 yards from the British fighters. The German was evidently hunting Allied shipping in the Channel and had not yet spotted the Spitfires. Al ordered the rest of the squadron to continue the patrol and he took his flight of four aircraft in pursuit of the Dornier. As the Spitfires closed on the German bomber, its rear gunner finally saw them and began shooting at them. At 300 yards Al returned fire and his initial burst caught the bomber's port engine. Edging closer for the kill, Al was startled as bullets began slamming into his own engine and a cloud of glycol erupted from the holed header-tank, eliminating his forward visibility. The severity of damage to his coolant system meant there would be no chance of getting back to England. The big Merlin engine would soon seize and he would come down. He quickly considered whether to ditch the Spitfire in the sea or try to land her on the nearby beach. Seeing no ships in the vicinity and thus no likelihood of imminent rescue, he decided on the beach and directed the other pilots of his flight to eliminate the Dornier. He slid back the cockpit hood and was immediately engulfed in thick black, oil-smoke. Switching the engine off improved his visibility as he began to side-slip towards the nearest stretch of beach. The Spitfire settled onto the shoreline in the most shallow part of the surf and, as it slithered along on its belly, a spray of water and wet sand struck Deere in the face. When she came to a stop it was more violent than he had anticipated and his forehead struck the edge of the windscreen knocking him unconscious.

As he came to he realized that the hissing, popping Merlin engine was on fire and he needed to get out of the cockpit and away from the aircraft immediately. Nauseated, covered in oil and wet sand and bleeding from the gash in his forehead, he managed quickly to release his harness and climb from the wrecked fighter. The light rain continued to fall and in a few moments a Belgian soldier appeared. The Spitfire was now fully engulfed in flame.

By 0500 hours Al had been taken to Oost-Dunkerke, a small town about half way between Ostend and Dunkirk where he had the pleasure and good fortune to be cared for by a young Belgian girl who washed him and dressed his head wound. She even provided him with a letter to a relative of hers, an official at the port of Ostend, who would help him to arrange passage there to England. What neither of them knew was that the Germans were already in the process of occupying Ostend and had, in fact, compressed the area still occupied by the British Expeditionary Forces to a rather small area around Dunkirk. With no knowledge of this, Al began walking to Ostend. In gratitude for her help, he left his bright yellow 'Mae West' life jacket with the girl. It bore Flying Officer Deere in red letters on the front.

As he neared Ostend he was caught up in a mass of refugees, all heading westwards away from the town. He soon learned of the chaos in Ostend and chose to move west with the refugees. He was able to catch a ride on a bus that was slowly making its way along the crowded road heading towards Dunkirk. When the bus became mired in the traffic he left it and found an abandoned bicycle which he used to get as far as a small village on the outskirts of Dunkirk. At a café there he ran into a few British soldiers and explained that he was an RAF pilot trying to get back to his unit in England. They said that they were heading for Dunkirk where they understood there was transport back to England and he was welcome to ride along with them. It was the first moment when he realized how desperate the situation had become for the British Army. As they neared Dunkirk further travel by vehicle became impossible as most roads were blocked by debris and downed power lines. Abandoned Allied military vehicles lay everywhere and as they walked towards the port itself the enormity of the black smoke plume from the still raging oil storage tank fires was a staggering sight. Al recalled:

The sight that greeted me on arrival at the beach, I shall never forget. My outstanding impression was one of discipline and control despite the obvious exhaustion and desperation of the thousands of troops who, arranged in snake-like columns, stretched from the sand dunes down to the water's edge. This was the British Army in defeat and, by jove, they were still able to appreciate that, no matter how desperate the situation, their chances of rescue were dependent on order and discipline. The spirit of the Tommy may have been dampened but it was not dead, as proved by the soldier who, having secured an unlimited supply of Craven A cigarettes from an unknown source, was careering in a truck up and down the lines of troops tossing cartons to all and sundry shouting as he did so 'Here we are lads, all free and with the compliments of the NAAFI. Take your pick.'

On the beach Al encountered a naval officer who was directing troops through the surf onto some of the many civilian 'little ships' gathered to do their part in the massive evacuation of the British Army. The officer promised to help Al find passage back to England but urged him to wait for the next Royal Navy destroyer to arrive, in order to make the trip more quickly. Several hours later a destroyer did arrive. While waiting to embark, the soldiers were soaked in the unrelenting rain which at least temporarily kept the German dive-bombers at bay. As the weather began to improve, however, the enemy returned and resumed their attacks on the beaches. Many of the British troops there wondered where their highly touted RAF was. It certainly did not seem to be defending them in their present predicament. But the pilots of Fighter Command were there, above the cloud cover in considerable numbers, engaging the aircraft of the enemy and, unfortunately, out of sight of the men on the beach whose morale needed much bolstering.

The naval beach commander led Al to the east mole where the destroyer was loading for the return voyage to England, but before he could reach the ship the loading operation was completed and the vessel departed. Quite soon another destroyer approached the mole and Al joined the queue to board it. Once on board, his identity checked, he was taken down to the small wardroom where he was met with stony silence from the other officers there. It was clear that the RAF was the victim of an underserved and wide-spread reputation among the members of the British Expeditionary Force at Dunkirk.

Throughout the Channel crossing the Royal Navy destroyer was attacked by German dive-bombers whose bombs exploded near enough to shake violently the ship from bow to stern causing her to list severely to port time and again before eventually returning to an even keel. During the zig-zagging three-hour journey Al was called upon by the ship's commander to come up on deck and assist the gunnery personnel in aircraft identification, a job he was both well-equipped for and keen to take on. It was a welcome distraction from the terror of being a bombing target, an experience he hoped fervently never to have again.

When the destroyer docked at the port of Dover, Al was determined to catch the next train leaving for London. He headed for the railway station. 'The question of purchasing a ticket never entered my head. I had no money or means of identification – RAF pilots flew without either – but reasoned that I had earned the right to a free train ride back to my unit.' He settled in a carriage and immediately fell asleep but was soon awakened by a guard hollering 'tickets please'. He explained his situation to the ticket man who was then punching the ticket of a high-ranking Army officer sitting opposite Deere. The wholly unsympathetic guard told Al that he would have to leave the train at the next stop and, overhearing this, the Army officer spoke up: 'It's obvious the boy is telling the truth, guard. Can't you see he's all in, and genuinely anxious to get back to his unit. How do you suggest he does it, walk?' The guard shrugged and gave up. Months later, when the air fighting of the Battle of Britain was at its most intense, Al was reminded of this incident. It was 2 September and Al had just been cleared by the station medical officer at Hornchurch to return to operational flying after having been injured during a bombing raid on the airfield. He was about to take off in the lead of his section to the forward field at Rochford where the squadron would operate for the day. A flight sergeant arrived at Al's aircraft and handed him a note from Al's friend and fellow flight leader, George Gribble. In the rush to get airborne there was no time to read the note and he had to wait until arriving at Rochford. Gribble was not flying on this day and Al assumed the message had something to do with his pilots. When he finally read the note he had to laugh. The envelope also contained a railway warrant with Hornchurch written as the station of arrival and the departure station left blank. The note read: 'Thought you might need this, Al.'

The Dover train arrived at London's Charing Cross station and Al then caught a tube train out to Elm Park station near Hornchurch, where the station commander and the squadron medical officer were enthralled listening to the tale of his adventure in France.

In the brief but intense air activity over the Dunkirk region, the pilots of Fighter Command, with practically no prior combat experience, took on the far more experienced pilots of the German Air Force in an arena much more advantageous to the Germans. In these unfavourable odds it was no surprise that the British lost 229 fighter aircraft, 50 per cent of their front line strength at the time, as well as 128 pilots, the bulk of them highly-trained flight and section leaders. It left Fighter Command in such a precarious position that the result of the coming Battle of Britain might have been very different had the

Germans pressed on with their air campaign in England immediately after the evacuation of the BEF at Dunkirk.

*   *   *

No. 54 Squadron was being rested briefly at Catterick in North York-shire when Al Deere returned to Hornchurch. On their departure they left behind two unserviceable Spitfires which, by the evening of Al's arrival at the Essex base, had been repaired and were awaiting air testing and delivery to the pilots up at Catterick. Al requested and received permission for himself and another pilot to fly the two 'Spits' north the following day to rejoin the squadron. The flight north was uneventful. In fact, the performance of the Spitfire Al had brought so pleased him that on landing, he asked the ground NCO in charge of the aircraft to have his New Zealand Kiwi emblem painted on it, with a roman numeral 'II' after it, as he wanted to keep the aeroplane for his own use to replace the Spitfire he had left near Dunkirk.

Among the first pilots with whom Al was reunited at the Yorkshire base was fellow New Zealander Colin Gray and they were soon in-volved in a lively discussion about the downing of the Dornier bomber whose rear gunner had shot Al down. It led to Gray expressing a view that had become that of many No. 54 Squadron pilots,

> It's absolutely useless having our guns harmonized to produce a rectangular cone of fire at 450 yards as at present. All this guaran-tees is a few hits by the indifferent shot; the good shot, on the other hand, is penalized. It just makes it impossible for those who are prepared to get in close, and can kill when they get there. I've always understood concentration of fire was a principle of war. Perhaps the slide-rule experts who worked out our present harmonization pattern haven't heard of it. We must get point harmonization at 250 yards or even less if the Spitfire guns can be brought to bear at that range. We'll get results then and a damn sight less ammunition will be used to achieve them.

'Sailor' Malan, of No. 74 Squadron, was probably the best shot in Fighter Command, in Al's opinion. Malan not only agreed entirely with the view expressed by Colin Gray; he simply went ahead on his own volition and had the guns of his aircraft re-harmonized to 250 yards, a move that would shortly become official Fighter Command policy for all its day fighters.

In another move to help the performance of the RAF fighter pilots, a new incendiary ammunition was slowly coming into use. It was called De Wilde and was distinguished by the fact that on impact it produced a small yellow flash providing perfect confirmation of the aim and strikes of the RAF pilot on the enemy aircraft. Unlike other 'tracer' rounds, the De Wilde bullets left no flame or smoke trace. Again, it was 'Sailor' Malan who was among the first Allied fighter pilots to recognize and enthusiastically promote the adoption of the combination of 250-yard gun harmonization with the use of the De Wilde ammunition as a virtually assured means of significantly increasing the kill rate.

* * *

The reconnaissance patrols continued for No. 54 Squadron, which was temporarily operating from the airfield at Rochford in Essex. Then, one day in late June, a message came through that Al was required at Hornchurch to attend the visit of a VIP on the station. When he arrived there he learned that the visitor was His Majesty The King and that a small formal parade was to be held at which honours were to be presented to himself, Sailor Malan, and Bob Stanford Tuck. Deere:

> The ceremony was carried out with a minimum of fuss, the normal activities of a station at war carrying on undisturbed. The parade was held on a small square of tarmac between two hangars and appropriately adjacent to the parked Spitfires of 65 and 74 Squadrons. For me it was a memorable occasion. As a New Zealander brought up to admire the Mother country and respect the King as her head, it was the honour of a lifetime, an ultimate milestone of my flying ambitions – the Distinguished Flying Cross presented by the King, in the field of action.

* * *

In conversations with this author, Al Deere indicated that, in the view of most of the participating pilots of RAF Fighter Command, the Battle of Britain actually began on 3 July 1940 when several German bombers, taking full advantage of the heavy cloud cover over the English Channel, began a series of attacks on Allied shipping in those waters. From that day onward the pilots in the fighter squadrons of No. 11 Group were almost constantly alerted, ordered off and involved in combat with the enemy throughout that dramatic summer and autumn. German Armed Forces documentation recovered after the war has confirmed that the duties assigned to the *Luftwaffe* in the resumption of operations preparatory to the planned invasion of Britain by the Germans involved: (1) Interdiction of the Channel to merchant shipping by means of attacks on convoys, and the destruction of harbour facilities; and (2) The destruction of the Royal Air Force. But poor weather conditions persisted in the Channel area through the first ten days of July, making the large-scale bombing operations that the Germans intended unfeasible.

Al recalled that Fighter Command entered the Battle of Britain with only about 300 serviceable Hurricanes and Spitfires and it was not until mid-August that that force numbered closer to 600 (the British Air Staff had estimated the number of fighters required for the defence of the British Isles against the German enemy at a minimum of 1,200). The availability of operational fighter pilots at that time was even more dire, and the strength of the *Luftwaffe* fighter force was greater than at any other point in the war, as was the morale of its pilots.

*   *   *

Among the first lessons learned by the fighter pilots of No. 11 Group that July was that the British RDF system (as the radar chain was then known) was limited to the extent that it was unable to provide sufficient information about approaching enemy air raids early enough to make the interception of the raiders viable before their attacks on coastal and shipping targets. To counter this deficiency, it quickly became policy to send a flight of fighters from each sector station every day to operate from a forward airfield in that sector. Thus, the Hornchurch squadrons sent aircraft over to Manston on the Kent coast. After their first week of operating from Manston, the daily deployment was increased to squadron strength and each day one of the Hornchurch squadrons took off to fly its sorties from the forward airfield and then return at last light to their Essex base. In those early July days the forward fields were frequently under bombing attack by the *Luftwaffe*, which destroyed many of their facilites and made take-offs and landings exceptionally hazardous for the pilots of Fighter Command.

The pressure was mounting on Deere and No. 54 Squadron pilots on 9 July as they continued to fly convoy patrols. Late in the day Al was leading a flight near Dover when he was ordered to investigate unidentified aircraft five miles east of Deal. He sighted the intruder, a silver seaplane with what appeared to be civilian markings. Almost simultaneously another of his pilots spotted several grey-painted Messerschmitt Me 109 fighters in a strung-out formation behind, above and ahead of the seaplane. Al decided that the seaplane was therefore enemy and dispatched a section of his fighters to deal with it while he led the rest of the Spitfires in an attack on the Me 109s. The Germans saw the approaching Spitfires and immediately broke into two rapidly separating sections. The British pilots were outnumbered six to one.

Al was soon aligned on one of the enemy planes and pressed in close before taking his shot which sent several sparkling yellow De Wilde bursts bouncing along the fuselage of the Me 109, which seemed to sag slightly under the impact of the rounds. Before he could add to the problems of his adversary, two Me 109s pulled in tightly behind his Spitfire and he was forced to break off his attack to try and manoeuvre out of the situation. Remembering how effective a tight, climbing spiral turn had been in a previous encounter with an Me 109, he tried it again and was delighted to see both of his pursuers stall out and fall from the climbing chase.

Recovering quickly, Al noticed another Me 109 about 3,000 yards out. The German had obviously seen him too and was turning onto a collision course with Deere. Al used both hands on the control column to steady the little fighter before opening fire on the rapidly closing German. Both pilots began firing at the same moment and continued firing until a few seconds later when their aircraft collided. Al was conscious and relatively alert. The violence of the impact had shoved him forward into his restraining straps and ripped the control column from his grip. He realized what had happened and that he was alive and relatively unhurt. He saw clear sky ahead of him. Increasing smoke and flame were pouring from his damaged engine which had started vibrating badly enough to make it nearly impossible to keep hold of the control column. His mind was clear as he moved to close the throttle and shut off the ignition switches, but just as he reached for them the big Merlin engine seized and the propeller slammed to a stop, its blades bent back radically by the collision. Al Deere's combat report of the incident included:

I was leading 'A' Flight on a patrol over Deal at 6,000 feet when I sighted a silver seaplane approaching Deal at 100 feet. Four Me 109s were flying above and in front. I ordered Yellow Leader to attack the seaplane with his section. I led my section towards the Me 109s, but on doing so saw another twelve 109s flying in loose formation close to the water.

I ordered my section into line astern, but apparently the order was not received, as pilots broke away to engage the enemy. I attacked the tail end aircraft of the original four from above and behind. It dived straight into the sea after I had given two bursts of fire. I then pulled up, climbing for height, and reported to home station that the seaplane had landed in the water, ten miles east of Deal.

I then dived down to attack the seaplane, but saw an Me 109 endeavouring to position itself on my tail. I turned towards him and opened fire at about 1,000 yards head-on. He was also firing and I could hear his bullets striking my fuselage. We both held our fire and apparently my propeller hit some of his fuselage as he passed by, because two tips were bent right back and my hood had been pushed in. The engine vibrated tremendously and then stopped dead; smoke then began to come out.

I was heading landwards at the time of collision and carried on for an open field. Flames then appeared at 1,000 feet and I was unable to see ahead, eventually crash-landing in a field. The air-craft was burning fiercely, but I managed to break the hood open and get out with slight injury.

Heavy, acrid smoke had filled the cockpit. Al groped blindly for the hood release toggle which he found but could not activate. He had struggled with the recalcitrant switch for what seemed an age, to no avail. Putting all of his considerable strength into the effort, he had tried to force the hood to slide back, but it wouldn't budge.

Barely able to see in the choking environment, and trapped by the jammed canopy hood, Al determined to head for the nearby coast and try to glide the crippled plane into an open area. Using full back pressure on the control column, he was just able to maintain the Spitfire in a relatively controlled gliding attitude. With minimal visi-bility he descended until ground objects were flashing past. A post rushed by one wing-tip and the fighter slammed onto the ground, briefly becoming airborne again before hitting hard and sliding through a series of what appeared to be fence posts bordering a field of corn. Again his restraining harness was cutting into his flesh and panic was starting to overtake him as he worked to free the harness release pin. With the engine blazing and threatening to destroy the aircraft and himself within seconds, he continued to bang on the resisting hood until it finally gave way with a splintering crack. He then scrambled to escape from the fuming cockpit. Once a safe distance from the ruined Spitfire, he took stock of his injuries. Both knees were badly bruised, both hands cut and bleeding profusely; he had a cut lip and his eyebrows were singed, but he was otherwise unharmed. His injuries, while somewhat painful, were not serious. He realized that the 'posts' he had noticed during his crash-landing had in fact been anti-invasion barriers intended to thwart landing German gliders. He noted too a number of local residents who were arriving to gape at the furiously burning Spitfire and its lucky young pilot. As they gathered near the wreck some of the machine-gun ammunition began exploding and Al addressed the little crowd of witnesses, 'I advise you to stand well clear of the aircraft. There is plenty of high-octane fuel in the tanks and an explosion is a distinct possibility.' His listeners quickly moved back from the flaming wreckage. As they moved away, a woman came forward and told Al that she had just telephoned the Manston airfield to notify them of his crash-landing. She added that an ambulance and fire engine were on the way to the crash site there at Gunstan

Farm, near Ash, about five miles from Manston. The lady then asked Al to come to her nearby farmhouse for a cup of tea. 'Thank you, I will, but I would prefer something stronger if you've got it.' She said that she thought there was some whisky in the house. He apologized for messing up her fields.

In the 1980s Al discovered that the German fighter he had collided with that July day in 1940 had been flown by *Oberfeldwebel* Johann Illner, a member of 4/JG 51. Illner had also survived the collision and was able to bring his Messerschmitt fighter across the Channel to a safe landing at his French base. The German ace had claimed Al as his victim that day and finished his wartime career credited with seven aerial victories. He was himself shot down in November of that year and became a prisoner of war for the remainder of the conflict. The Heinkel He 59 seaplane attacked by Al's squadron on the 9th had been forced down at sea on the Goodwin Sands. The four-man crew were all captured and the aircraft was towed by a British lifeboat to Deal where it was beached.

When Al was able to rejoin the squadron the next day, he learned that, in the previous ten days of action, the unit had lost six pilots with two more injured. Thirteen of their Spitfires had been lost or damaged and the surviving pilots were all at the point of exhaustion. But there would be no immediate rest for them. Down at dispersal Al found that there were actually only four serviceable aircraft. He would at least have the rest of the morning off before it would be his turn to fly again. He asked the intelligence officer if he knew anything about the civil-marked seaplane the pilots had encountered in the action of the day before and was told that the Air Ministry was investigating. A few weeks later the AM issued a report on the incident:

It has come to the notice of His Majesty's Government in the United Kingdom that enemy aircraft bearing civil markings and marked with the Red Cross have recently flown over British ships at sea and in the vicinity of the British coast, and that they are being employed for purposes which His Majesty's Government cannot regard as being consistent with the privileges generally accorded to the Red Cross.

His Majesty's Government desire to accord ambulance aircraft reasonable facilities for the transportation of the sick and wounded, in accordance with the Red Cross Convention, and aircraft engaged in the direct evacuation of sick and wounded will be respected, provided that they comply with the relevant provisions of the Convention.

His Majesty's Government are unable, however, to grant immunity to such aircraft flying over areas in which operations are in progress on land or at sea, or approaching British or Allied ships.

Ambulance aircraft which do not comply with the above requirements will do so at their own risk and peril.

*   *   *

Keenly recalled by Al Deere among his early victories in the Battle of Britain was that of 24 July when No. 54 Squadron was scrambled at noon to patrol near Deal on the Kent coast.

The squadron had been airborne twenty-five minutes and was flying at a height of 7,000 feet when they sighted a formation of about forty German bombers with a substantial fighter escort near the Thames estuary. From the combat report of Al Deere:

> There were three Me 109s and a further twelve above and in cloud. I told Blue Leader to go for the first three and I would take my section above after the other nine. At that moment nine He 113s came from behind and I saw them in time to avoid being shot at. I managed to stall turn into their tails and fire a burst into the centre of the formation, which then broke up. Other 109s then came down and a dogfight ensued. I had general wild bursts at various aircraft, but was unable to get a decent bead on any of them, because of constant attacks from behind. I managed, however, one decent long burst of fire at a 109 at close range and he went down with glycol pouring from his machine.

*   *   *

War inevitably brings the loss of friends and comrades and in late July Al returned to the forward airfield at Rochford and was told of the death of Johnny Allen, a fellow pilot of 54 Squadron who had flown many missions with him. The friendship and mutual respect had been one of special significance to them both and Al felt the loss deeply. According to Johnny's wingman, who witnessed Allen's Spitfire being hit by a Bf 109 during the initial attack of the British fighters on enemy bombers that day: 'I followed him down as he glided towards the coast. Just as he crossed in, his engine appeared to pick up again and he turned towards Manston hoping, no doubt, to get it down safely there. The next moment fire broke out in the engine and at once the aircraft flicked on to its back and dived into the ground on the outskirts of Foreness.'

By the end of July 54 Squadron had lost the bulk of its best and most experienced pilots. Of the seventeen on operational status at the time of the Dunkirk action, only five had survived. The relentless strain of the several weeks since Dunkirk, the nearly constant readiness and the enormous number of combat sorties flown in the period, left the remaining pilots physically and mentally exhausted. That, coupled with the very real if rarely mentioned fear factor, had reduced their fighting efficiency and morale. Deere:

> I know only too well the almost overpowering urge either to break off an engagement, or participate in such a way as to ensure one's safety, when surrounded and outnumbered. On many an occasion in July I had to grit my teeth and overcome fear with determination in just such circumstances or, alternatively, when I became temporarily isolated from the main battle, to talk myself into going back. I refuse to believe that there are those among us who know no fear. Admittedly, there are those who show no fear and again others who are demonstratively more brave than their comrades in arms; but everyone in his innermost heart is afraid at some time. The dangerous state is reached in battle when one is so tired mentally and physically that the ever present urge of self-preservation overrules the more normal urge to do one's duty.

The need for an immediate rest and refit was paramount if the squadron was to be effective in the even more demanding actions to come over the rest of the summer. Someone higher up was looking out for them and that evening orders arrived for the squadron to fly up to Catterick for a spell of rest and recuperation. The timing of the respite could not have been more auspicious. As the *History of the Royal Air Force* states:

> ... In the month (July) preceding the Battle of Britain ... the flying effort forced on Fighter Command by the daylight attacks was very large, amounting to some 600 sorties per day; and since the fighter escorts with our ships were of necessity small, and the warning usually too short for further squadrons to reach convoys before they were attacked, most of the combats found our pilots at a grave disadvantage. Over and over again a mere handful of Spitfires and Hurricanes found themselves fighting desperately with formations of 100 or more German aircraft ...

The men of No. 54 Squadron enjoyed a full ten days time out of war at Catterick during which the unit was replenished of both aircraft and pilots. The new minimum strength of twenty-two pilots was achieved. In fact, Air Chief Marshal Dowding, C-in-C Fighter Command, had decreed that minimum squadron strength should be twenty-nine pilots, but that level was not to be reached during the 1940 Battle. Their return from Catterick to Hornchurch in early August coincided with the beginning of the next phase of the Battle of Britain, the attacks on the RAF airfields and the radar stations. In these operations the

Germans employed all their bomber types, protecting them with large fighter escort forces. More than three decades after the Battle, Deere recalled:

> We had just settled down to the inevitable game of cards in our dispersal hut at Manston (Pontoon was the normal relaxation between operations) when the telephone shrilled warningly. How we hated the dispersal telephone; its very note was abnormal and the unexpectedness with which it rang had the immediate effect of producing an awful sick feeling in the pit of one's stomach. A pin could have been heard to drop as, with cards poised and eyes turned expectantly towards the orderly as he reached for the receiver, we strained to hear the message from the now faintly urgent voice which came over the wire. 'Hornet squadron scramble.' There was no need to hear more – the orderly would pass the full message to 'Prof' as he strapped himself in his cockpit – table, cards and money shot into the air as first one and then all the pilots dived headlong for the door.

The order to take off and intercept the incoming enemy raiders had come too late. The Spitfires of No. 54 Squadron could not achieve the needed height to engage the *Luftwaffe* on any sort of reasonable terms before the enemy fighters bounced them. The encounter was relatively brief and within a few moments the British pilots received an order from the Controller to land at their home base. The Spitfires were regrouping between Deal and Ramsgate and, looking down to their right, the pilots were fascinated by the sight of the Manston airfield, largely enveloped in smoke and heavily pocked with bomb craters. Manston, their frequently used forward operating field, would receive several bombing attacks during the following week. 'Hell's Corner', as that part of southern England had recently come to be known, was the object of considerable attention now by the bombers of the *Luftwaffe* and the Fighter Command airfields at Hawkinge and Lympne, as well as the nearby coastal radar stations, were also hit hard that first day of the new enemy campaign. But the ingenuity and determination of the ground personnel at Manston got the field back in use later that afternoon, in time for No. 65 Squadron, another Hornchurch outfit, to divert there. Their stay was brief, however, as the second German bombing raid of the day was about to strike the Kent airfield. Fortunately for the British, all the pilots of No. 65 Squadron managed to get their Spitfires into the air before the arrival of the first enemy bombs of the afternoon.

Later in the afternoon the pilots of No. 54 Squadron landed again at Manston after their second operation of the day, to find the place in ruins. Ground staff had laid out twin rows of yellow flags to mark out a relatively safe landing path for the fighters. Chaos reigned with ground personnel wandering the field, many of them wounded. After two days of the airfield attacks, Manston was in a dire state. Its phone cables were damaged, limiting contact with command, the power supply had been cut and the hangars and administrative buildings badly damaged. The situation there was bad, but the action of the day was not yet over. Deere:

> I was leading the squadron, two sections of four aircraft each and one section of three, on a patrol west of Dover. We were at 21,000 feet when we received a report of a German raid at Manston. I spotted a force of about fifty bombers over North Foreland turning from west to east. Then Blue Leader called a Tally-Ho to his aircraft near Dover. I told him to stay with me and we would attack the raiders at Manston, which did not seem to have an escort. Blue Leader did not hear my order and, in company with Yellow Section, attacked the bombers over Dover. It was not until I was within striking distance of the east-bound enemy bombers about ten miles off North Foreland, that I realized Blue Leader had left me. Now Messerschmitt 109s were on my left as I approached the German bombers. I ordered my section to break and engage the 109s. Coming out of a quick turn I saw a 109 shoot a Spitfire down in flames and I managed to get on the tail of the German. I chased him down from about 17,000 feet to 11,000 feet firing short bursts at him from a distance of about 250 yards. The Messerschmitt burst into flames and fell in a vertical dive towards the sea. As I was returning to base I encountered twelve Messerschmitt Me 110s about mid-Channel. I caught them by surprise and fired a long burst into them. They immediately turned back for France. With deflection I fired two more long bursts at one of the 110s, which settled onto the sea. I saw a crewman climb out and onto a rubber dinghy. Another 109 then appeared and shot the hell out of me. I quickly retired and headed for base.

One of the worst days of the Battle was yet to come, 15 August. It began with an initial wave of sixty Junkers Ju 87 Stuka dive-bombers escorted by about sixty Messerschmitt 109 fighters heading for the airfield at Lympne. The pilots of No. 54 Squadron were assigned to intercept the raiders and caught them at the coastline at 1120 hours, between Dover and Dungeness, near Folkstone. Grossly outnumbered, the British pilots had no hope of preventing the bombing, but threw themselves among the Stukas in such a way as to upset their plans to some extent. Still, the enemy dive-bombers were able to punish their target, but not without suffering themselves. One of their number fell to Al Deere's guns. He then headed for a landing at Manston, having no ammunition remaining. But as his Spitfire settled into the yellow-flagged 'safety lane' on the field, with flaps and under-carriage down, a most vulnerable condition, it was suddenly caught up in ground fire from an airfield defence Bofors gun crew who were trying to bring down an attacking Me 110 which was down at low level having just dropped its load. Al reacted instantly, raising his under-carriage and flaps and streaking off inland and out of the situation. For the next fifteen minutes he remained low, circling away from the action at Manston, while waiting for an all-clear indication so he could try again to land there. Six times that day Al had been airborne, with each sortie lasting around forty minutes. The Germans had sent 2,000 aircraft sorties against targets all over the southeast of England. The end of the day meant a respite for the bone-weary pilots of the squadron, but not for Al Deere. On his last sortie of the afternoon, he was shot down and spent the next five hours in the back of an RAF ambulance being jostled agonizingly across Kentish fields finally to arrive for treatment that evening at the Queen Victoria Cottage Hospital, East Grinstead, in West Sussex.

Prior to that final operation of the day, the pilots of 54 Squadron had been told by their commanding officer that, if they were ordered into the air again that afternoon, they were to land back at their home base of Hornchurch. The exhausted flyers were mostly slumped in well-worn wicker chairs, too tired to read or even to chat with one another, wishing only for the demands of the day to end and to be released for a beer and a bed. That would have to wait, however, for within minutes the warning bell sounded at their dispersal and yet another squadron scramble was under way. The nine Spitfires of the squadron that were still operable lifted off from the surface at Manston under orders to head for Dover where they were expected to arrive in time to meet some seventy plus enemy aircraft between Dover and Dungeness. It would be the first occasion in which the Spitfires were to be specifically assigned to engage the German escort fighters. As they reached the point where the Controller expected them to encounter the enemy raiders, the British planes had climbed through 25,000 feet, 5,000 feet higher than Control had ordered, yet barely level with the enemy fighters then coming into view. They would have no height advantage over the Germans, but at least would not be jumped this time. In fact, the Spitfire pilots were able to approach the enemy fighters from behind with at least a partial element of surprise and two 109s fell immediately to the guns of 54 Squadron, one of them a victim of Deere. Al then turned onto the tail of another 109. The German pilot had not yet seen him and he remained in the blind spot of his adversary, hidden by the Messerschmitt's tail unit. Chasing the

German fighter towards France, Al finally came within shooting range as they crossed the French coast. The German began a dive towards the airfield at Calais-Marck, which, at that moment, had a number of other 109s in the landing circuit. Two of the enemy planes left the circuit in pursuit of the intruding Spitfire. Al turned and made a run for England with the two Germans in hot pursuit and gaining rapidly. The first of the German pilots caught up with Al and lined up for an attack. Al turned into him and the German broke off his approach without firing. The extraordinary fatigue after the long day of action was now telling on the British pilot, who was finding it ever more difficult to concentrate and perform well in the situation. And then one of the Germans was able to position himself for a proper shot at the Spitfire. His bullets hem-stitched the British fighter, some of them smashing the cockpit hood and instrument panel. Al was saved by the armour plate behind his seat. He managed to turn into several successive attacks by the 109s, minimising their effect, but still the hits kept coming. Finally the big Rolls-Royce Merlin engine began to vibrate. The Spitfire's oil tank had been pierced and pitch-black oil spattered the windscreen to the extent that Al's forward visibility was greatly reduced. His defensive manoeuvring was at an end. All he could do now to save himself was violently to kick one rudder pedal and then the other in his attempts to ruin his enemy's aim. He now had the white cliffs of Dover in sight. As the three aircraft neared the English seacoast, the German pilots evidently decided that the area was just too dangerous for them with the little fuel they had remaining and elected to break off and return to their French base.

The Spitfire was still marginally controllable and responded when Al climbed to 1,500 feet. His instruments were nearly all shattered and useless, but he didn't need gauges to know that his engine was about to seize and stop. In anticipation, he jettisoned the cracked canopy hood, ready to try a forced landing in the next few moments. With that the engine erupted in flames. Baling out was his only option now and he rolled the Spitfire inverted after having released his Sutton harness. He shoved the control column forward and was sucked from the cockpit and immediately halted again as his parachute pack caught on something. The aircraft was losing altitude rapidly and his efforts to free himself from it were hampered by the airstream forcing him backwards from the cockpit. The ground seemed terribly close when he finally got free. Hurled back into the tailplane, he suffered a painful wrist injury but was able to release his parachute in time for it to open quickly and provide enough support to cushion his almost immediate landing less than 100 yards from the flaming wreckage of his Spitfire.

It seemed only seconds before two young airmen appeared and informed Al that they were ambulance attendants on the way to RAF

Kenley. They had seen the Spitfire crash and stopped to see if they could be of some help. Al asked them for a lift to Kenley where, he reasoned, a medical officer could look at his arm which he feared might be broken. Al fell asleep quickly on one of the stretchers in the back of the vehicle and awoke hours later wondering where they were. The attendants said that they had become lost and were now, they thought, nearing the hospital at East Grinstead. For Al, the pain of his arm was now severe. When they arrived at the hospital a nursing sister gave him a sedative to help him sleep. An X-ray of his arm would have to wait until morning. Before falling asleep he asked the sister to phone the Duty Officer at Hornchurch please to say that Al was safe at the hospital in East Grinstead. The next morning he learned that she had been unable to get through to Hornchurch due to poor phone connections and that his parents in New Zealand had already been notified that he was missing in action.

Later in the morning Al's arm was X-rayed and no broken bones were found. He then determined to be released and to return to Hornchurch as quickly as possible. During an air raid alarm he slipped out of the hospital and caught a train that brought him back to base by early afternoon. Back at Hornchurch the effects of the Battle were apparent. Fighter Command was losing pilots at an untenable rate with 154 killed, missing, or severely wounded in the preceding ten days of air fighting. Their replacements amounted to just sixty-three. Replacing the lost and written-off aircraft was not much of a problem thanks mainly to the brilliance of Max Aitken, Lord Beaverbrook, at the Ministry of Aircraft Production. New Spitfires and Hurricanes were being delivered to the front-line squadrons on the same day as they were requested. Deere:

> The pilot picture was not so rosy. Not only was the replacement problem serious, but the growing strain on those who had been in action continuously, with only brief rests, was also beginning to tell. Small things which earlier would have been laughed off as irrelevant, now became points of bitter contention. At this stage of the Battle, pilot losses far outstripped the replacements and it was only a question of time before the serious position became a grave one.

Al recalled that between August and early September, the critical pilot shortage was exacerbated by the fact that replacement pilots were arriving on the Spitfire squadrons without ever having flown Spitfires, there being no conversion units in existence at that time.

> They came straight to us from the training establishments. Some of them did have a few hours on Hurricanes, but not on the Spitfire. For example, two young New Zealanders, Charlie Stewart

and Mick Shand, were sent to my flight. They had been six weeks at sea coming over to Britain and had been trained on an obsolete aeroplane called a Wapiti, back in New Zealand. In Britain they had each had two trips in a Hurricane and were then sent directly to us on the squadron. We were pretty busy then. We gave them what was known as a cockpit check. We gave them one trip in our Miles Master monoplane and then one of our pilots would take them up to see how they handled it. We would then brief them on the Spitfire and send them up for one solo flight. Then we'd send them off into battle. They didn't last long. In about two trips they were shot down, both of them ending up in Dover hospital. All I could really tell the new boys was 'Stick with your leader. Don't do anything by yourself. Just watch and learn. Stay out of trouble until you get a feel for things.' It was pretty hard on them. What usually happened was that they would follow their leader and then the next thing they knew, they'd been shot down by a 109 they never saw who had got up behind them.

Referring to this aspect of the Battle, the *History of the Royal Air Force* states:

The replacement of casualties was the most serious aspect of the pilot problem, but it was not the only one. There was also the growing strain on those who survived ... The long hours at dispersal, the constant flying at high altitudes, the repeated combats, the parachute descents, the forced landings – all took their toll, even where the harm was not at once apparent. The growing tiredness of those who had been most actively engaged was a factor which Dowding could neglect no more than his casualties. Fighter Command was still successfully resisting the enemy. Its own strength was being steadily sapped in the process.

It was at this point that Air Vice Marshal Keith Park, Air Officer Commanding, No. 11 Group, reached the conclusion that it was essential to utilize selected Spitfire squadrons to draw away the German escort fighters from their bomber formations and thus improve the prospects of the Hurricanes for shooting down the enemy bombers. Operating under the new rules, the pilots of No. 54 Squadron brought great distinction to themselves and their unit on 18 August when, in the course of four separate combat engagements with the *Luftwaffe*, they destroyed fourteen enemy aircraft with no losses of their own. Their actions of the day brought this commendation from the Chief of the Air Staff: 'Well done, 54 Squadron. In all your hard fighting this is the way to deal with the enemy.'

*　　*　　*

One of the more bizarre experiences to befall Al Deere in the Battle of Britain occurred in the early afternoon of 28 August. In response to the second large-scale *Luftwaffe* raid of the day, a formation of Dornier bombers and their equally large fighter escort approaching the North Foreland area, the pilots of No. 54 Squadron were scrambled and climbing towards the 20,000 foot altitude of the enemy bombers. Al was caught up in a wild exchange of fire among several 109s and Spitfires in which he apparently failed to score any meaningful hits. Then, according to his combat report of the incident, while climbing through 23,000 feet, 'I was shot down by a Spitfire (no markings observed). My control wires to the rudder were shot away and I had to bale out.'

He had no difficulty exiting his crippled fighter this time and remembered having the time and opportunity to enjoy the magnificent view of the Kentish fields below during his ten-minute descent from around 10,000 feet where he deployed his parachute. His only (minor) injury was incurred as he crashed through a plum tree in an orchard near the airfield at Detling, leaving him with some scratches and bruises. He was greeted angrily by the farmer who, wielding a shotgun, ordered Al to stay where he was. When Al managed to convince the man that he was not a German pilot, the farmer put down his gun but was still angry. 'Why did you have to land on my prize plum tree?' he grumbled, after which he led Al to the farmhouse and provided a telephone so the Detling airfield could be notified to send transport for the downed RAF pilot. Three hours later Al was back at his Hornchurch dispersal.

For the men of No. 54 Squadron, 31 August was certainly among the most memorable days of the Battle. Four large enemy raids were detected by British radar, assembling over the French coast in the early morning. When they turned towards England it was clear that one formation was heading for Dover. The others appeared to be going towards the Thames. Within minutes it was evident that the key targets of the raids were to be the Fighter Command airfields at Manston, Biggin Hill, Hawkinge, West Malling, Lympne, Debden and Hornchurch. Hornchurch was among the last of the fields to be hit, its sirens sounding at about 1300 hours. The warning had not come in time for the Spitfires of No. 54 Squadron to become airborne. The pilots were taxiing out for take-off and the ground personnel were running for the shelters as the orders rang over the Tannoy sound system. The enemy bombers were already raining their loads down on the airfield when the Spitfire pilots were still struggling to reach the take-off end of the field. Squadron Leader James 'Prof' Leathart was lucky. He got his Spitfire into the air scant seconds before the first of the bombs hit. Some of the other pilots, including Al, were not so fortunate. Al was at the head of his three-plane section:

> We had been ordered to take off. Then the order was cancelled. The radar reporting chain was only effective up to the coast. Inland it was up to the Observer Corps and there was a bit of an overlap. If they couldn't actually see the enemy planes, there could be some confusion and indecision. It was the early days of the system, which took some time to iron itself out.
>
> We were ordered to Readiness and then to Stand-by, sitting in our cockpits, strapped in and ready to go. Then we were told to go back to Readiness. We got out and were walking back to dispersal when the phone rang and someone at dispersal yelled, 'Scramble as quickly as possible.' We ran back to the aircraft and that's when we were caught taking off. The Germans were already overhead dropping their bombs. I was leading and was being held up by a new pilot who had got himself stuck in the take-off lane and didn't know where to go. 'Get to hell out of the way, Red Two,' I yelled. By the time we got him sorted out I was the last one off.

After a few seconds' delay, Al led the section off at full take-off power and noted the rest of the squadron retracting their landing gear as the Spitfires cleared the far hedge and began to climb away from the field.

As Al was about to become airborne a bomb exploded immediately ahead and to his left. His recollection of what happened next was of a:

> ... great blast of air, carrying showers of earth, striking me in the face and the next moment thinking vaguely that I was upside down. What I do remember is the impact with the ground and a terrifying period of ploughing along the airfield upside down, still firmly strapped in the cockpit. Stones and dirt were thrown into my face and my helmet was torn by the stony ground against which my head was firmly pressed. Finally the aircraft stopped its mad upside down dash, leaving me trapped in the cockpit, in almost total darkness, and breathing petrol fumes, the smell of which was overpowering. Bombs were still exploding outside, but this was not as frightening as the thought of fire from the petrol seeping into the ground around my head. One spark and I would be engulfed in flames. I had caught the bombs. I was blown sky high. All three of us were, but we all got away with it. My Spitfire was blown up and I was pretty badly concussed. I finished up on the airfield in a heap. My No. 2 had his wing blown off. Our No. 3 had ended up a mile away. I was shaken up and the top of my

scalp was badly torn from my head scraping along the ground when the aircraft had careered upside down along the ground.

Pilot Officer Eric Edsall, was kneeling by the inverted cockpit, asking Al if he was alive. 'Yes, but barely. For God's sake get me out of here quickly.' Edsall asked if Al could reach the release wire on the small cockpit door. Working together the two men were able after a few minutes to force the door outwards. Al's next problem was how to free himself from his parachute harness. Unless he could manage that he would not be able to squeeze through the cockpit door aperture. After another few moments of struggle he wriggled out of the trap and into blessed fresh air. It was Edsall who then required Al's help. He had sustained an injury to his leg in the incident and had had to crawl over to help rescue Deere. The two men hobbled as quickly as they could between the many bomb craters away from the wreck of Al's Spitfire to the relative safety of a nearby hangar. Later, at the station sick quarters, the pair found a long queue of injured airmen awaiting treatment. Al deposited Eric there and dragged himself back to the officers' mess where he washed his head wound and went to bed where he waited for the Medical Officer who was due to arrive at lunch time. His injuries included a bloodied three-inch patch on the right side of his head, many small cuts and a terribly stiff neck. He learned from his friend and fellow New Zealand pilot Colin Gray, that the port wing of Al's Spitfire had been blown off by the bomb blast, causing the plane to flip onto its back. The big Merlin engine had evidently been torn off its mount as the machine skidded along the ground and finished up several yards away from the wrecked airframe. A wide furrow more than 100 yards long ended at the inverted fighter. Al realized how fortunate he was to have lowered the seat all the way down in the Spitfire for take-off. Had it been positioned any higher he almost certainly would have suffered a broken neck.

> The doctor bandaged me up and told me to get some rest and report back in forty-eight hours. I took the night off and was back flying the next day, all bandaged up.

In recording the events of the day the operations book of No. 54 Squadron stated:

> Hornchurch bombed. The miraculous escape of three of our pilots who were bombed out of their planes. The station bombed a second time.
>   At 13:15 a large formation of enemy bombers – a most impress-ive sight in Vic formation at 15,000 feet – reached the aerodrome and dropped their bombs (probably 60 in all) in a line from the

other side of our original dispersal pens to the petrol dump and beyond into Elm Park. Perimeter track, dispersal pens and barrack block window suffered, but no damage to buildings was caused and the aerodrome, in spite of its ploughed condition, remained serviceable. The squadron was ordered off just as the first bombs were beginning to fall and eight of our machines safely cleared the ground; the remaining section, however, just became airborne as the bombs exploded. All three machines were wholly wrecked in the air. The survival of the pilots is a complete miracle. Sergeant Davis, taking off towards the hangars, was thrown back across the River Ingrebourne two fields away, scrambling out of his machine unharmed. Flight Lieutenant Deere had one wing and his prop torn off; climbing to about 100 feet, he turned over and coming down slid along the aerodrome for 100 yards upside down. He was rescued from this unenviable position by Pilot Officer Edsall, the third member of the section, who had suffered a similar fate except he had landed the right way up. Dashing across the aerodrome with bombs still dropping, he extricated Deere from his machine. 'The first and last time, I hope' was the verdict of these truly amazing pilots – all of whom were ready for battle again the next morning.

* * *

It was on 20 August that the Prime Minister, Winston Churchill, addressed the British House of Commons in a speech that included the now famous words:

> The gratitude of every home in our Island, in our Empire, and indeed throughout the world, except in the abodes of the guilty, goes out to the British airmen, who, undaunted by odds, unwearied in their constant challenge and mortal danger are turning the tide of world war by their prowess and devotion. Never in the field of human conflict was so much owed by so many to so few.

Deere recalls:

> I remember clearly hearing the BBC announcer repeating them with commendable emphasis in a late news bulletin. I was listening with George Gribble who said, 'It's nice to know that someone appreciates us, Al. I couldn't agree more with that bit about mortal danger, but I dispute the unwearied.' Despite the flippancy of George's remarks such encouraging words from a most inspiring leader were a wonderful tonic to our flagging spirits. To me, and indeed I believe to all of us, this was the first real indication of the seriousness of the Battle, and the price we would have to pay

for defeat. Before, there was courage; now there was grim determination.'

* * *

At the end of the day, 3 September, Al's squadron was withdrawn from combat operations in the Battle of Britain and was relieved at Hornchurch by No. 41 Squadron. During the period of No. 54 Squadron's participation in the Battle, Al claimed and was credited with the destruction of eleven enemy aircraft, ten of them Messerschmitt 109s and one a Messerschmitt 110. From the Hornchurch diary:

> In the late afternoon, 54 Squadron left us for a period of rest and recuperation at Catterick. During the previous fortnight, they had been bearing the brunt of the work in the Sector for they had to hold the fort while the various new squadrons arrived and settled down into the Sector routine. With the exception of two very short breaks, they had been with us continuously during the first year of the war, and in this period had destroyed ninety-two enemy aircraft.

No. 54 Squadron was the highest scoring Fighter Command squadron at the time.

As one of RAF Fighter Command's most successful and prominent pilots, Al Deere flew and fought in the Battle of Britain with great courage and high achievement, and he was not shy about expressing his sometimes controversial views on the British conduct of the Battle. He certainly concurred that the criticality of the pilot shortage in Fighter Command as the Battle wore on was real. Referring again to the *History of the Royal Air Force*, 'By the opening week of September Dowding's squadrons had, on the average, only sixteen operational pilots out of their full complement of twenty-six.' Deere: 'When we consider quality as well as numbers, the gravity of the pilot position becomes even more apparent. The newcomers, though magnificent material, did not match their predecessors in flying experience nor in their knowledge of the technicalities of air fighting.' In general, Al praised Dowding's management of his resources in the Battle, noting that his own squadron was rested [stood down from combat operations and sent north to Catterick for rest and recuperation] at precisely the right time on two occasions before finally being withdrawn from the Battle. On the third and final occasion, however, he believed that the squadron should have been withdrawn sooner than it was, but acknowledged the dilemma Dowding faced, as many of his squadrons were being both exhausted and depleted by late August, and his resting and re-forming squadrons were not yet ready to replace them on the front-line. He further supported Dowding's decision to retain some of

his squadrons for operation in areas of England outside of No. 11
Group's operational area, the hottest combat arena of the Battle. He
reflected on those who, over the years, have criticised Dowding for
failing to employ the concept of his No. 12 Group AOC, Air Vice-
Marshal Trafford Leigh-Mallory, who advocated the concentration of
all available Fighter Command forces in the most threatened area
through the utilisation of L-M's 'Big Wing' formation.

> What would have been the outcome of the strong German raids
> against the north-east coast on August 15th had there been no
> forces in position to meet them? It is easy to be wise after the
> event, but I suggest that had these raids been unopposed, or met
> by only token forces, there would have been an outcry against
> Dowding from the Air Staff and the Government. The vital
> question affecting Dowding's whole outlook was: How long is the
> battle going to last? No one could give him the answer: only time
> would tell and time was working on the side of the enemy with his
> numerically superior forces.

As a Spitfire pilot operating in No. 11 Group under the command of
Air Vice-Marshal Keith Park, Al has stated that he knew of no pilots
in the squadron or the group who did not enthusiastically support
Park's policy of assigning certain Spitfire squadrons the task of drawing off the enemy escort fighters to make it easier for the other Fighter
Command squadrons of both Spitfires and Hurricanes, to deal more
effectively with the German bombers. This, in spite of the fact that
implementation of the policy meant a much more demanding role for
the pilots of No. 54 Squadron and the other Hornchurch squadrons.
He recalled occasions in which he witnessed the greatly improved
results by the Hurricanes in particular, when assisted by Spitfires in
that new assignment.

Al was adamant in his opinion of Leigh-Mallory's 'Big Wing' tactic.
Actually, the concept was that of another famous pilot of the Battle,
Douglas Bader. Deere: 'The truth was, at that stage of the war, the
kind of information provided by the radar chain system was both
incomplete and insufficiently reliable to enable the successful use of the
Big Wing policy.' As an example, he recalled that though the building
up of an enemy bombing raid over the French coast was initially
reported by the radar system, the information provided was sketchy at
best and was incapable of accurately determining the strength or com-
position of the striking force. 'Was it 200 bombers? Was it 30 bombers
and 170 fighters? Or, was it just 200? There was no way of telling. It
would have been blind folly, therefore, to have hurled masses of
defending fighters into the air on each and every occasion that a build-
up occurred.' The penalties for operating with such tactics, he believed,

were grave, citing hypothetically the effect of other simultaneous attacks on targets in a distant part of the country, Portsmouth, for example, with no defending forces left to meet the attackers. He noted too that, in his entire experience of the Battle, there were few if any occasions in which it would have even been possible to scramble two or more No. 11 Group squadrons and assemble them into a big wing in time to intercept effectively the enemy bombers before they attacked their target. He pointed out that virtually all interceptions by Bader's Duxford big wing were actually made over or just short of the bombers' target and often after the bombs had been released, indicating the vital significance of the time squandered in assembling the big wing and travelling to the target in large formation.

Al readily drew attention to a comparison between the situation faced by the German Air Force fighter arm against the American daylight heavy bombers in 1943, and that of RAF Fighter Command in the summer of 1940. Even though the Germans went up against the American bomber streams as far more experienced air fighters, operating within a much more advanced and sophisticated radar control system; even though they had far greater early warning of raids heading towards their homeland and thus much more time to form and focus their defensive formations as they wanted them, they ultimately came to rely on small, relatively mobile fighter formations that operated independently. This after having experimented with massive defensive formations. In these exercises the Germans found that they were sacrificing an essential flexibility of action for their individual fighter pilots and denying them most of the opportunities that aggressive airmen need for success in air combat. Through the course of the war, Al found that two squadrons were the most that could be controlled efficiently in combat, three fewer than had frequently been launched by Bader and Leigh-Mallory in No. 12 Group during 1940 and 1941.

Al reaffirmed that the stated purpose of the *Luftwaffe* in the Battle of Britain was the destruction of RAF Fighter Command in the air and on the ground to open the way for a sea-borne invasion of England and that Dowding's job was to prevent the destruction of his forces and, simultaneously, to inflict the maximum destruction on the enemy air forces. Both Dowding, and his commander of No. 11 Group, Keith Park, fully realized that they lacked sufficient resources to destroy the *Luftwaffe*. Al noted that the soundness of Dowding's and Park's strategies was confirmed in late August, the point by which, according to *Luftwaffe* estimates, Fighter Command would be defeated, the front-line squadrons of No. 11 Group were still powerful and fully engaged in the punishment of the German enemy. He also pointed out that captured German documents have dispelled any doubt that the

Germans would have invaded England had the *Luftwaffe* won the Battle of Britain. Finally, he recalled that, while Dowding and Park won the Battle, they were cast aside in their finest hour, as Winston Churchill was in the post-war polls.

* * *

During their third and last rest period at Catterick, in early September 1940, the pilots of No. 54 Squadron were near to complete exhaustion. James Leathart's term as head of the squadron had come to an end and he was reassigned to the Air Ministry for the next year. No. 54 Squadron was now a training squadron and Al found himself in the role of grooming promising new aviators to become effective fighter pilots. He went up with them on practice flights and gave them the benefit of his considerable combat experience. The turn of Sergeant Howard Squire to fly and learn from Al came on 28 December when the two of them took off to practice dogfighting. Al had noticed that Squire was a better than average pilot and looked forward to the flight. Squire had, in fact, been the charge of Al's deputy on that morning's training roster, but the deputy awoke with the flu and the assignment passed to Deere.

The first series of tail-chases ended with the two aircraft down around the 3,000-foot level. Deere: 'OK, Red Two, I'll climb up again to 10,000 feet and we'll have another go. You are doing fine, but please keep your distance at about 250 yards, you are getting far too close.' Squire acknowledged the order and drifted back to the required separation. When they reached 10,000 feet they resumed the dogfighting exercise. Squire was good and Al found it difficult to keep track of the other Spitfire, which the new man was keeping nicely behind and below Al's aircraft. The limited rearward visibility from his Spitfire made Al's job tougher and, following a succession of demanding manoeuvres that finished in a tight turn, Al had lost sight of Squire. In order to determine if he had succeeded in eluding the new pilot, Al instantly reversed his turn. In the next second Squire's aircraft was on top of his. The two Spitfires collided and Squire's propeller destroyed Al's tailplane, sending his fighter into a savage spin. The Spitfire was now out of control and Al was pinned to his seat by centrifugal force.

Somehow he managed to jettison his cockpit hood and release himself from his Sutton harness and R/T lead, preparatory to baling out. The Spitfire was plummeting earthward as well as spinning and Al was rapidly running out of time and space. He strained, pushing with his hands, to break the grip of the force holding him firmly in the seat, to no avail. And then, miraculously, the force let up for an instant and he was released from the Spitfire, but his freedom lasted only about two seconds. The slipstream slammed him into the ruined tailplane, where he became ensnared. After another bout of exhaustive effort he twisted free of the wrecked tail.

Automatically, Al reached for the rip-cord handle to open his parachute. He couldn't find it and then realized that the parachute pack was partially detached and was spinning above his head as he tumbled toward the earth. In yet another apparent miracle, his parachute somehow deployed with no help from Al, an event that seemed to occur within only a moment of his hitting the ground, which, fortunately was a farmer's cess-pool. He had arrived at Town End Farm, near Kirk Leavington in North Yorkshire. He had landed horizontally and the foul effluent had cushioned his impact sufficiently. Once again he had cheated death. He was, however, in great pain from his back and suffered considerably as he crawled from the mess. Help soon arrived in the presence of a passing motorist who assisted Al into his car and drove him the seven miles back to the base at Catterick. From there he was immediately driven in the station's ambulance to a nearby hospital where an X-ray established that he had a chipped bone at the base of his spine as well as a severely strained back which would require several days bed rest back at the base. Howard Squire's aircraft had caught fire after the mid-air collision with Al's plane and the sergeant had baled out and survived the incident without injury. For the rest of his life Al would suffer acute back pain and endure many sleepless nights as a lasting result of the bale-out.

Howard Squire had joined No. 54 Squadron's A Flight under the command of Al Deere on 1 December 1940. At that point he had 150 hours flying time recorded in his logbook, with just ten hours and fifteen minutes of that time on Spitfires. He had been a member of the RAF Volunteer Reserve and was chosen for pilot training after being called up when the war started in September 1939. By 28 December, the day he and Al Deere went up for that bit of air-fighting practice, he had accumulated a grand total of twenty-two flying hours on Spitfires, including sessions of formation flying, aerobatics, air-fighting, and three actual combat patrols. He was pleased to be a part of No. 54 Squadron and to be among its illustrious personnel and was well aware of the reputations of Deere, Colin Gray and the others. As a Sergeant Pilot, he especially appreciated the easy-going atmosphere and commeraderie of A flight and the way the officer and NCO pilots worked and related to each other.

The 28 December had dawned cold, clear, crisp and cloudless. His only instruction from Deere had been to put more distance between himself and the aircraft of his instructor in the dogfighting exercise. His memory of the collision included that of the heavy crash sound as his Spitfire caught and mangled Deere's tailplane and then passing under the other aircraft. His own cockpit hood was torn off in the impact and his engine had begun to vibrate alarmingly. His aircraft was still relatively stable though severely damaged. The degree of damage seemed to him sufficient that he was not likely to make it back to base and he elected to bale out. Unlike Al, Squire was able to dive clear of the aircraft. Being still at relatively high altitude he delayed opening his parachute for several seconds. When he finally pulled the ripcord, the psychological relief of the spreading canopy over his head was offset harshly by the discomfort caused as the improperly adjusted 'chute straps tore into his groin. Grabbing for the shroud lines, he was soon able to improve the adjustment. As he neared the ground he tried to avoid a large fence and, in doing so, crashed through the upper branches of a stand of trees, slightly shaken but unhurt. He then gathered up his parachute and headed off for a nearby country house whose mistress was pleased to entertain him with tea, cake, and a large whisky while he awaited transport back to the airfield. In time an ambulance arrived from the base and he directed the driver to the still smoking crash site where Al's Spitfire had impacted. Al had long since been rescued and removed from the scene. Squire was soon back at base and dreading his impending encounter with Al and his other superiors re the mid-air collision for which he fully expected to be held responsible. When all was said and done, however, Al and the other A Flight pilots gathered to work out a convincing explanation which they felt would satisfy the top man. The commanding officer was, in fact, neither convinced nor amused by their attempt, but limited his response to a mere reprimand. Squire was back on operational status that same day and was forever grateful to Al for obviously exerting his influence in the matter, helping to keep Squire on the squadron.

After a week in bed Al was anxious to get back in the air in a Spitfire, but his first flight proved too much for him. 'I felt most unsafe and whenever another aircraft came near me I broke out in a cold sweat.' At the end of a week of such experiences he realized that his nerves were shot and he went to see the squadron commander who sent him to the Station Commander. This understanding officer arranged for Al to have a week away from the base before taking up his next duties as a controller in Station Operations, a temporary non-flying assignment. The controller job was notable for Al only due to the intense boredom it brought him, which was broken briefly after a month in the job when he was ordered to attend a ceremony at Buckingham Palace where the King presented the Bar to Al's Distinguished Flying Cross, an honour and occasion he would always remember with gratitude.

* * *

In late February 1941, No. 54 Squadron was returned to both its former status as an operational fighter squadron and to Hornchurch, the Essex air station that had served as its home base for so much of its history. Now Fighter Command was on the offensive and the new role of the squadron included the raids known as Rhubarbs, low-level nuisance attacks mainly over France on targets of opportunity. No. 54 Squadron departed the snow-covered field at Catterick on 23 February for Hornchurch – without Al Deere. His affiliation with the organization ended that day for the duration of the war. The late December incident during the dogfighting exercise with Howard Squire had cost him plenty in terms of his self confidence. The period in which he was serving as a controller did much to help restore him to his former confidence and competence. By late March he had had quite enough operational down-time and applied to the Station Commander for a return to combat operations. He had benefited from and, to some extent, enjoyed his time as a controller, but was now driven to get back to the action.

While awaiting a new assignment Al met the girl with whom he would spend the rest of his life. Joan Fenton was living with her parents in Harrowgate, near Darlington, North Yorkshire, and had recently applied to join the American Ambulance of Great Britain, a volunteer group of British girls who drove ambulances which had been paid for with funds raised in the United States. Al and Joan had known each other for a short but happy time when he was summoned to see the Station Commander. 'Deere, you have been posted as a flight commander to No. 602 Squadron with effect from May 7th'. So, it was with mixed emotions that he telephoned Joan to inform her of the posting.

*   *   *

In the morning of 5 June, Al and the pilots of No. 602 Squadron had taken off on a practice mission. In the preceding six months, Fighter Command had followed a precedent set by Adolph 'Sailor' Malan of No. 74 Squadron. In the Battle of Britain, Malan had observed and understood a distinct advantage held by the *Luftwaffe* fighter pilots, who flew in sections of four aircraft as elements of three such sections, and fought in two-plane elements. He introduced these tactics in his squadron and they soon became standard practice for the fighter pilots of the RAF. On this particular morning Al and the others were climbing to 30,000 feet to practice the relatively new procedures. While passing through 10,000 feet, his Rolls-Royce Merlin engine suddenly began vibrating excessively. He immediately throttled back while scanning his gauges. The oil pressure reading was severely down and in the next instant Al heard and felt a great 'bang'. Thick black oil began beading back over the cowling and onto the windscreen. He switched off the engine and twisted in the seat as he checked his distance to the

English coast. He reckoned it lay about ten miles from his present position and considered whether his 10,000 feet of altitude would be sufficient for him to glide to a safe forced landing as opposed either to baling out or ditching the Spitfire out at sea. The Air Ministry had not yet begun issuing seat-pack dinghys for its fighter pilots and Al saw no ship traffic of any kind in the vicinity. The stories he had heard about ditching experiences with Spitfires led to a quick decision. He would try for the coast and, should he run out of air at the last moment, would ditch as near to the beach as he could. At his present rate of gliding descent he estimated that he was losing about 1,000 feet of height for each mile of distance he covered as he headed towards the shoreline. It would be a close call.

Once again his luck held as he barely managed to clear the clifftops near Ayr and began searching frantically for a reasonable field in which to put the crippled fighter down. The fields immediately beneath him were all small and divided with deadly stone fences. He was quite low by this time and had virtually no time to debate with himself about which field to choose. Not that he had the luxury of manoeuvring. He was committed to a largely straight-in landing and it certainly looked as though he would end up in tangled wreckage against one of the stone walls. His only choice was to shove the control column forward and drop the little fighter onto the ground at ninety miles per hour. It scraped through the thousands of potatoes that littered the field until finally pitching forward, up and over onto its back in the soft, black earth. What saved Al was his tightly fitted Sutton harness which contained him firmly in the seat and prevented him breaking his neck. Alert and evidently unhurt, he was aware that there was no smell of petrol and knew that he had long since switched off the engine and the danger of fire was minimal. Able to move his arms enough to release the small side door of the cockpit, he thought as he hung upside down by the harness, about how to release it safely without allowing the weight of his body to injure either his neck or his back, an unfortunate after effect experienced by some fighter pilots in similar situations. He gently released the harness and suffered only a minimum of discomfort in the act, and soon was able to squirm through the tiny cockpit door and the ground clearance. Freed, he reflected on the fact that he was quite alone with no one in sight and wondered how long he might have been trapped upside down in the inverted Spitfire before help would have arrived.

He noticed a building in the distance and headed for it. It was the clubhouse of the golf course at Girvan and there he was offered the usual cup of tea after explaining that he had left his Spitfire in the potato field adjacent to the links. Al was soon collected by the Station Commander himself, Group Captain Loel Guinness, who drove him back to the aerodrome. A subsequent investigation by Rolls-Royce personnel established that Al's engine had thrown a connecting rod through the engine block.

Leading No. 602 Squadron which had been moved to RAF Kenley, near London, in the summer of 1941, Al took them on many offensive fighter sweeps into northern France, as well as Circuses, which were combined fighter and bomber sorties, Ramrods, bomber forces escorted by the fighters, and Rodeos, fighter sweeps without bombers. These activities were flown to destroy German military targets and *Luftwaffe* fighters and to tie up as many *Luftwaffe* aircraft and pilots as possible in France to take some of the pressure off the RAF Bomber Command raiders on targets in Germany. The Fighter Command pilots were being used as a kind of bait to draw German fighter defences onto them and, over time, the Germans learned to exploit the British tactic and were ready and waiting for the Spitfires, making them pay a heavy price for their attacks.

* * *

At the end of April 1942 Al Deere arrived at North Weald in Essex to take command of No. 403 (Royal Canadian Air Force) Squadron, which had incurred heavy losses in the preceding weeks, losing its commanding officer during a sweep over northern France on 27 April. No. 403 Squadron shared the North Weald base with Nos. 121, 222 and 331 Squadrons and the wing there was commanded by David Scott-Malden, an old friend of Al from No. 54 Squadron and the Battle of Britain period.

An especially demanding day for the squadron was to be 2 June. They were assigned to operate from the forward airfield at Southend, taking off and forming up with the other North Weald squadrons over Chatham. Over Hastings they were to rendezvous with the squadrons of the Hornchurch wing and head off *en masse* at wave-top height for Cap Gris Nez, where they would then climb to 25,000 feet and turn east for a sweep across St Omer, emerging at Le Touquet and returning to England. The mission was carried out as planned and No. 403 Squadron brought up the rear of the large formation as it crossed over Le Touquet turning for home base. Approaching from the south was a force of between fifteen and twenty Focke-Wulf Fw 190 fighters. Al turned the squadron into the attacking German planes and as they banked he spotted a further fifteen plus Fw 190s dropping on them from above and behind. More Fw 190s were now arriving from the south and in seconds the Canadians of No. 403 Squadron were facing upwards of fifty enemy fighters. In the next seconds Al used up his cannon and machine-gun ammunition in short, quick bursts. In the confusion he happened to see two aircraft crash into the sea about ten miles off Le Touquet and noticed a single parachute descending nearby. At this point he was being pursued by an Fw 190 and was unable to call in a position fix on the downed pilot or pilots. Fortunately, the German fighter broke off the chase and headed back to France just as Al sighted another Spitfire pilot baling out. This time he was able to call in the position report and ask for rescue boats to be sent out.

One of the Spitfire pilots that Al had seen brought down was Flight Sergeant G.D. Aitken, whose combat report for the mission read:

I was Blue 4 and heard Pilot Officer Hurst (Red 3) shouting over the R/T that there were six enemy fighters behind. I looked back, following Blue 3 (Pilot Officer Parr), and heard the CO say, 'Break'. We broke left and I saw a German, which I think was a 109F, attacking Pilot Officer Parr from quarter port astern. I turned slightly to port and gave the German a long burst sweeping him along the fuselage as he crossed my sight with cannon and machine-gun. I then felt bullets hit the armour plate at my back and bullets perforate my cockpit hood. My aircraft gave a lurch and the radio was suddenly useless. I went into a steep turn and levelled out and started weaving. I saw nothing more of the aircraft in my section.

Then an enemy aircraft appeared on my starboard side, some 500 feet above and approximately 400 yards away. I took a hasty look around and saw another on my port above and about 500 yards away. The enemy fighter on my starboard side dropped his port wing slightly, so I figured he was coming in to attack. I turned towards him and opened fire from a range of 200 yards. He fired as he came down and I saw his tracer pass underneath me. He then broke away; I continued a steep turn right and levelled out at 10,000 feet and headed for home.

I then saw tracer pass on both sides and saw cannon hits on both my wings. I went into a steep dive, but levelled out again at 5,000 feet. I throttled back and reduced boost and then looked around to see what damage had been done and whether I could make it to Hawkinge airfield. The nose of the aircraft wanted to go up, so I trimmed fully forward, which took most of the pressure off the control column. The engine then started to sputter, puffs of white smoke and flames started to come from the exhausts and gasoline was leaking out into the cockpit as the aircraft began to lose height.

I then decided it was about time I got out. Holding the stick with my left hand, I undid the straps and slid the hood back. I then changed hands and removed my helmet with my left hand, opened the door and throttled back and pulled the nose up, then held onto the stick and put my left leg onto the wing. I then pulled the ripcord and fell backwards out of the aircraft. My parachute opened and almost got entangled on the tail. This all happened at 1,000 feet. As I went down I saw my aircraft hit the deck with a hell of a bang and sink immediately. I inflated my Mae West and turned the quick release as I hit the water. I had hold of my dinghy strap as I could not swim, and gave the strap a hard jerk to free the dinghy from the parachute. It inflated and I climbed in, found the paddles and looked for the shore. I saw a Spitfire circling and this was Squadron Leader Deere; later several more aircraft arrived and one I recognised as David Scott-Malden's, the Wing Leader. I was picked up 25 to 30 minutes later by a rescue launch, given a big drink of scotch, rubbed down and put to bed and eventually landed at Dover.

Al had been airborne for two hours and ten minutes and was nearly out of fuel when he landed, this time at the coastal airfield, Lympne, just west of Folkstone. There he learned that six of his twelve pilots had failed to return from the mission.

On 16 June No. 403 Squadron was ordered to move north to Catterick for a rest period. Al was perplexed by this action and requested a meeting with Air Vice Marshal Trafford Leigh-Mallory, AOC, No. 11 Group, who received him cordially at the Uxbridge headquarters. When Deere questioned him pointedly about No. 403 Squadron remaining in the group, however, the AVM hardened and commented on Al's leadership of the unit with particular reference to the early June incidents and the losses the squadron had suffered, 'You are rather too fond of getting into a fight and taking unnecessary risks.' Al remained composed but countered that when suddenly attacked from above by superior enemy forces fighting was unavoidable. He'd had no option but to fight. Leigh-Mallory closed the subject and the meeting.

*   *   *

On 14 March 1943, Al Deere was posted to Biggin Hill as Wing Leader there, replacing Richard Milne, who had been shot down on 18 March in combat with Fw 190s near Hardelot. Milne had baled out over the Channel and been picked up by an enemy patrol boat. He was a prisoner of the Germans until the end of the war.

The station commander at Biggin Hill then was Al's long-time friend, 'Sailor' Malan, who greeted Al warmly and was quick to express his confidence in Al's judgement and leadership. He gave Al free reign to devise and implement the tactics he believed to be appropriate for the Biggin wing, which included: All squadrons and sections in the wing formation would be independent, but also remain interdependent when the need arose; that he would lead the wing and would have total control over the formation, routes and critical timings on operations; the squadron and section leaders could use their own judgement in event of enemy attacks, but they must inform him before going into action; that all squadrons must be relied upon to take equal responsibility when the wing was undertaking escort for a raid and, if the event arose, they might be called on to take over the lead, if the other squadrons were engaged in enemy attacks. He stressed the need for their fighters not to be restricted by the bombers they were to escort (the German High Command had tried this procedure during the Battle of Britain, with disastrous results). The Spitfires would always be in sight of the bomber formations, but would not be tied to their speed.

*　*　*

A part of the work of the Biggin Hill Wing under Al Deere's command was the escorting of American bombers of the US Eighth Army Air Force. In October 1943, Al received a communique from Lieutenant General Ira Eaker, Commander, Eighth US Army Air Force:

Under the provisions of Army Regulations 600-45, 8th August 1932, as amended, and persuant to authority contained in Section I, Circular 36. *The Distinguished Flying Cross* is awarded to the following officer. *A.C. Deere* Wing Commander, Royal Air Force. For extraordinary achievement, while leading his Wing as fighter escort for medium bombers of the Eighth Air Force on more than fifteen missions over enemy occupied Europe. Wing Commander Deere devoted untiring energy assisting in the development of new, untried tactics for medium bombardment aircraft. In order to observe the effectiveness of the new tactics, he personally led his Wing as cover for the bombers on the first mission. The successful bombing of heavily defended target without loss of an aeroplane is in a large measure due to the planning, skill and leadership of Wing Commander Deere. His actions reflect highest credit upon himself and the Armed Forces of His Majesty's Government.

After the American award, Al was asked to give an interview on the BBC Overseas Service on his time as Biggin Hill wing leader:

I came to Biggin Hill early this year as supernumerary squadron leader, attached to one of the Spitfire squadrons. A supernumerary squadron leader is one who, after six months off operations, is required to go back to a squadron and to act as a stooge until he gets his hand in again. Then you normally get command of a squadron; I got command of the Biggin Hill Wing.

For six weeks after I arrived at the station, I flew as No. 2 and No. 4 positions. These are the stooge positions in a fighter squadron. On two or three occasions I was following sergeant pilots who were leading my section, and during the attacks I often had to follow my sergeant pilots in to attack the Hun. One day when the wing was flying at 32,000 feet near St Omer, I spotted and reported fifteen enemy aircraft. They were about 10,000 feet below. I received permission from the wing commander to attack, and followed the section leader, who was a flight sergeant. When the leader of the enemy formation saw me, he dived to the ground. This is a typical Hun evasive tactic, but knowing their tactics I followed him eventually showing about 480 miles an hour on the clock. When my first burst hit him, great chunks flew off and after the second burst, it was all over. To make sure I gave him a further burst. He completely disintegrated.

Our most recent activities have been concerned with escorting the American Flying Fortresses. It is a wonderful sight to see, this great gaggle of Fortresses flying in formation. I remember quite clearly going out to pick up these Fortresses returning from their first daylight raid on the Ruhr. We met some 200 of them coming back as if they had been on a pleasure cruise. It was a breathtaking sight. We could see them about sixty miles away. Somewhere south of Rotterdam we met them. They were in boxes of about twenty strong, and the whole distance covered by this formation was something like twenty miles. It took this formation fifteen minutes to pass a given point – twenty miles of four-engine bombers. When I saw them I felt sorry for the Hun fighter pilots, who are ordered to attack these formations, as the Fortresses' fire power is deadly.

To get back to the wing again, I must say I enjoy being with the Biggin Hill Wing very much, particularly as it has such a record. We have a French squadron who are looking forward to the day when they shall all be back in France, fighting from their own soil and fighting over Hun territory. We are a fairly mixed wing at Biggin. The group captain, as you probably know, is a South African; I am a New Zealander, Jack Charles a Canadian. There are also Czechs, Poles, and Australians – in other words, pilots from all over the British Empire including our Allies. I was asked the other day at Biggin by an American pilot if I would like to fly a Flying Fortress. I think my reply was typical of every pilot on this

A dramatic view of vapour trails formed during aerial combat over Lewes, East Sussex, at the height of the Battle of Britain. *(All photos from the collection of the Author.)*

R.A.F. Fighter Command Spitfires in perfect formation over England during the Second World War.

Messerschmitt Bf 109 fighters during the Battle of Britain.

Heinkel He 111 bombers on their way to attack a target in England in September 1940.

A captured German airman who has just arrived in England by parachute.

Al Deere, far right, and pilots of A Flight, 54 Squadron, Hornchurch, Essex, in June 1940.

Al Deere with his Spitfire, Kiwi 1, at R.A.F. Hornchurch, Essex, during the Battle of Britain.

A Cuthbert Orde drawing of Al Deere, 54 Squadron, Hornchurch.

Air Commodore Al Deere, a New Zealander who served with 54 Squadron at Hornchurch during the Battle of Britain.

A line drawing of Geoffrey Page, 56 Squadron, as he looked in the spring of 1940.

A fine Cuthbert Orde drawing of Group Captain Adolf 'Sailor' Malan, an outstanding fighter leader at 74 (Tiger) Squadron, Hornchurch, during the Battle of Britain.

'SAILOR'

Group Captain Peter Townsend in a Spitfire during the filming of the motion picture Battle of Britain, at Duxford, Cambridgeshire, in 1968.

A Cuthbert Orde drawing of Wing Commander Peter Townsend, then commander of 85 Squadron at Debden, Essex.

Group Captain Brian
Kingcome commanded No.
92 Squadron at Biggin Hill.

Brian Kingcome (in cockpit) and other members of 92 Squadron at R.A.F. Biggin Hill in summer
1940.

A Cuthbert Orde drawing of Flight Lieutenant Brian Kingcome, of 92 Squadron, Biggin Hill, Kent.

A pilot of one of the R.A.F. Polish squadrons with his Spitfire.

Robert Stanford Tuck, served with 65 Squadron at Hornchurch, 92 Squadron at Biggin Hill, 257 Squadron at Debden, and as Wing Commander at Biggin Hill.

A Cuthbert Orde drawing of J. C. Mungo-Park, who became Commanding Officer of 74 Squadron in April 1941, having served with the squadron under 'Sailor' Malan for nearly two years. He was killed in June 1941 in a fighter sweep over France.

Pilots of 92 Squadron running to their Spitfires in a 'scramble' during the Battle of Britain.

A British fighter pilot is hauled aboard a Supermarine Walrus amphibian of R.A.F. Air-Sea Rescue Squadron while a Lysander circles until the operation is completed.

A Junkers Ju 88 bomber that was shot down over England in 1940.

Pilots of JG.52 with a Messerschmitt Bf 109 in France during 1940.

Heinkel He 111 bombers taking off from a base in Northern Germany to attack a target in the Netherlands in May 1940.

Crewmen of a Dornier Do 17 that crashed on the beach at Folkstone, Kent, on August 31st 1940. (courtesy Fox Photos)

James 'Ginger' Lacey, the highest-scoring British ace of the Battle of Britain, with his Hurricane fighter.

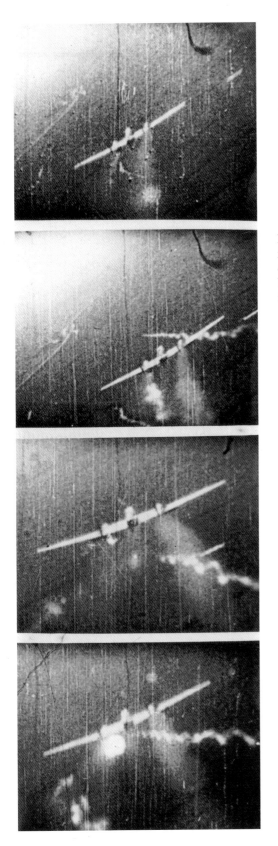

Partial gun-camera
footage showing the
destruction of a German
bomber by an R.A.F.
fighter pilot late in 1940.

An early mark Supermarine Spitfire fighter.

station. Give me a single-engine aircraft any day – preferably a
Spitfire.

All we New Zealanders over here hope that before long, and
I'm sure it won't be long, we shall be out in the Pacific operating
our Spitfires from Australia or New Zealand, giving the Japs a
beating, until the great day comes when the Armistice arrives.

*   *   *

Just prior to the Allied invasion of the European continent at
Normandy in June 1944, Al Deere was requested by the Free French
Air Force to lead their wing of Spitfires into France, having commanded two French squadrons as Wing Leader at Biggin Hill. He was
sent to lead them up to and including D-Day.

I remember the tears running down the faces of those gallant
Frenchmen when I briefed them about the invasion. The weather
on D-Day was bad and we didn't see much along the beachhead.
We flew as cover over the British beaches, but the weather was
too bad for the German Air Force and they hadn't reacted. The
French pilots were very good, but could sometimes be a bit excit-
able in the air. If we got into combat and they sighted something,
they used to get a bit carried away and I would have to tell them:
'You are not to use the R/T unless it is an emergency.' But I got on
really well with them although I could not speak a word of
French.

*   *   *

In his long and colourful career as a fighter pilot, Alan Christopher
Deere claimed the destruction of seventeen enemy aircraft, the shared
destruction of one, the unconfirmed destruction of two and one
shared, three probably destroyed, and seven damaged with one shared.
He flew as a member of five Royal Air Force fighter squadrons and
was leader of the Biggin Hill Wing, and he flew a total of fifty different
Spitfire aircraft including the Mk.1A, Mk.1, Mk.IIB, Mk.Vb and
Mk.IX.

With the end of the war Al Deere remained in the RAF and received
a number of prestigious appointments including that of Station Commander, RAF Duxford, near Cambridge, in December 1945. In
September he and Joan were married. His final air force posting came
in November 1965 when he was made commandant of the famous
Aircraft and Boy Entrant training establishment, RAF Halton, in
Buckinghamshire, near Wendover, where Al and Joan had made their
home. Alan Deere died on 21 September 1995, following a long illness.
His last wishes were that there be no funeral service for him and that he

be cremated and his ashes scattered over the Thames Estuary from a Spitfire. In his foreword for Al's autobiography, Lord Dowding wrote: 'He will always stand to me as an example of the best type of fighter pilot, whose endurance and determination brought this country of ours through the greatest immediate danger, which had threatened it since Napoleon's armies stood along the Channel shore.'

CHAPTER TWO

Geoffrey Page

W hen RAF Wing Commander Alan Geoffrey Page died in August 2000, Air Chief Marshal Sir Christopher Foxley-Norris said of him: 'Even by Battle of Britain standards, he was the bravest of the brave. Geoffrey was one of my oldest and dearest friends. The most modest and self-effacing of men, he had to live his life in nearly constant pain that stemmed from the horrific burns and injuries he sustained as a pilot during the Battle of Britain and later in the Second World War. If ever anyone had what has become known as "the right stuff", he did.'

*   *   *

Born at Boxmoor, Hertfordshire on 16 May 1920, Geoffrey Page was educated at Dean Close School in Cheltenham and London University. Knowing that my wife and I lived in the Cheltenham area, on more than one occasion he encouraged this author to give his old school the two-fingered salute for him whenever we passed it. I still honour his request.

Like so many young men and boys of the late 1930s and early 1940s, Geoffrey loved aeroplanes and flying and let everyone in his family know of this fascination with aviation. He first became interested in aeroplanes at age five and at nine was hugely disappointed by the inaccuracy of a flying model aircraft he was given for his birthday, which caused him to modify it making it look like the real thing. It flew well, leading him to believe that he had an instinct about flying.

His uncle, the aircraft manufacturer Sir Frederick Handley Page, tried to discourage him from becoming a pilot, warning that 'pilots are two a penny.' His father said to him,

I have spoken to your uncle at length about your desire to be a pilot and he has advised me strongly against it. Hundreds of pilots are chasing a handful of jobs. Some of the best and most experienced have applied to join his firm. So what makes you think you'll be any better than they are and can walk straight into a job?'

Geoffrey tried to explain that what he wanted was a permanent commission in the RAF and a flying career in the air force. But his father was adamant,

> 'Your uncle is prepared to find you a place in the Company if you qualify as an engineer. And that is precisely what I would do if I were in your shoes. Of course, if you insist on going to Cranwell, you'll have to pay for it yourself, as I don't intend to provide the money for such stupidity.'

Geoffrey later learned that the main reason his father and uncle were so opposed to his becoming a pilot was that their younger brother had been one and was killed. Reluctantly Geoffrey entered London University where he studied engineering, to the satisfaction of his father. There, however, he also found that if he could pass a strict medical examination he could enrol in the University Air Squadron and be afforded an opportunity to learn to fly with free RAF training. He joined and never looked back, spending at least as much time on his flying lessons at Northolt airfield in London as he did on his academic work. The mission of the University Air Squadrons was twofold: to encourage undergraduates to choose the Royal Air Force for their career and to create a reserve of partially-trained officer pilots who could quickly be brought up to operational standards in the event of war.

Geoffrey was becoming a competent pilot but his studies were suffering. By the summer of 1939 he was faced with an ultamatum from his parents – to continue his studies in engineering without the distractions of flying, or leave the University to make his own way in the world. Then Hitler moved on Poland and Geoffrey was called up for flight training at RAF Cranwell when war broke out in Europe.

Before reporting at Cranwell, Geoffrey was required to report to the newly opened Aircrew Receiving Centre at Hastings on the Sussex coast where he and several hundred other University Air Squadron members from Oxford, Cambridge and the London Universities came under the power of non-commissioned officers whose job it was to whip the new men into shape in days rather than months. Another part of the Hastings experience was the visit to the Medical Branch where the typical series of inoculations was administered. 'Just a little prick' was the hilarious remark issued by one of the two medical orderlies before giving each man his shots. Geoffrey admitted to having made the error of watching the man in front receive his injection. His next recollection was of being lifted off the floor by the two orderlies and wondering if he really was cut out to be a pilot, let alone a cool, efficient killer.

Nineteen year-old Officer Cadet Page had a personal hero and inspiration, the famous Royal Flying Corps pilot of the Great War, Captain Albert Ball. Ball had been renowned for penetrating far behind enemy lines alone as he hunted for their aircraft. He had shot down forty-seven German planes before he was himself shot down and killed. Geoffrey knew all about Albert Ball and maintained a life-long interest in the aviator and Victoria Cross winner.

At Cranwell Geoffrey performed with distinction during his advanced flying training, rather too well in fact, for against his wishes he was assigned as a flight instructor on graduating, having been rated 'exceptional'. He recalled being stunned when he read the sheet on the notice board listing where each graduate pilot was being posted. After his name it read: Training Command. He later had the opportunity to discuss his posting with the Chief Flying Instructor at the college who told him:

> You must remember that to be sent to central flying school to be trained as an instructor for future instructors is about the highest compliment the Air Force can pay a pilot. We didn't give you an exceptional assessment just to get you shot down! And another thing to remember, you're not going to like this, but good pilots are often bad fighter pilots. A fighter pilot needs to be very ham-fisted on occasions and you're just not made that way. Sorry!

Soon, however, Norway and then France fell to the Germans, and the Royal Air Force needed fighter pilots desperately. To Geoffrey's delight, in May 1940 the Air Ministry posted him to No. 66 Squadron, a Spitfire outfit stationed at Horsham St Faith, now the Norwich airport. At Horsham he met the Squadron Commander who asked him what aircraft he had trained on. When Geoffrey replied, 'Tutors, Harts and Hinds, Sir', the commander said, 'No, I mean since those types.' Geoffrey said: 'Nothing, sir. Hinds were the last.' And the commander roared: 'Christ! What will they be sending us next? For a start we may as well establish the fact that you're a damned nuisance. I think it might be wiser if I sent you away for a conversion course.' Geoffrey protested and the CO finally agreed to let him have a go in a Spitfire,

> I had been sitting in the cockpit for half an hour memorizing the procedures for take-off, flight and landing. An airman climbed onto the wing behind me to help me with my parachute and harness. Word spread swiftly that an unusual first solo on type was taking place and soon ground and air crews were gathering to watch with morbid interest.
>
> As soon as I was properly strapped in, the squadron commander climbed onto the wing for a final word. 'Don't forget, taxi

out quickly and turn her into the wind – do a quick check and then get off. If you don't, the glycol will boil and so will my blood. Good luck!'

I responded with a nervous smile, closed the tiny door and turned to face the mass of dials, buttons and levers. For a moment panic seized me and the temptation to undo the straps and get out was very great.

The enquiring voice of the airman standing by the starter battery reminded me of the engine starting procedure, and my nervous feeling passed with the need for concentrated action. Throttle about half an inch open – gas on – nine full strokes in the KI-gas hand priming pump for a cold engine – propeller in fine pitch – brakes on – stick held back – press the starter button. I raised my thumb, the waiting airman replied with a similar sign, and I pressed the starter button firmly – the propeller began to rotate . . .

A trickle of sweat ran down my forehead. Suddenly the powerful engine coughed loudly, blew a short stream of purpley-white smoke into a small cloud and roared into life. Remembering that I had little time to spare before the temperature reached the danger mark of 110 degrees, I waved my hands across my face. The waiting airman quickly ducked under the wing and pulled away the restraining chocks. Glancing down, I was alarmed to see that the glycol coolant temperature had risen from 0 to 70 degrees. Releasing the brake, I eased the throttle open and the surge of power carried the aircraft forward rapidly over the grass.

Was everything ready for a quick take-off? I figured I'd better call up Flying Control and get permission to take off immediately. Pushing over the switch on the VHF box, I tried to transmit. 'Idiot!' I said to myself, switch the damn thing on. Another glance at the temperature showed 95 degrees and still a long way to go before turning into the wind. The radio came to life with a whine, and contact was made with a fellow human being. The controller's voice was soothing and for the first time since strapping into the narrow cockpit, I relaxed slightly. But I was still none too happy.

The temperature now read 105 degrees and there were still a few yards to go, plus the final check. Softly I prayed for help. Temperature 107 degrees . . . Now for the drill: R-A-F-T-P-R – the radiator – God alone knows how many times I'd vainly tried to open it beyond its normal point to try to keep the temperature down. A – airscrew in the fine pitch – that's okay. F – flaps. Temperature 109 degrees.

I abandoned the remainder of the cockpit drill and, opening the throttle firmly, started the take-off run. The initial kick from the rapid acceleration drove the worry of the engine temperature away for a while. Working the rudder hard with both feet to keep the sensitive little machine straight, I was too busy for other thoughts. Easing the stick forward, I was startled by the rapidity with which she responded to the elevator controls. The long nose in front of me obscured the rapidly approaching end of the airport, but by looking out at an angle, I was able to get an idea of how far away it was. If the glycol boiled now at this critical stage, the aircraft would be enveloped in a cloud of white smoke that would prevent me from seeing the ground when the inevitable engine seizure and crash landing followed. Looking back into the cockpit again, I saw the hated instrument leering at me – 110 degrees.

Accompanying the feeling of fear was a new sound. The wheels had stopped drumming and a whistling note filled the air. The Spitfire soared gracefully into the air, thankful, as I was, to be away from her earthly bonds.

Inside the cockpit I worked desperately to get the undercarriage raised. The CO had explained to me that because the starboard aircraft leg hung down in front of the radiator when the wheels were lowered, this affects the cooling effect by the airstream. By raising the wheels the air would pass unhindered through the radiator to do its work. But here I fell into trouble again. To raise the wheels, I had to move the selector lever and this was on the right hand of the seat. I then had to pump them up with twenty movements by a long handle, also on the right. To do this while flying the very sensitive aircraft meant using my left hand for the control column, while the right hand struggled with the undercarriage mechanism.

The Spitfire was now about twenty feet up, gaining speed rapidly and skimming over the trees and hedges. I selected 'wheels up' and gave the handle a first stroke. The engine cut out for an instant and the nose plunged earthwards. Being unused to the technique of keeping my left hand absolutely still while the right one moved forward, I had inadvertently pushed the control column forward simultaneously with the first pumping stroke, thus causing the machine to dip suddenly. The negative G placed on the carburettor had caused a temporary fuel stoppage. Some trees flashed by alongside the aircraft as a frightened pilot hauled back on the stick, and soon I was soaring skyward again, pumping frantically after removing my left hand from the control column. At this stage it was obvious that the Spitfire could handle herself better than I could. After this nightmare, the green light finally shone on the instrument panel, indicating that the wheels were in the locked up position, and the engine temperature gauge showed a healthy fall. I took a moment to utter another silent prayer, this time of thanks.

Now I had some breathing space, so I was able to look about and concentrate on the other aspects of flying the airplane. Throttling back the engine and placing the propeller in coarse pitch, I allowed myself the luxury of relaxing slightly and looked down on the beauties of the Norfolk Broads. However, the pleasures of the English countryside didn't last long. Glancing down and behind me, I was horrified to discover that the airport was nowhere in sight. The swiftness of the Spitfire had soon taken me out of sight of the landing ground, and although homing facilities were available over the R/T, pride stopped me from calling the flying control tower for assistance. Instead, a worried young man flew about the sky in circles anxiously peering down for a sign of home. Ten minutes later, relief flooded through me when the unmistakable outlines of Norwich Cathedral appeared out of the summer haze, and from there the airport was easy to find. A minute later the graceful plane was banking round the circuit preparatory to landing.

Again I recalled the cockpit procedure given to me by the squadron commander: R-U-P-F – radiator, undercarriage, pitch and flaps. This time the pumping down of the wheels came quite simply, and the other essential procedures prior to the final touch-down followed. The exhaust crackled delightfully as the engine was throttled back and the plane came in gliding fast over the boundary hedge. In the cockpit, I eased the stick back and the long streamlined nose rose up and cut out the forward view of the landing run. Looking out to the left, I carefully judged the height as the Spitfire floated gracefully a foot or two above the green grass, then losing speed she settled down on the ground to the steady rumble of the wheels. As soon as the machine had come to a halt I raised the flaps and thankfully undid the tight-fitting oxygen mask. The pool of sweat that had collected trickled down my neck. With a newly born confidence, I taxied the machine back towards the waving airman near the hangar. Just as I removed my helmet and undid the confining harness and parachute straps, Dizzy Allen walked up. 'Back in one piece, I see. How'd you get on?' Trying to appear nonchalant, I replied, 'Loved every minute of it. She certainly handles beautifully.' The feeling of achievement obliterated the memory of the fear I'd felt during most of the flight, and now I felt justified in taking a place among my fellow fighter pilots.

*   *   *

Not many days after that first flight in a Spitfire, Geoffrey learned that a mistake had been made when he was posted to No. 66 Squadron. He was meant to go to No. 56 Squadron, a Hurricane outfit stationed near London at North Weald, Essex, near the Epping Forest.

He had barely learned to fly the streamlined, fast and agile all-metal Vickers-Supermarine Spitfire fighter and before he could accrue much flight time in the aeroplane, he was posted to No. 56 Squadron which was operating the slighter slower and less attractive, but still most exciting Hawker Hurricane, 'a lovely great fighter,' as Geoffrey referred to it. At first the idea of flying the Hurricane depressed him, after being introduced to the glamourous Spitfire, but he knew the Hurricane was a good aeroplane and he also liked the idea of becoming a member of No. 56 Squadron, the same unit in which his idol, Captain Albert Ball, had served during the Great War.

On arriving at North Weald, Geoffrey learned that the squadron had been sent up to Digby for a few weeks of gunnery practice and were not due back for three more days. He walked over to the hangars hoping to find a Hurricane he could sit in to familiarize himself with, and there, between two hangars sat two of the Hawker fighters, brand new examples. He compared the machines to the Spitfire, thinking of the latter as having the grace and speed of a greyhound. The Hurricane, on the other hand, while slower, was more solidly built, rather like a bulldog.

*   *   *

Young Pilot Officer Page was asked one day by his flight commander, 'Minny' Ereminski, to collect an aircraft from the hangar area and taxi it over to the B flight dispersal. Ereminski, who looked Nordic but was actually Russian, told Geoffrey that he would be flying as his No. 3 on their first mission of the day. Geoffrey collected the Hurricane, one of the two new aircraft he had noticed the day he had arrived at the station, and prepared for the sortie. After emptying his pockets he put on his yellow Mae West life jacket. At the dispersal hut he stuffed maps into the tops of his black leather flying boots. The maps would come in handy should he be shot down in enemy territory. Out by the Hurricane he realized that it would be at least an hour and a half before he would have an opportunity to urinate. It seemed that every pilot in A and B flights had the same thought at that moment. That taken care of he climbed into the cockpit and was immediately assisted by an airman who passed the parachute and Sutton harness straps over Geoffrey's shoulders. Next came the leather flying helmet with the oxygen mask clipped across his face. He primed the engine and awaited the signal from his flight leader. When it came the engines of the B flight fighters burst into life. The Hurricanes of A flight were already taxiing from their dispersal pens to the upper end of the airfield. The taxiing machines reminded Geoffrey of large brown beetles crawling across the grass in follow-the-leader formation.

The B flight aircraft now arrived at the take-off end of the field. Minny turned his machine into the wind, followed immediately by his No. 2 and No. 3, 'Dopey' Davis, so nicknamed because of his resemblance to the last of the Seven Dwarfs, and Geoffrey, respectively. Minny opened his throttle smoothly, the others followed suit and the three olive-and-earth-camouflaged fighters began to roll. In seconds they were all airborne, climbing rapidly and retracting their undercarriages.

Suddenly life was serious. They crossed the English Channel and Geoffrey's thoughts were of the way civilians in the neighbouring towns and villages perceived him and his fellow young pilots, quite unaware that the extraverted, rowdy behaviour of these pilot officers was merely masking the jagged nerves and fatigue that were making them old before their time. It seemed to him that they were getting almost no sleep and precious little rest. He prayed that would not negatively affect their flying or their actions in combat. As they crossed the Channel, he began to understand the folly of wearing a collar and tie in the fighter. The constant swivelling of one's neck while scanning the sky for enemy aircraft left his neck chafed and sore. No wonder fighter pilots tended to wear scarves when they flew. It was much more than an affectation. Flying the Hurricane with one hand, he groped beneath the encumbrances he wore and managed to remove the offending collar and tie. Sliding the hood back he offered them to the slipstream.

Little of consequence happened during the remainder of his sortie to France. Just beyond Abbeville the flight passed through a dense black smoke cloud from a fire at an oil tank farm and when he emerged from the cloud, the other two Hurricanes had disappeared. He searched for several minutes to no avail and eventually rolled the fighter onto its back and dived towards the calm sea where he headed back for North Weald. A few days after this uneventful flight, Geoffrey saw someone killed. He recalled it as one of those stupid accidents that have destroyed pilots since the earliest days of flying. He was standing beside the dispersal hut when he heard a shout from one of the ground crew. He then noticed three Hurricanes diving low over the field. From the letter codes on the sides of their fuselages he knew they belonged to No. 151, the sister squadron of No. 56 Squadron there at North Weald.

The three planes pulled up steeply, the two outside Hurricanes breaking away from their leader as they climbed. The right-hand aircraft then began to roll as it broke away, but when it was inverted it dropped rapidly and dived into the ground in a great explosion,

Appalled by the scene, the onlookers stood transfixed while a hideous column of fire rose from a field beyond the airfield boundary. Then we all began to run like wild men, crashing through the long grass and weeds. Overhead the remaining two airplanes circled like puzzled birds watching one of their own kind after it had plummeted to earth. Logic penetrated through my brain and I stopped running. Common sense exerted itself and refused to accept any possibility of survival. The deed was done and all the running in the world wouldn't piece together the pulp that had once been a human being.

In the distance the clanging bells of the fire engine and ambulance sounded as they bounced across the airfield. I didn't really know what it was that drove me on towards the crackling funeral pyre. The pilot hadn't been a particular friend of mine, but somehow there was this insatiable desire to look at the bits and pieces.

The ambulance went by, the bell clanging of its own accord as the clapper rocked back and forth with the effect of the uneven ground. Passing through a gateway in the hedge it swayed its way over the field and came to rest near the wreckage. Arriving muddy and breathless, I joined the impotent group that watched the medical officer and orderlies, assisted by the firemen as they kicked the smoking pieces of metal aside in search of ghastly remains.

After I'd stood there for a while I was aware of two definite reactions to the scene before me. The first was one of slight nausea from the combined smell of charred wreckage and burnt flesh. The other sensation was more powerful than that of a queasy stomach. I realized with surprise that the death of this recent companion didn't disturb me very much. It was as if a wave of shock radiated out from the mangled debris, but just as it approached, the wave passed by on either side leaving the senses high and dry on a little island, erected by nature to protect the occupant from the drowning effect of the horror of the event.

In the bar we practiced the noble art of medicine. We knew the sickness and the remedy. Ailment – death of a close friend or companion; remedy – wash the brain wound well with alcohol until the infected area becomes numb to the touch. Continue the treatment until the wound closes. A scar will remain, but this will not show after a while. The two doctors carried out the treatment until the probing shadowy fingers of twilight reached along the dewy grass, and caressed the jagged edges of the manmade fissure in the gentle English field.

* * *

To say that the pilots of No. 56 Squadron were carrying an exceptionally high fatigue factor during the Battle of Britain period was to understate the fact. In one bitterly cold dawn the six pilots of B flight walked wearily among their aircraft in a desperate attempt to warm up. The damp grass and the cold, drafty hut floor offered no possibility of rest for their tired bodies. But gradually, the rising sun promised and slowly began to deliver the day's first rays of warmth.

Minny Ereminski had been killed in action and replaced by Flight Lieutenant E.J. 'Jumbo' Gracie, a portly fellow whose haemorrhoids occasionally left him in a foul mood. They were his main topic of conversation on the ground. In the air it was a different matter. Gracie and the other B flight pilots responded instantly to the crack of the Verey flare pistol, covering the short distance to their waiting Hurricanes. Someone at one of the dispersal hut windows yelled, 'Scramble B flight, Angels ten', and in less than two minutes they were off with Jumbo in the lead. Roaring off the North Weald grass, Geoffrey and Barry Sutton followed him closely. Getting himself and his fighter ready for action, Geoffrey switched on the gunsight, camera gun and twisted the brass firing button on the spade grip of the control column to 'fire'.

If he needed awakening at that early hour, the excited voice of the ground controller barked over the R/T: 'Ninety bandits approaching from Calais. Yorker Blue Leader. Twenty plus at about Angels six, remainder Angels twelve, over.' Jumbo acknowledged the message and immediately called for the two sections of B flight to go into line astern formations behind their respective leaders. Geoffrey's main thought then was 'Six of us against ninety, hardly fair odds for someone going into his first fight. Why the devil don't they send up another squadron to give us a helping hand?'

'Bandits eleven o'clock above and below . . . Yorker Green One, you take the gaggle below and we'll look after the lot up top . . . Blue Leader over' yelled Jumbo. Almost at the same moment Geoffrey spotted the formation of twenty Heinkel He 111 bombers and their escort of about thirty Me 110 twin-engine fighters. Seconds later he saw the higher escort of forty Bf 109s. Geoffrey and the other two Hurricane pilots of his flight had now climbed above the flight level of the Me 110s but were still lower than the Bf 109s. Oddly, he thought, the Me 110s were forming into a defensive circle to protect themselves from the swiftly approaching enemy fighters. As he closed on the circle, Geoffrey selected two Me 110s and fired at them. He was firing and then diving through the centre of the circle. As he passed through it he was being fired on by the rear gunners of several of the Me 110s and found himself in a cone of tracers. Once safely through the circle he climbed again to make another attack, head-on this time from the opposite direction of the Me 110s flight.

For the next few moments the battle was chaotic with the top-cover Bf 109s dropping down to take on the RAF fighters. Geoffrey managed what he believed to be good shots at a few of the Bf 109s, but with no apparent strikes. Many years later, with the publication of *The Luftwaffe War Diaries*, by Cajus Bekker, he learned that he had indeed been successful in the encounter. An extract from the book describes the combat between Geoffrey and the German pilot whose name was Dau:

> Dau, after shooting down a Spitfire, had seen a Hurricane turn in towards him. It then came straight at him, head-on and at the same height. Neither of them budged an inch, both fired their guns at the same instant, then missed a collision by a hair's breath. But while the German's fire was too low, that of the British pilot, 'A.G. Page of 56 Squadron' connected. Dau felt his aircraft shaken by violent thuds. It had been hit in the engine and rudder and he saw a piece of one wing come off. At once his engine started to seize up emitting a white plume of steaming glycol. 'The coolant temperature rose quickly to 120 degrees,' he reported. 'The whole cockpit stank of burnt insulation. But I managed to stretch my glide to the coast, then made a belly landing close to Boulogne. As I jumped out, the machine was on fire and within seconds ammunition and fuel went up with a bang.'

* * *

A few days later Geoffrey Page was to achieve his first recorded aerial victory. In their almost constant state of physical exhaustion the pilots of B flight faced two enemies, the Germans and the dispersal hut telephone. 'Telephonitis' is what he called it. When that phone rang, even if they were asleep in the hut, they heard it and tensed until the click of the receiver being replaced followed. If no summons to action resulted from the call, they could enjoy perhaps another thirty minutes of sleep, if they were lucky. Often they were not. On this particular day the sleep-deprived men of B flight lurched to their feet when the shrill cry 'scramble!' filled the hut. There was no time for tea.

The new CO was Squadron Leader Manton. He ignored the long, unmilitary hair and the rumpled uniforms of the pilots gathered around him and quickly briefed them for the patrol they were about to fly. The weather for most of that spring and summer had been gloriously warm and sunny with little rainfall or storm cloud to interfere with operations. Today, however, there was heavy cloud cover and its base was at 10,000 feet over the south coast. The twelve Hurricanes cruised back and forth along the coastline between Dover and Dungeness just under the cloud base. They sighted the final action of a sea battle between motor torpedo boats of the Royal Navy and enemy 'E' boats near the French coast and then the R/T crackled with 'Forty bandits approaching from the south – they are most likely after our friends down below.' Two Royal Navy destroyers were racing out from Dover to assist the withdrawing MTBs.

As the Hurricanes neared the enemy formations, the British pilots noted that a dozen Ju 87 Stuka dive-bombers were in the lead of a large formation of Bf 109s. Clearly, the Stukas were about to attack the destroyers. Manton ordered A flight to take on the fighters and B flight the Stukas. Geoffrey and the other five pilots of B flight dived on the Stukas, reaching them just as they were beginning their own dives on the warships. With great courage and restraint, the sailors aboard the destroyers withheld their anti-aircraft fire to let the Hurricane pilots deal with the German dive-bombers.

Having to cope with the pursuing British fighters, all but one of the Stuka pilots missed their targets. The lead Stuka scored a direct hit on one of the ships. Now the Stukas had resumed level flight down almost at sea level and were struggling to reach their French base. Moved by his anger at the sight of the stricken destroyer, Geoffrey dived on the ragged flock of Stukas and chose one as his target. He closed to within 100 yards as the machine-gun fire of the enemy plane's rear gunner sent orange tracer rounds flashing past him. The old admonition, 'short bursts and make them count', was forgotten as he pressed and held the gun button on the control column until the Stuka was a fireball filling his windscreen.

The achievement had left Geoffrey dazed and the image of that furiously burning enemy plane kept returning as he headed back to his own base. Having destroyed that aircraft, and almost certainly its two-man crew, had left him both horrified and fascinated and he reeled at the impersonality of this air fighting game. He was a newly-blooded fighter pilot and he couldn't help wondering if he might also be a murderer hiding behind the shield of official approval. One thing was becoming clear to him – in this game, which they sometimes referred to as 'Juggling with Jesus', only death could win, but it was fun while it lasted.

*   *   *

A small registered package arrived for Geoffrey one day in July. It contained a handsome silver hip flask, a present from his mother. He filled it with Three Star brandy in the Mess bar that night and declared to the others of his flight that the flask was to be used for emergencies only.

On 12 August the sky was cloudless, a clear, blue day like nearly all in the past few weeks. After an early lunch, the squadron was ordered to fly down to Rochford and relieve another squadron following its morning shift at the forward airfield. At Rochford, No. 56 Squadron occupied the spartan facilities of the old Southend Flying Club, which amounted to a large bell tent and a field telephone. There were no chairs, tables, camp beds or any other items of furniture.

The twelve Hurricanes landed and were immediately refuelled. Rochford was a satellite of the North Weald sector station. Its only features were a low line of hangars and other structures at the opposite end of the field from where the fighters of No. 56 Squadron were parked, and a distant grouping of barrage balloons protecting the town of Southend. As the pilots sat or lay around on the grass near the bell tent, the only sounds that afternoon were the thump-thump of the petrol bowsers fuelling the aircraft and the bird songs. A tea wagon arrived and delivered heavy Thermos flasks of the beverage along with hunks of buttered bread and a jar of jam. In the midst of the sprawled airmen sat the black field telephone. It rang and was quickly answered by Jumbo Gracie who then roared, 'Scramble ... seventy plus apporaching Manston ... angels one-five.'

Page was up, on his feet and covering the fifty yards to his waiting Hurricane. He had had the name 'Little Willie' painted on the fuselage just under the left rim of the cockpit. He put his right foot into the extended stirrup step, his left foot onto the wing and was lowering himself into the cockpit as a rigger helped him with the parachute and Sutton harness straps. Then, in rapid succession, leather flying helmet on with oxygen mask clipped in place, oxygen on, engine primed, switches on, thumbs up, press the starter button and his Rolls-Royce Merlin engine comes to life just as the engines of the other Hurricanes of 56 Squadron fire up along the airfield perimeter. The prop wash flattens the grass behind them. Jumbo starts to taxi out with the other fighters in trail. He is to lead the squadron today as Manton has been given a one-day respite. Geoffrey will fly on Gracie's right with Bob Constable-Maxwell on the leader's left. In seconds the squadron is climbing swiftly from the Rochford grass.

It was a classic scramble. The voice of Wing Commander John Cherry, the North Weald controller, sounded over the R/T: 'Hullo, Yorker Blue Leader, Lumba calling. Seventy-plus bandits approaching Charlie Three, angels one-five.'

The day was hot and so were the pilots of 56 Squadron. Geoffrey slid the cockpit hood back during the climb. The wind quickly cooled the cockpit, drying the sweat of his brow. They climbed through 10,000 feet while crossing Kent to intercept the German raiders heading for Manston and Margate. Passing through 11,000 feet Geoffrey closed the hood. The Hurricanes were in relatively tight Vic formations of three planes each, but were spread a bit to allow the pilots constantly to scan the sky for the enemy aircraft without having to concentrate on maintaining precise formation. It was called battle formation.

Geoffrey had exceptional eyesight and was among the first to spot the dark cluster of specks several thousand feet above the Hurricanes. As the gap closed he realized that the enemy formation was made up of about thirty Dornier Do 215 bombers escorted by about forty Bf 109s. Jumbo: 'Echelon starboard – go!' Before engaging in air combat it was Geoffrey's habit to pull the sliding hood back and lock it in position to facilitate a quick exit from Little Willie, should that be necessary.

As they approached it, the German formation began a turn to the north out over the sea. The much faster escort of Bf 109s weaved above their bombers, ready to drop on British fighters which were now turning northwards in pursuit of the Germans. Like the British planes, the Dornier bombers were flying in echelon starboard as the Hurricanes arrived at the same flight level. Geoffrey recalled:

> To my surprise I saw that Jumbo was intending to attack the leading aircraft in the bomber formation. This necessitated flying past the aircraft behind the leader's, and also meant running the gauntlet of their rear gunner's fire.
>
> Slowly we overhauled the heavy *Luftwaffe* machines, and I had the impression of an express train overtaking a slower one. There was time to inspect each other before passing on to the next one up the line. Instinctively I glanced above and behind, but for some strange reason the 109s were still sitting aloft. The sweeping movement of my trained eyes showed that Bob no longer stood between me and the enemy. Momentarily reassured that nothing lethal was sitting behind my aircraft, I settled down to the task of firing at one of the leading machines although it was still about 600 yards ahead.
>
> Then the enemy rear gunners started firing ...
>
> Analyzing it later I realized that the fire power of the whole group was obviously controlled by radio instructions from a gunnery officer in one of the bombers.
>
> One moment the sky between me and the thirty Dornier 215s was clear; the next it was criss-crossed with streams of white tracer from cannon shells converging on our Hurricanes.
>
> Jumbo's machine peeled away from the attack. The distance between the German leaders and my solitary Hurricane was down

to 300 yards. Strikes from my Brownings began to flash around the port engine of one of the Dorniers.

The mass of fire from the bomber formation closed in as I fired desperately in a race to destroy before being destroyed.

The first bang came as a shock. For an instant I couldn't believe I'd been hit. Two more bangs followed in quick succession, and as if by magic a gaping hole suddenly appeared in my starboard wing.

Surprise quickly changed to fear, and as the instinct of self-preservation began to take over, the gas tank behind the engine blew up, and my cockpit became an inferno. Fear became blind terror, then agonized horror as the bare skin of my hands gripping the throttle and control column shrivelled up like burnt parchment under the intensity of the blast furnace temperature. Screaming at the top of my voice, I threw my head back to keep it away from the searing flames. Instinctively the tortured right hand groped for the release pin securing the restraining Sutton harness.

Dear God, save me ... save me, dear God ... I cried imploringly. Then, as suddenly as terror had overtaken me, it vanished with the knowledge that death was no longer to be feared. My fingers kept up their blind and bloody mechanical groping. Some large mechanical dark object disappeared between my legs and cool, relieving fresh air suddenly flowed across my burning face. I tumbled: sky, sea, sky, over and over as a clearing brain issued instructions to outflung limbs. 'Pull the ripcord – right hand to the ripcord.' Watering eyes focused on an arm flung out in space with some strange meaty object attached to its end.

More tumbling – more sky and sea and sky, but with a blue clad arm forming a focal point in the background. 'Pull the ripcord, hand,' the brain again commanded. Slowly but obediently the elbow bent and the hand came across the body to rest on the chromium ring but bounced away quickly with the agony of contact.

More tumbling but at a slower rate now. The weight of the head was beginning to tell.

Realizing that pain or no pain, the ripcord had to be pulled, the brain overcame the reaction of the raw nerve endings and forced the mutilated fingers to grasp the ring and pull firmly. It acted immediately. With a jerk the silken canopy billowed out in the clear summer sky.

Quickly I looked up to see if the dreaded flames had done their work, and it was with relief that I saw the shining material was unburned. Another fear rapidly followed. I heard the murmur of fading engines and firing guns, but it was the sun glinting on two pairs of wings that struck a chill through my heart. Stories of pilots being machine-gunned as they parachuted down came flashing through my mind, and again I prayed for salvation. The two fighters straightened out and revealed themselves to be Hurricanes before turning away to continue the chase.

It was then that I noticed the smell. The odor of my burnt flesh was so loathsome that I wanted to vomit. But there was too much to attend to, even for that small luxury. Self-preservation was my first concern, and my chance for it looked slim. The coastline at Margate was just discernible six to ten miles away. Ten thousand feet below me lay the deserted sea. Not a ship or a seagull crossed its blank, grey surface.

Still looking down I began to laugh. The force of the exploding gas tank had blown every vestige of clothing off from my thighs downwards, including one shoe. Carefully I eased off the remaining shoe with the toe of the other foot and watched the tumbling footwear in the hope of seeing it strike the water far beneath. Now came the bad time.

The shock of my violent injuries was starting to take hold, and this combined with the cold air at the high altitude brought on a shivering attack that was quite uncontrollable. With that the parachute began to sway, setting up a violent oscillating movement with my teeth-chattering torso acting as a human pendulum. Besides its swinging movement it began a gentle turn and shortly afterwards the friendly shoreline disappeared behind my back. This brought with it an *idée fix* that if survival was to be achieved, then the coast must be kept in sight. A combination of agonized curses and bleeding hands pulling on the shrouds finally brought about the desired effect, and I settled back to the pleasures of closing eyes and burnt flesh.

Looking down again I was surprised to find that the water had come up to meet me very rapidly since last I had taken stock of the situation. This called for some fairly swift action if the parachute was to be discarded a second or two before entering the water. The procedure itself was quite simple. Lying over my stomach was a small metal release box which clasped the four ends of the parachute harness after they had passsed down over the shoulders and up from the groin. On this box was a circular metal disc which had to be turned through 90 degrees, banged, and presto! The occupant was released from the 'chute. All of this was exremely simple except in the case of fingers which refused to turn the little disc.

The struggle was still in progress when I plunged feet first into the water. Despite the beauties of the summer and the wealth of warm days that had occurred, the sea felt icy cold to my badly shocked body. Kicking madly, I came to the surface to find my arms entangled with the multiple shrouds holding me in an octopus-like grip. The battle with the metal disc still had to be won, or else the water-logged parachute would eventually drag me down to a watery grave. Spluttering with mouthfuls of salt water I struggled grimly with the vital release mechanism. Pieces of flesh flaked off and blood poured from the raw tissues.

Desperation, egged on by near panic, forced the decision, and with a sob of relief I found that the disc had surrendered the battle.

Kicking away blindly at the tentacles that still entwined arms and legs, I fought free and swam fiercely away from the nightmare surroundings of the parachute. Wild fear died away and the simple rules of procedure for continued existence exerted themselves again. 'Get rid of the 'chute, and then inflate your Mae West,' said the book of rules, 'and float about until rescued.'

That's all very well, I thought, but unless I get near to the coast under my own steam, there's not much chance of being picked up. With that I trod water and extricated the long rubber tube with which to blow up the jacket. Unscrewing the valves between my teeth, I searched my panting lungs for extra air. The only result after several minutes of exertion was a feeling of dizziness and a string of bubbles from the bottom of the jacket. The fire had burnt a large hole through the rubber bladder.

Dismay was soon replaced by fatalism. There was the distant shore, unseen but positioned by reference to the sun, and only one method of getting there, so it appeared. Turning on my stomach I set out at a measured stroke. Ten minutes of acute misery passed by as the salt dried about my face injuries and the contracting strap of the flying helmet cut into the raw surface of my chin. Buckle and leather had welded into one solid mass, preventing removal of the headgear.

Dumb despair then suddenly gave way to shining hope. The brandy flask, of course. This was it – the emergency for which it was kept. But the problem of undoing the tunic remained, not to mention that the tight-fitting Mae West covered the pocket as another formidable barrier. Hope and joy were running too high to be deterred by such mundane problems, and so turning with my face to the sky I set about the task of getting slightly tipsy on neat brandy. Inch by inch my ultra-sensitive fingers worked their way under the Mae West towards the breast pocket. Every movement brought with it indescribable agony, but the goal was too great to allow for weakness. At last the restraining copper button was reached – a deep breath to cope with the pain – and it was undone. Automatically my legs kept up their propulsive efforts while my hand had a rest from its labours. Then gingerly the flask was eased out of its home and brought to the surface of the water. Pain became conqueror for a while and the flask was transferred to a position between my wrists. Placing the screw stopper between my teeth, I undid it with a series of head-twists and finally the great moment arrived – the life-warming liquid was waiting to be drunk. Raising it to my mouth, I pursed my lips to drink. The flask slipped from between wet wrists and disappeared from sight. Genuine tears of rage followed this newest form of torture, which in turn gave place to a furious determination to swim to safety.

After the first few angry strokes despair returned in full force ably assisted by growing fatigue, cold and pain. Time went by unregistered. Was it minutes, hours or days since my flaming Hurricane disappeared between my legs? How could I steer towards the shore if I couldn't see the sun? How could I see the sun if that rising pall of smoke obscured it from sight?

That rising pall of smoke … that rising pall of smoke. No, it couldn't be. I yelled. I splashed the water with my arms and legs until the pain brought me to a sobbing halt. Yes, the smoke was coming from a funnel – but supposing it passed without seeing me? Agony of mind was greater than agony of body and the shouting and splashing recommenced. Looking again, almost expecting that smoke and funnel had been an hallucination, I gave a fervent gasp of thanks to see that whatever ship it was, it had hove to.

All of the problems were fast disappearing and only one remained. It was one of keeping afloat for just another minute or two before all energy failed. Then I heard it – the unmistakable chug-chug of a small motor-boat growing steadily louder. Soon it came into sight with a small bow wave pouring away to each side. In it sat two men in the strange garb peculiar to sailors of the British Merchant Service. The high revving note of the engine throttled back. Slowly the boat circled without attempting to pick me up. A rough voice carried over the intervening water. 'What are you? A Jerry or one of ours?'

My weak reply was gagged by a mouthful of water. The other man tried as the boat came full circle for the second time. 'Are you a Jerry, mate?'

Anger flooded through me. Anger, not at these sailors who had every reason to let a German pilot drown, but anger at the steady chain of events since the explosion that had reduced my tortured mind and body to its present state of near-collapse. And anger brought with it temporary energy. 'You stupid pair of fucking bastards, pull me out!'

The boat altered course and drew alongside. Strong arms leaned down and dragged my limp body over the side and into the bottom of the boat. 'The minute you swore, mate,' one of them explained, 'We knew you was an RAF officer.'

The sodden dripping bundle was deposited on a wooden seat athwart ships. A voice mumbled from an almost lifeless body as the charred helmet was removed. One of the sailors leaned down to catch the words. 'What did you say, chum?'

The mumble was more distinct the second time. 'Take me to the side. I want to be sick.'

The other man answered in a friendly voice. 'You do it in the bottom of the boat, and we'll clean it up afterwards.'

But habit died hard and pride wouldn't permit it, so keeping my head down between my knees, I was able to control the sensation of nausea. Allowing me a moment or two to feel better, the first sailor produced a large clasp knife. 'Better get this wet stuff off you, mate. You don't want to catch your death of cold.'

The absurdity of death from a chill struck me as funny and I chuckled for the first time in a long while. To prove the sailor's point the teeth chattering recommenced. Without further ado the man with the knife set to work and deftly removed pieces of life jacket and tunic with the skill of a surgeon. Then my naked body was wrapped up in a blanket produced from the seat locker.

One of them went forward to the engine and seconds later the little boat was churning her way back to the mother ship. The other sailor sat down beside me in silence, anxious to help but not knowing what to do next. I sensed the kindness of his attitude and felt that it was up to me somehow to offer him a lead. The feeling of sickness was still there from the revolting smell of burnt flesh, but I managed to gulp out 'Been a lovely ... summer, hasn't it?'

The man nodded. 'Aye.'

No further efforts at conversation were necessary as by now the tall sides of the old tramp steamer were looming above the little boat as they lined the rail looking down at me. A voice hailed us. 'What you got there, Bill? A Jerry?'

The man with the knife cupped his hands and called back, 'No, one of our boys.'

Swiftly a gangway was lowered and two pairs of strong arms formed a hand chair and carried me to the deck aloft. The grizzled captain came forward to greet me with outstretched hand. Clasp knife spoke quietly. 'He can't, Skipper. Both hands badly burned.'

'Bad luck, lad,' the captain said. 'But never mind, we'll soon have you fixed up.' To the sailors he said, 'Bring him into the galley.'

They carried me down the gently heaving deck and through a door into the galley. The warmth of the room struck me immediately and I asked to be allowed to stand. Reluctantly they deposited me on my feet and a brew of hot ship's tea was held to my lips. New life began to course through my frozen body as the fluid and the warmth of the room took effect. The captain, who had disappeared, came back with a metal first aid kit. 'We'll have you fixed up in a jiffy, and the Margate lifeboat's on its way out here to take you ashore. Right, off with the blanket.' Naked and unashamed I stood there while the old man cast a swift look over my body. 'You got shot in the leg as well.' The skipper shook his head sadly. Surprised, I looked down and for the first time became aware of the bleeding wound in my left calf.

Quickly the captain cut up large squares of pink lint, and made fingerless gloves for my injured hands. Another strip of lint was tied across the raw forehead. 'That's the best I can do, I'm afraid,' the old man said.

My thanks were cut short by a hail from the deck. 'Lifeboat alongside, Skipper.'

With the blanket back around my shoulders they led me out through the door in time to meet the coxswain of the lifeboat. Two of his crew followed carrying a stretcher. A quick exchange of information took place between the two captains, then the coxswain bade me lie down on the stretcher. Feeling rather much the admired hero, I refused at first, but the common sense of the two skippers prevailed, and I lay down. The instant my head touched the canvas I knew how exhausted I really was.

Warm blankets were tucked about me and soft coverings placed round my hands. A sensation of swaying followed by tilting, the lapping sound of water, and then the gentle lowering of the stretcher into the centre of the long boat.

'Smoke, chum?' My head nodded weakly. 'Afraid it's only a Woodbine.'

Lying on my back looking up at the blue sky through swollen watery eyes, I became aware of the cigarette placed between my lips. Deeply inhaling the smoke, a sense of complete relaxation prevailed and for the first time my tired muscles relaxed.

However, the sensation of well-being passed almost as quickly as it had arrived. The warmth of the galley and the steaming tea had brought back life and feeling, and feeling brought with it the intense pain of burnt hands.

Roughly the crew attempted to console me as whimpers of suffering escaped through my lips. It was obvious that their inability to ease the suffering was causing them acute mental discomfort.

Nature offered her own relief-valve, and for a few minutes I escaped into unconsciousness.

When I came round again the boat was only half a mile away from the quayside and I insisted on being propped up to watch our arrival. Apart from a group of about a dozen people, the town had an air of desertion about it that struck me immediately. Behind the group on the quayside stood a white ambulance. On coming alongside the stone steps that led from the water's edge to the promenade, the same query was called down to the boat. 'Is it a Jerry?'

Dimly I wondered what would have been my chances of survival had I been an officer of the *Luftwaffe*. British people were kind-hearted, but there was a snapping point after they had been goaded too far.

The reception committee was waiting at the top of the steps. The blurred image of a figure stooped over the stretcher which made polite sounds about being the Mayor, and that he would be only too delighted to help in any way. The figure was replaced by two uniformed representatives of the lay offering more practical suggestions of help. 'Would I like my unit and next of kin informed, and where were they to be found?'

Dim recollections of an ambulance ride, the outside of the general hospital, followed by a long journey down endless corridors on a trolley, a heave, and I was lying on top of a comfortable bed in a small private room. Soon blessed relief from pain was injected into my arm. The matron bustled in and displayed her singular charm. Pride at being one of the nation's heroes rose in my breast, but an instant later the 'hero' was mortified to hear that he was to receive an enema before being wheeled into the operating room. Such was the price of glory.

In spite of my protestations about keeping singularly good health, the procedure was insisted upon. It was pointed out to me that burns ran a grave danger of septicemia and that the blood must be kept cleansed.

After the indignity had been completed by a singularly pretty nurse – just to make matters worse – I was trundled away to the operating room on a trolley. The surgeon, anaesthetist and a gowned nurse comprised the skeleton staff for surgical cases. All three helped to lift me onto the table beneath the huge over-hanging light.

The nurse and surgeon disappeared to scrub-up and the anaesthetist prepared his hypodermic syringe.

A sudden desire to know the extent of my facial injuries absorbed me and I pleaded for a glance in a mirror. Sensibly the second doctor refused the request and changed the subject to safer topics.

The masked and gloved surgeon returned with his assistant. Neatly the anaesthetist tied a rubber cord round my bicep and searched the hollow of the elbow joint for a suitable vein. Not wishing to see the needle enter the skin, I looked away and up-wards, catching sight of myself in the reflector mirrors of the over-hanging light. My last conscious memory was of seeing the hideous mass of swollen, burnt flesh that had once been a face.

The Battle of Britain had ended for me, but another long battle was beginning.

The nursing sister arrvived with her kidney dish containing another hypodermic and blessed escape. She lifted his head to give him a drink of lemonade and said: 'I'm sorry to trouble you Pilot Officer Page, but I'm afraid I've got to get one or two particulars from you. I should like to know the address of your next of kin, and your religion.' He replied: 'I'm going to disappoint you I'm afraid, Sister. I'm going to live.'

With consciousness there was only pain. With the morphia there was blissful unconsciousness. But often when Geoffrey slept the nightmare of the burning Hurricane cockpit returned. Between the conscious pain and the nightmares he dozed fitfully until the air raids began with the violent discharge of the anti-aircraft gun positioned much too close to his window. The raids continued for three days and finally, when he could no longer tolerate the great pain, the noise of the gun and the danger of the bombs falling nearby, he implored the matron to have him moved to a quieter place. She made the arrangements and the next day he endured a five-hour ride to the Royal Masonic Hospital in Hammersmith, a facility which had been recently taken over for use by the Royal Air Force.

The familiar pattern of drug-induced sleep with its attendant night-mares of being in the burning aircraft, and the pain and misery of awakeness gradually gave way to a more normal routine. The pain was still there, though less severe, but slowly Geoffrey began to return to the land of the living. His primary nurse noticed the change immediately and remarked to him, 'You've been a sick boy. Hungry?' 'I could eat a horse', he replied. She laughed and said, 'It's highly likely your wish will be granted.'

When their operational commitments permitted, Jumbo, Barry Sutton and Bob Constable-Maxwell came to visit and told Geoffrey of the pilots of No. 56 Squadron who had been killed since he had been shot down. The news depressed him, but later the appearance of one of the prettiest girls he had ever seen brightened his day considerably. She was a VAD Red Cross nurse and she personified the angel of mercy until he saw the expression of horror and disgust she registered at the sight of his ghastly burns. The girl was assisting Geoffrey's regular nurse in changing his dressings and suddenly she became sickened by the experience and rushed from the room. This upset Geoffrey and he asked his nurse for a mirror. He had not yet been allowed to look at the damage that had been done to his face and now was determined to see it. The nurse politely refused his request which then became a demand. She stood her ground firmly, 'You will be allowed to look in a mirror, Pilot Officer Page, when I see fit to permit it and not before.'

As soon as the nurse had left his room, Geoffrey began an agonizing effort to free himself from the tightly restraining bedding so he could cross to the mirror over the washbasin. With only the use of his elbows, it took him five minutes of exhausting work to throw off the sheet and blanket. Dizzyness seemed about to overwhelm him as he slid to the cold floor and he broke out in an icy sweat as he struggled across the short distance to the washbasin. There he saw reflected in the mirror the grotesquely burnt face swollen far beyond normal size. The shocking image, coupled with the extreme effort to see it, caused him to faint just as the nurse re-entered his room.

* * *

September 1940 – as the Battle of Britain was winding down, the blitz bombing of London was starting and Geoffrey learned of a plan to evacuate the RAF pilot-patients from the hospital to another one in the country. A few days later the matron came by to say that he had a visitor, a Mr Archibald McIndoe, the consultant plastic surgeon to the Royal Air Force. The man entered his room and Geoffrey was reminded of Harold Lloyd, the movie comedian. McIndoe pulled a chair next to the bed and sat down. He pulled a sheet of paper and a pencil from his briefcase and gently asked a few questions.

'Hurricane or Spitfire?'

'Hurricane.'

'Header tank?'

Geoffrey laughed. 'Yes. The wing tanks in my machine were self-sealing, but some bright type forgot to treat the tank in front of the pilot.'

'Just can't trust anyone, can you?'

McIndoe then asked if Geoffrey had been wearing goggles and gloves, how long he was in the water, and how soon afterwards was the tannic acid treatment given. The visit was brief. 'Good-bye, young fellow. See you again.' Little did Geoffrey realize how often he would be seeing McIndoe.

The German bombing raids on London worsened in October and the hospital authorities ordered that the patients be evacuated to the RAF Hospital at Halton, a pre-war establishment famous for its department devoted to the curing of airmen with unpleasant social diseases. At Halton, Geoffrey was under the care of Wing Commander Stanford Cade, a soft-spoken Polish surgeon whose manner and handling of Geoffrey's painfully sensitive hands was patient and compassionate. He carefully snipped at the tannic acid-covered leathery skin, exposing the raw flesh beneath and gave instructions for the continuing treatment with saline dressings. Geoffrey's hands throbbed with nearly constant pain and, finally, the doctor decided to remove surgically the tannic covering. When Geoffrey awoke after the operation, his two pink, unbandaged hands were so sensitive that the slightest draught across the ward brought sharp pain. It reminded him of the way an indrawn breath hurts on the exposed nerve of an aching tooth.

Each day his strength and stamina increased, but the condition of his hands continued to deteriorate. The tendons were contracting, bending the fingers downwards until the tips were touching the palms. As they healed the hands formed a tough, leathery scar tissue and the surgeon told Geoffrey that a series of skin grafting operations would be needed unless treatment by molten wax baths improved the condition. The hot wax treatment was started that afternoon.

Every day the dreaded hot wax bath, followed by electric shock therapy, brought renewed agony, but it all failed to produce the results Doctor Cade had hoped for. The thickening skin of Geoffrey's poor, tortured hands became like heavy leather and the surgeon arranged for the patient to come under the care of Archibald McIndoe at the Queen Victoria Cottage Hospital, near East Grinstead.

On arriving at the neat, one-story facility that also served as the hospital for the West Sussex town, Geoffrey was greeted by Sister Hall who said that Mr McIndoe would be doing his rounds that evening. She showed him to his bed and had a nurse help him to unpack. The ward was divided into three small sections divided by glass partitions. A few of the other burn patients introduced themselves and another, a tall man in a dressing gown with his head thrown right back so that he seemed to be looking along the line of his nose, greeted Geoffrey with 'Ah, another bloody cripple! Welcome to the home for the aged and infirm!' Two great orange circles surrounded the horizontal slits of his eyes. His hands were wrapped in large lint covers and a thin wisp of smoke rose from a long cigarette holder between his teeth. This was Geoffrey's introduction to Richard Hillary, who, during his stay at the cottage hospital wrote one of the finest books of the Second World War, *The Last Enemy*.

* * *

Archie McIndoe slowly examined Geoffrey's hands and said that he would have to operate on them '... many times, I'm afraid. But you'll be all right in the end.' The day of McIndoe's first operation on Geoffrey brought the usual unpleasant preparations for the patient, and his first meeting with one of the great characters of Geoffrey's wartime experience. 'I'm John Hunter, better known as the Gasworks ... which reminds me, have you heard the story about the girl called Virginia ...?' The other members of the team in the operating room giggled and Hunter began the yarn as he readied his syringes, vials and other tools of the anaesthetist's work. Then he stretched and tied a piece of flexible tubing around his patient's left bicep to raise a vein. 'Just a little prick, if you'll pardon the expression,' said Hunter cheerily. He was also known as the Knock-Out King. He was a big, ebullient bear of a man with a reputation for being able to drink anyone under the table and it is said that McIndoe had arrangements with the publicans of East Grinstead to give Hunter a glass of tonic water when he asked for gin.

The days and weeks passed with Geoffrey enduring surgery after surgery and in the periods of unmedicated consciousness there was throbbing agony, worse than any that had gone before. All the rest of the time he spent under the spell of the morphia. In the operations he received grafts of skin taken from the inside of his thigh to replace the thick, scaly keloid scars that McIndoe removed from Geoffrey's knuckles to his wrists.

'Get the hand into the bath, Sister. Let it soak for half an hour, then the usual dressings – plenty of sulphanylamide powder. The rest of the stitches can come out tomorrow' instructed McIndoe.

... a message came that McIndoe was sending one of the resident Air Force surgeons to remove the stitches. I felt like a small child that is deprived of its mother's protective nearness. I did not wish to have my dressings done by this strange doctor, and in my mind began to think up excuses to cause a postponement. While my brain was frantically searching for a reason, Sister Hall re-appeared accompanied by the surgeon. Feebly I began to suggest that perhaps the following day would be more propitious, but my pleas fell on deaf ears. Soon the bandages were peeled away, leaving the greasy tulle-grass strips lying next to the sensitive flesh.

Deftly these were lifted off with forceps, their fatty nature not causing them to stick to the raw exposed areas.

Fascinated despite myself, I followed the quick, trained movements of the surgeon's hands. The pattern remained the same – surgical tweezers gripped the suture firmly and raised and raised it sufficiently for the next action; a quiet but distinct snip as the stitch scissors cut through the black gut and the tweezers coming to grips again to lift clear the neatly tied little bows.

Life altered at the seventh stitch.

A nurse at the far end of the ward dropped a luncheon tray as the scream rang out. Heads raised themselves off pillows in curiosity. The RAF doctor looked up from his task in surprise at his ashen-faced patient.

'Sorry, did I hurt you?'

It was a moment before my quivering lips could form an answer. 'The stit ... stitch must be through ... through a nerve. Just like a red hot needle being pushed up my hand and arm.'

Again the surgeon bent to his task, speaking as he poised his instrument for another attack. 'Take a grip of yourself and it'll be over in a second.'

Again the cry rang out, this time sounding like a medieval victim being stretched on the rack. The surgeon looked up impatiently, anger furrowing his brow.

'You've got to stand a little pain you know!'

The words came hissing from between my bloodless lips. 'You swine ... you bloody filthy butchering swine. Get away from me and stay away.'

The Sister's voice rose above the heavy racking sobs that followed. 'I think perhaps he's had enough for one day, sir.'

Without a word the irate uniformed doctor departed.

With my face buried in the pillow, I began to kindle up hatred for the first time in my life. I began by hating the surgeon for causing me the physical suffering, and this in turn extended to everyone about me. Then, as my mind and body calmed down, the hatred went back to original causes and the Germans became the focal point of my loathing and bitterness.

The seed was sown.

As Geoffrey slowly improved he was able to spend more and more time in the company of his fellow patients and join in their conversations. This comradeship through their shared misfortune led to the formation of the Guinea Pig Club. The terribly disfigured men of Ward 3, Queen Victoria Cottage Hospital (QVCH), understood that they were special, not in a self-serving way, but as individuals who were required to find or develop in themselves special qualities in order to survive their ordeal. In Archie McIndoe they saw a man who also was special through his pioneering techniques and successful treatment of some of the most traumatic burn cases in medical history. So, one day in 1941 a handful of them decided to form the Guinea Pig Club, initially an élite drinking society and later much more.

The official objects of the club were to promote good fellowship among and to maintain contact with approved frequenters of Queen Victoria Cottage Hospital. There were three classes of membership, all having equal rights:

1. The Guinea Pigs (patients);
2. The Scientists (doctors, surgeons and members of the medical staff); and
3. The Royal Society for the Prevention of Cruelty to Guinea Pigs (those friends and benefactors who, by their interest in the hospital and patients, make the life of a Guinea Pig a happy one).

Geoffrey Page and the other founding members elected Flying Officer Bill Towers Perkins their first secretary and Pilot Officer Peter Weeks their first treasurer. Perkins had no hands with which to write the minutes and Weeks could not walk and so could not abscond with the funds. For their first president they chose the man they most admired and to whom they owed their futures, Archie McIndoe, whose often-stated goal was to return every patient to a full and active life as a worthwhile member of the community. As Ben Bennions, one of the early Battle of Britain pilot patients at QVCH, or 'the sty' as the Guinea Pigs referred to it, said of McIndoe:

> He was a God. Really, a remarkable man. Nothing was too much trouble for him when he was caring for the needs of the aircrew he was looking after. He could have got us to do anything.
>
> He hated red tape. He used to cut through it – and that didn't make him popular in Whitehall. He frequently had arguments over his insistence that we, and he, had the facilities that he needed. Once, he threatened that, if he didn't have more money and equipment, he'd mobilise all of us, wheelchairs, crutches, and all, and march us down Whitehall to shame the power-that-be. We'd have done it for him, too.

Archibald McIndoe maintained his London Harley Street practice throughout the Second World War providing elective cosmetic surgery to affluent Britons which helped subsidize his work at East Grinstead, rebuilding the faces, hands and limbs of Britain's fighter pilots, whose injuries came to be known as 'Hurricane Burns'. Richard Hillary described his first meeting with him:

Of medium height, he was thick-set and the line of his jaw was square. Behind his horn-rimmed spectacles a pair of tired, friendly eyes regarded me speculatively. 'Well,' he said, 'you certainly made a thorough job of it, didn't you?' He started to undo the dressings on my hands and I noticed his fingers – blunt, capable, incisive. He took a scalpel and tapped lightly on something white showing through the red, granulating knuckle of my right fore-finger. 'Bone,' he remarked laconically.'

One of the things his patients at East Grinstead liked most about McIndoe was that he was always straight with them, always told them frankly about the treatment they were to receive. They appreciated and respected him for that and loved him for his humanity.

The Guinea Pig Club membership grew during the war to around 640. For a long time the 'Pigs' met regularly. In the post-war years they met once a year, in September, for a dinner and dance at a hotel near East Grinstead. It was always referred to as the Lost Weekend. The drink and conversation flowed and they were comfortable exchanging information about their medical, disablement, financial and social problems. In the early years these bright, alert, formerly handsome young men talked about coping in the normal world of people who were not burned and disfigured, about the daily chores of living, about finding and attracting a nice girl, and about finding and holding down a decent job in a business community that didn't understand them or their problems. Guinea Pig Tom Gleave used to say,

No Guinea Pig shall ever be selling matches from a tray on the street corner. We would move heaven and earth if we ever found it happening. In fact, the biggest single achievement of the Guinea Pig Club is to have helped every member to save his face. His 'other' face, that is, in a psychological sense, so that he could securely take his place once more in society.

Ward 3 was one of the old 'temporary' at the cottage hospital. During the war it was decorated in the dark green and cream colour scheme favoured by the Ministry of Works. In that time the central feature was a piano that Archie McIndoe played when he could spare the time. The second most prominent furnishing was a barrel of beer on tap. There was also a very large bathtub with strange attachments. It provided the saline baths that soothed and helped in the burn healing process. Anyone could help themselves to a beer whenever they wanted. Someone saw to it that the barrel never ran dry. Many of the former Ward Three patients remembered it as a rather jolly, convivial place when one wasn't in too much discomfort to relax and enjoy the atmosphere. Geoffrey Page described the ward as 'a cross between

Emergency Ward 10, The Red Lion and a French bordello.' McIndoe made a point of choosing the prettiest nurses he could find to work with his patients. They had a big job to do, way beyond normal hospital routine. They had to know how to handle a man whose despair at his condition reached its lowest ebb in the middle of the night.

The young airmen patients of the ward operated with their own unwritten code. If a man was terribly ill and having a really rough time, you didn't disturb him. When he had passed through the awful period, he was then fair game for practical jokes and the social life of the ward. Their irreverant vernacular included references to their experiences in a burning aircraft (being fried), having an operation (going under the knife), and the operating table (the slab). They were expert at discerning a patient who was feeling a bit too sorry for himself and soon set him straight, and they demonstrated genuine sympathy and understanding for anyone deserving it.

In Ward 3's first year of operation most of its patients were Battle of Britain pilots like Geoffrey, national heroes who had earned and paid dearly for the special treatment they received in Archie McIndoe's capable hands. As the war went on, however, a great many Air Force burn patients arrived there for treatment, not all of them Britons. There were also Poles, Czechs and Commonwealth airmen. The Guinea Pig Club grew substantially, but retained its exclusivity, restricting membership to air crew only.

As the Pigs progressed and gradually improved, many were able to spend some of their time away from the hospital. Many of these had lengthy periods of rest between surgical procedures and wanted to do something constructive, something to help the war effort, during these periods. So, to take advantage of their aviation training, workshops were established at Saint Hill Manor near East Grinstead, and at Marchwood Park in Hampshire where the men were put to work in the manufacture of items used in aircraft navigation. The quality of their work was judged to be of a consistently higher standard than that produced by able-bodied people producing similar items in other factories.

In his determination that his patients at the cottage hospital receive all possible assistance in returning to useful lives in society, Archie McIndoe went round to talk with the townspeople of East Grinstead, to explain his approach to the treatment of the Guinea Pigs and to ask for their help. They were only too pleased to help and did so in a variety of ways. The manager of the Whitehall, a combination pub-restaurant-cinema in the town centre, for example, made sure that the Pigs were always treated with consideration and tolerance. Others in the town invited patients individually to their homes for dinner and conversation. These vital connections to the community helped greatly in the restoration of the patients' social confidence. Later, when a German bomb fell on the Whitehall cinema, McIndoe was able partially to repay the kindnesses of the community towards his patients by treating many of those injured in the explosion.

* * *

The founding members of the Guinea Pigs recalled that, of them all, Geoffrey Page was McIndoe's favourite patient. They had a special kind of relationship that was a mixture of father/son and elder brother/ younger brother. Of the surgeon, Page said,

> A normal human being with a great insight into human frailties. He was capable of what, to Air Force officials, must have seemed inexcusable skulduggery. The regulations of the day stated that, if a member of air crew was off active duty for more than eighteen months, he was automatically invalided out of the service. If any of his patients had ambitions to return to flying, and because of their operations were going to be out of action for eighteen months or more, McIndoe would pull every string he could to find the man a job. Usually a fake job, too. So that, theoretically, the pilot had gone back to work, but he was probably sitting with his feet up in a pub, doing nothing at all, waiting for the next oper-ation. Provided you had three months working at your hypo-thetical job, you were then free for another eighteen months before the regulations began to apply again.

It was two years from the day that Geoffrey was shot down in flames until he was able to return to flying. He recalled that the worst time for him at the East Grinstead hospital was during the summer of 1941 when he was able on occasion to sit in the sunshine and watch as squadrons of Spitfires passed overhead on their way to fly fighter sweeps over northern France. He yearned to be up there with them and determined to return to combat flying as soon as he could. In bitterness he vowed to destroy one enemy aircraft for each operation he under-went.

Geoffrey had spent most of the past two years in Ward 3 and had endured fifteen operations. One more and McIndoe would discharge him from the hospital. There would be many more operations over the coming years, but for the time being they would stop. He and Richard Hillary would both soon be discharged and both wanted desperately to fly again. Both knew too, that Archie McIndoe was deeply opposed to their doing so and they began a campaign of badgering him until he reluctantly agreed to support their ambition. 'If you're determined to kill yourselves, go ahead, only don't blame me.' On 8 January 1943,

Richard Hillary died in the crash of his Blenheim bomber. He was twenty-three.

When Geoffrey reported to the Central Medical Establishment in London's Middlesex Hospital, the adjutant read his file, '... third degree burns, hands, face and legs; gun-shot wound, left leg,' and said 'You should get your bowler hat without any trouble.' Page replied, 'I've come here to get a flying category, not to be invalided out.'

'Forget about it, you haven't a chance. You still have to undergo a full medical examination for us to discharge you. They'll call you from the waiting room.'

After another hour his name was called and the examination proceeded. After a further wait he was summoned to the Air Commodore's office. The officer told Geoffrey that, apart from his injuries, he looked fit. He asked what Geoffrey wanted him to do, invalid him out or give him a limited category? Geoffrey asked about the limited category and was told it meant fit for ground duties in the United Kingdom only. He said that he wanted a flying category and went on to talk the man into passing him 'fit for non-operational single-engine aircraft only.' 'At the end of three months you will be boarded again, and if you've coped all right, we'll give you an operational category. Good luck, and don't let me down.'

*　　*　　*

No. 3 Anti-Aircraft Cooperation Unit was based at Cardiff Municipal Airport in Wales, then a small grass airfield on the edge of the city. The station commander was a self-important man in his forties with no apparent interest in flying. He was universally disliked by his junior officers who were bored rigid by their assignment; flying Masters and Lysanders back and forth along prearranged routes at set altitudes, to allow anti-aircraft units to train their gun crews. All conversation was dominated by complaint. Morale and the general atmosphere were dismal. Never mind. Geoffrey was there to put in his required three months before taking and passing his next medical board. Then on to ops.

The three months of anti-aircraft cooperation seemed like three years. He took and passed the second medical board and was given an A1.B flying category, the highest obtainable, and requested posting to a fighter squadron.

His request was granted and he was sent to fly Spitfires at Martlesham Heath, near Ipswich. His delight in flying the elegant fighter was tempered during his first month at Martlesham by the boring convoy patrols he was required to fly, back and forth along the east coast, work not unlike his chores at Cardiff. After a month of the convoy patrolling, Geoffrey approached his squadron commander with an idea he was eager to try. He intended to attack a German encampment located between Dunkirk and Nieuport in the early morning when most of the enemy troops would be moving back and forth from the canteens. The CO agreed and at dawn on a filthy grey and wet November morning three Spitfires left Martlesham for France with Page in the lead. His intention was to cross the French coast about five miles south of the target, proceed inland and then turn back towards the target to approach it from an unexpected direction.

In a few moments the Spitfires made landfall, but not where intended. They roared low over sand dunes and Geoffrey knew that they had missed their entry point by several miles, but then he spotted a canal with a barge puffing along it to the north. It was an approved target and he led the other fighters down towards it. Switching the gun button on his control column from 'safe' to 'fire', he watched his cannon shells track the canal surface like a string of fountains until they slammed into the barge's wooden hull.

Flashing low over the canal the three fighters soon came upon a group of barges that were being loaded from a granary on the bank of the waterway. Each of the planes made two cannon runs, leaving large holes in all of the heavily-laden barges. The Spitfires continued northward along the canal until they spotted a train stopped near a rural siding. The engine driver and the fireman were walking along the track towards the locomotive and began running in the opposite direction when they saw giant holes opening in the boiler of the iron horse, releasing absurd clouds of steam in all directions.

Geoffrey and the others flew on northwards along the rail line and approached a large town. He noticed the steam emerging from another locomotive, this one attached to a long passenger train which was standing at the platform of a large railway station. Passengers were milling about on the platform. He brought the Spitfires around to an ideal angle on the locomotive and they all fired on the hissing engine, causing the passengers to flee from the station. Climbing away Geoffrey now realized that they were flying over the centre of Dunkirk, a town heavily defended by anti-aircraft batteries. As the three fighters passed over the sea wall, the sky around them immediately filled with flak bursts from the shore guns. But the speed of the Spitfires quickly took them out of range as they headed back to their Martlesham base.

After the action of the past half hour, Geoffrey reflected that, while they had probably not killed any Germans, they had done significant damage to their transportation system. A few weeks later he discovered the reason for the navigation error that had caused the Spitfires to miss their intended landfall in France by such a wide margin. Geoffrey had been carrying a long knife inside one of his flying boots and the magnetic properties of the blade had affected the compass in his aircraft.

A few weeks after the Dunkirk raid, Geoffrey was posted to the RAF Air Fighting Development Unit at Wittering, a non-operational organization involved in the evaluation of all types of fighter planes, both Allied and captured enemy aircraft. Another pilot assigned to the AFDU at that time was Squadron Leader James MacLachlan, a one-armed flyer who had recently finished a tour of night intruder operations. The missions had required him to loiter in the dark skies near enemy airfields, awaiting the return of German bombers from their nightly raids on British targets. When the bombers entered the landing pattern, MacLachlan would pounce on them. After such exciting nights out, he quickly tired of the evaluation duties. His enthusiasm returned, however, when the unit was supplied with a pair of North American Mustangs, reputed to be the fastest low-level fighters in existence at that time. He was able to persuade Fighter Command to let him carry out a lone raid into German territory in one of the new planes. His intention was to get into enemy areas where Allied aircraft had not yet been seen in daylight at low altitude, penetrating the German fighter defences. He had the Mustang camouflaged to blend with the French countryside and spent many hours in low flying over England to perfect his low-level navigation.

Days later, Geoffrey was one of those listening in the Mess as MacLachlan recounted his initial operation in the Mustang. Crossing the French coast he was spotted by German fighters. With the limited rearward visibility of the early-model Mustang, and the altitude efficiency limitation of its Allison engine, it would have been folly to continue in the presence of the Fw 190s. He was forced to abort the mission. Geoffrey then approached MacLachlan and from that conversation came a plan for two Mustangs operating together and protecting each other. But Geoffrey doubted that their commanding officer would consent to their use of a second Mustang. MacLachlan dismissed the concern. 'To hell with him. I'll get permission from Fighter Command, and then he'll have to lend us the second plane.' In the following week the permission was secured and the other Mustang was prepared. The camouflage paint was applied, the guns were synchronized, the sights harmonized and fuel consumption testing was accomplished. What came next was not nearly so matter-of-fact. The two pilots had to learn to fly with each other with great precision, in split-second teamwork at extremely low altitude. It had to be achieved without radio communication between them as the one-armed Mac was fully occupied flying the aeroplane and navigating without having to handle the push-buttons and transmitting switch of a VHF radio.

Their training took several weeks and then they had to wait for the right weather conditions. The missions would have them skimming the crops of the French fields and the enemy aircraft they sought would all be above them, so they needed a cloud layer at about 3,000 feet to silhouette the enemy planes even at great distance. Visibility had to be good and winds had to be minimal as they caused turbulence, adding to the fatigue the handicapped pilots would have to endure on the demanding flights.

When ready, Mac and Geoffrey flew their Mustangs from Wittering in central England, down to Lympne, an airfield on the south coast, where they would wait for the required weather conditions. While waiting, Geoffrey experienced a kind of fear he had not known before. It was nearly three years since he had been in combat with enemy aircraft. He had been shot down in flames and badly burned during the Battle of Britain and had spent two painful years in hospital. Soon he and Mac would face enemy flak as well as fighters, and he had repeated visions of his Mustang being hit and exploding in flames in the same way his Hurricane had done. Fire is the greatest fear of all airmen, and this time they would be flying very low level rather than at 15,000 feet with the possibility of baling out. Even the memory of the smell of his own burning flesh returned to nauseate him.

The day came when the weather favoured the mission and everything was ready. The plan called for a full squadron of Hawker Typhoon fighters to escort the two Mustangs across the Channel at wave-top height until the formation was about to cross the German-held French coast. The Typhoons would then climb and create a diversion while the Mustangs proceeded inland, skimming the treetops to the German nightfighter airfields south of Paris where the pair expected to find ample prey.

As Geoffrey and MacLachlan sat waiting in their fighters on the grass field at Lympne, the Typhoons taxied out in pairs, turned into the wind and took off. In a few minutes they were joining up in a squadron formation and circling the airfield. Mac and Geoffrey had started the engines of the Mustangs and rolled out to the take-off position. They became airborne and soon caught up with their escorts who shifted position to form on both sides of the Mustangs. The mass of fighters left the English coastline and gently descended to twenty feet above the waves. Settled in the formation, Geoffrey was again visited by memories of the day he'd been shot down and burnt. The business of flying forced the terrible thoughts from his mind. In the next moment the fighters were in the midst of hundreds of seagulls. A bird strike to a propeller at that height would likely bring down one of the planes – another unnerving thought for Page. They passed through the gulls without incident and the watery grey outline of the enemy coastline appeared dead ahead. All the aircraft increased their speed for the crossing in and the Typhoons started to climb away on their diversionary assignment, leaving the two Mustangs alone and unprotected.

Roaring across the French fields, the onus was now on Mac to navigate them precisely, a challenging role for a pilot with just one hand for flying and a map spread on his lap. Any lapse in concentration at their speed and altitude and he would be carving a trench in the countryside.

They raced over the rooftops of Beauvais, turning slightly to the south towards Rambouillet and passed over the River Seine and under a line of high-tension electric cables. Cruising about ten miles ahead at an altitude of 1,500 feet were three aircraft in tight formation. They appeared to be enemy planes and that was confirmed as Mac and Geoffrey rapidly closed on them. Switching his gun camera, gun button and gun sight to on, and the propeller to fine pitch, Geoffrey prepared for his first air combat in three years.

Mac fired on the port aircraft which instantly became a tumbling, flaming mass, descending at a rather slow pace into a house on the edge of the forest. With no other enemy fighters in sight, Mac and Geoffrey lit out after the two remaining enemy planes and dispatched them as efficiently as Mac had their companion. A few minutes later the English pair encountered another enemy aircraft and the four cannon of Mac's Mustang set it afire. Geoffrey then completed the destruction of the German fighter, observing its wreckage scattered across a large field.

As their Mustangs neared Bretigny, Geoffrey spotted a pair of German nightfighters that were apparently up for an air test. The Ju 88s were in the landing pattern at their base as Mac closed on one, blasting it with cannon shells. Again, Geoffrey finished the job. Incredibly, the second Ju 88 continued its landing approach, providing Mac with an irresistible target which he turned into a sheet of flame slithering down the length of the runway. The action had not escaped the attention of the flak gun crews protecting the German airfield. The gunners immediately threw up a barrage of deadly 'orange balls' that the Englishmen somehow managed to safely fly through. Their mission that day was more successful than either man had imagined possible. It brought Geoffrey a measure of satisfaction in his quest for vengeance after his years of pain and hospital confinement. But it also seemed to increase his need for revenge and his lust for killing the enemy.

With the success of that raid uppermost in their minds, Mac and Geoffrey set off again on a similar mission with the next favourable weather conditions. Again they were escorted by Hawker Typhoons whch departed as they neared France. As Geoffrey recalled:

Crossing in over the French coast Mac must have collected some machine gun fire. His aircraft climbed steeply from our treetop height, and at 1,000 feet his canopy opened. He presumably changed his mind about baling out, for the aircraft proceeded in a glide towards a small field. His approach speed was too fast, and the Mustang first touched the ground three quarters of the way across the field, with retracted wheels. Still moving rapidly, it ploughed into an orchard shedding its wings before it came to rest as a battered, dust-clouded wreck. I orbited the crash several times at a low height, but no sign of life emerged from the wreckage. For an instant I contemplated trying to land in the field to come to Mac's aid, but judgement ruled out the possibility of landing wheels down in such a confined area. Reluctantly I dived at the scene of the crash to register some camera gun photographs, and heartbrokenly headed for home. Years later I learned that Mac had survived the actual crash, but died three weeks later in the hospital. His body lies buried in a small French graveyard. It was the passing of a very brave man.

On the loss of MacLachlan, Geoffrey was posted briefly to No. 122 Squadron and then on to No. 132 Squadron. From there he was sent to a special dive-bombing course at a base called Milfield, near the Northumberland coast. At Milfield those in attendance were all young but highly accomplished and heavily decorated wing commanders and squadron leaders, present to learn of their role in the coming Allied invasion of Europe. After breakfast on their second day at the field, they were addressed by a young air commodore:

Good morning, gentlemen. As many of you may have guessed, the invasion of Europe is not far away. The Army and Navy will do their jobs and we will do ours. That is why you are here. For the next three weeks you will fire your guns and practice dive-bombing until it is second nature. On the beaches near here are convoys of brand new lorries of different sizes and shapes. There are also tanks. These you will attack with cannons and rockets followed by an inspection on foot of the damage caused. You will learn through trial and error the best angle of attack for thin and thick-skinned vehicles. On the bombing ranges you will obtain a proficiency previously thought impossible. You will set a standard for the pilots in your squadron, a standard that you must demand that they in turn attain. You will keep up the highest traditions of the Royal Air Force.

Geoffrey and his colleagues were now flying Spitfires and with each day becoming more proficient in the delivery of their deadly weaponry.

The young air leaders emerged from their course confident in their ability to do their part on the day of the invasion and in the days after. Page:

> One crisp, cold morning we were ordered to carry out a routine dive-bombing exercise. This particular day I was to fly as No. 2 to another pilot. This meant he was my leader for the sortie and I was to follow him at all times. We turned into the wind at the end of the runway which stretched ahead of us with three-foot snow-banks on either side. The ice on the runway gleamed in the early morning light.
>
> My leader raised his hand and commenced the take-off. Tucking my left wing close behind his right one I opened my throttle firmly to keep station. Our tails came up as we roared down the runway. Then I realized that a cross-wind was causing the other aircraft to veer in my direction as its wheels slipped on the icy surface. Naturally I had to ease over to the right as well to avoid collision.
>
> Just as we got airborne I was almost into the bank and the thought of hitting it with a 500-pound bomb under my aircraft was not an encouraging thought. Swiftly I moved the 'wheels up' lever, but too late. There was a thud beneath me and the aircraft gave a slight lurch. Knowing I was in trouble I turned away from my leader, but continued to climb. I then tried to figure out the situation. Firstly the two green lights on the instrument panel were not shining. As I thought, probably the right wheel had struck the snowbank and either the wheel and oleo leg had snapped off, or were hanging down in some distorted fashion.
>
> My eyes quickly took in the engine instrument readings, and were immediately arrested by the glycol coolant temperature. It was rising alarmingly, and soon the engine would stop through overheating. A dead engine meant a 'wheels-up' landing in a field with a deadly bomb attached to soften the impact! A quick look at the altimeter showed I was too low to bale out. Even if I could, perhaps the abandoned Spitfire and its lethal load might dive into one of the farms or houses scattered below.
>
> I had no choice but to turn my crippled aircraft seawards, and there jettison the bomb, provided the engine did not pack up beforehand. I throttled back to try and keep the temperature under control, but this meant eliminating the possibility of gaining more height. Painfully, slowly the coastline came towards me, and the temperature needle reached the danger mark. Thankfully, I limped over the beach and immediately afterwards pressed the bomb release button. Lightened of the load, the engine bore less

weight, and with a singing heart I returned to the airfield, there to execute a belly landing on the snow-covered grass. My first introduction to skiing!

After the course at Milfield, Geoffrey rejoined his unit at its new airfield, Ford, on the south coast of England. From Ford the pilots of 132 Squadron continued dive-bombing practice by attacking the secret German V-1 flying bomb launch sites in France on a daily basis. As squadron commander, Geoffrey was responsible for his pilots' navigation from Ford to the pin-point map references to his target locations, the correct identification of the targets from several miles away, getting all his aircraft into echelon formation for the attack, determining the best direction from which to launch the attack in order to avoid the complication of a cross-wind and then leading the attack in a dive from 8,000 feet to the precise bomb-release point. And leading his pilots through the diving attack meant exposing them to savage anti-aircraft fire from guns surrounding the target. Following the attack, it was his job to assess quickly the damage done to the target and re-form the squadron into a unit as fast as possible, while watching for enemy fighters.

*   *   *

The base commander, Group Captain Jamie Rankin, stood to the side of a large wall map of the Normandy coast. 'There are five main beaches. Three British – Sword, Juno and Gold, and two American – Omaha and Utah. The task of our three squadrons is to provide close cover over the two American beaches from first light tomorrow morning.'

On the airfield Geoffrey briefed his pilots. They were due to start engines in ten mnutes and rendezvous over Omaha Beach in forty-seven minutes. He told them that, on no account whatsoever was anyone to leave the beach area during their patrol period, even if there was a big, fat, juicy Hun a couple of miles inland asking to be shot down. Their job was to give cover to the troops below. 'The odds are that a lone Jerry is bait to get us out of the way while a big formation has a crack at the landing barges.' To the question of one pilot: 'What happens if we get engine trouble, sir?', he replied 'A forced-landing strip is being prepared here [indicating a map location]. It may not be ready for a day or two, so you'll just have to use common sense.'

In his Spitfire Geoffrey conducted the routine cockpit check. At the appointed time he and the other pilots of the squadron started their engines, the chocks were pulled from their wheels, and the twelve machines taxied out in six pairs to the take-off end of the runway. Airborne and observing as the other planes of the unit joined the circuit round the airfield, he watched them cut across his turning circle to close up on his fighter. Formed up, he took them across the Isle of Wight as the sky began to grow brighter in the east. He called for the squadron to open into battle formation and noted the roughness of the sea, sympathising with the thousands of troops below in their landing barges for the dreadful seasickness that many of them would be experiencing.

The Cherbourg Peninsula loomed to the right. Below, hundreds of warships, from giant battleships to tiny barges, sprawled across the sea surface; the battleships hard at the task of sending massive sixteen-inch shells onto the French countryside, their fire control aided by two circling Royal Navy Seafire fighters that were spotting the accuracy of the gunners and calling in firing corrections to them.

The squadron flew its patrol over Omaha and Utah Beaches. They encountered no reaction whatsoever from the German Air Force and, after sixty minutes in the area, reluctantly turned back for England.

Several days and many patrols later, Geoffrey's squadron was ordered to relocate from their field at Ford to a new and hastily pre-pared landing strip in a Normandy wheatfield. The 'runway' had been bulldozed right out of the tall wheat, leaving a reasonably level but extremely dusty landing surface. The dust got into everything, from clothes and food to intakes and the operating mechanisms of the air-craft machine-guns and cannon, often causing life-threatening stop-pages.

Once settled in Normandy, the squadron entered a period of intense activity that saw it ranging far beyond the German lines to attack any legitimate targets that were moving along the roads; trucks, armoured cars and motorcycles. The only vehicles immune to the attentions of the Spitfires were the heavily-armour-plated German tanks. These were easy prey for the RAF's rocket-firing Hawker Typhoon ground-attack fighters.

As busy as the pilots of Geoffrey's squadron were at the time, none was more eager for action against the enemy than he. Frequently he used the excuse of a 'necessary cannon test' to justify a hunting expe-dition in search of enemy aircraft. On one such trip he was accom-panied by two colleagues as they took their Spitfires southwest towards Lisieux. Approaching the town, and some thirty miles behind the German lines, they sighted a formation of thirty Messerschmitt 109 fighters on an easterly course. While diving on the enemy formation, they were spotted and the German fighters broke formation and began climbing to meet the three Spitfires head-on. Outnumbered ten to one, the British pilots soon found themselves on the defensive and fighting for their lives. Luckily for them, their Spitfires were capable of out-turning the 109s. But when the stresses of the g-forces caused Geoffrey to break the spiral and climb for the safety of the clouds a few thousand feet above, the German pilots swarmed after him in an effort to get in a deflection shot at the Englishman. In the turning climb one of the 109 pilots did manage a burst of cannon fire that caused an explosion aboard Geoffreys' aircraft, filling the cockpit with smoke and reminding him in graphic detail of his fiery experience in the Hurricane four years earlier. But miraculously the smoke cleared and so did his thought processes. The Spitfire was not actually burning. It had not yet reached the haven of the cloud layer and he knew then that it would not. He was also aware of blood running down his left leg and into his flying boot.

He instantly decided that his only chance lay in a violent, ham-fisted manoeuvre and he threw the Spitfire onto its back while pulling the stick hard into his stomach. With the engine and propeller turning at maximum boost, the plane roared downward as he attempted to shake off his pursuers. He knew that the German fighters could outrun him in a dive but saw his only hope in reaching the treetops and then jinking to throw the adversaries off his tail.

His wound had left his leg numb and useless. His plan was working until he descended through 2,000 feet and was jarred by the appearance of orange tracers flashing past his canopy. Making maximum use of his one good leg, he kicked desperately at the rudder bar while climbing and then diving to take as much evasive action as he could in his condition. The tracer continued to dog him as he neared the ground and he pulled the Spitfire up into a tight climbing turn. Looking back he was relieved to find that only a single 109 was still pursuing him. His pain and his deep-seated anger then brought a new resolve: 'I'll get you if it kills me, you bastard.'

What happened next left Geoffrey flabbergasted. The chasing German pilot knew that he could not out-turn the Spitfire. The Messerschmitt was on the edge of a stall as its pilot pulled the nose back sharply to set up a deflection shot. When he fired at the Spitfire, the recoil of his guns slowed the 109 sufficiently to cause it to flick over and slide inverted into the trees only twenty feet below. He had effectively shot himself down.

Geoffrey Page finished the war with seventeen aerial victories to his credit. Years later he reflected on the experience: 'I was given a lovely fast aeroplane to fly for nothing and was paid the glorious sum of five pounds a week to do it.'

A common, unconsidered man who for a moment of eternity, held the whole future of mankind in his two sweating palms, and did not let it go.

– Sir Christopher Foxley-Norris

CHAPTER THREE

Adolph 'Sailor' Malan

The Battle of Britain produced many airmen of great skill and accomplishment; high-achievers who made their mark in one of history's most memorable and demanding campaigns. But only a few of these men distinguished themselves in such a way as to become legends in their own lifetimes. Among the greatest of these was Sailor Malan.

Malan was thirty years of age during the Battle of Britain, old for a fighter pilot, but his maturity gave his leadership a firm authority.

* * *

Captain Cuthbert Orde was one of the great war artists of all time, creating powerful and moving drawings of many pilots in Royal Air Force Fighter Command during the Second World War. Orde was not a war artist in the traditional sense; he was something more. As Air Vice-Marshal J.C. Slessor, C.B., D.S.O., M.C. wrote of him at the height of that war, 'It would indeed have been difficult to find anyone more ideally qualified by temperament, experience and sympathy than 'Turps' – or 'the Captain,' as he is known to hundreds of Fighter boys – to draw pictures of the pilots of Fighter Command that will live as a permanent record of the sort of chaps they were and what they looked like. And I think in these drawings he has caught something of their characters, something of the essential selves of the men who have made the British Fighter squadrons incomparably the best in the world.'

Of then-Squadron Leader Adolph G. Malan, D.S.O. (and bar), D.S.C. (and bar), whose portrait Captain Orde made on 29 December 1940, the artist wrote: 'All would agree that 'Sailor' Malan is the outstanding Fighter pilot of the war. He is our top scorer with twenty-nine confirmed victories. I have seldom been more impressed by anyone than by him the first time I saw him. A very strong face, a very quiet manner, and an air of authority made it obvious that here was a leader of great determination and ability, with a very sincere personality. 'Sailor' was in the South African Merchant Service for eight years, and joined the RAF about nine years ago. He is married and has a son, to

93

whom the Prime Minister recently stood godfather. I mention that because when I was painting him he told me that having a wife and son had been of the greatest moral help to him during the Battle of Britain, that it gave him an absolutely definite thing to fight for and defend, and that this was his constant thought. His skill, courage, and fighting qualities may be taken for granted: they're obviously facts and are shared by many others, but his character is shared by few. I do not think that Malan could join a squadron without improving it, however good it was. Not by sword-waving, but by a strength of mind and integrity that are at once recognizable and effective. Don't imagine from this that he never laughs; but he has a serious mind and is intent on winning the war.'

> Sailor Malan was the best pilot of the war, a good tactician; above average pilot and an excellent shot. In the end it comes down to being able to shoot. I was an above average pilot, but not a good shot, so the only way I could succeed was to get closer than the next chap. This wasn't easy. The Spitfire's guns were harmonized to about 450 yards, but this was spread too far across. Sailor trimmed his own guns down to 200–250 yards, and we all followed suit. The best shot in the Air Force, I think. Malan was the best. A great shot and a splendid Wing Leader. He had the maturity of years and experience behind him. Others were good but he was the greatest. He was the best fighter tactician and leader produced by the RAF in World War II.
> –Air Commodore Al Deere, C.B.E., D.S.O., D.F.C.

*   *   *

For his smiling, cherubic look, his fellow teenage sea cadets aboard the South African training ship *General Botha* called him 'Angel Face.' In his early days with the RAF, his sea-faring background led to his fellow pilots referring to him as 'The Admiral.' To his wife Lynda, throughout their marriage he was always 'John', but to everyone else then and since, he was 'Sailor'.

Born in 1910, from early childhood Adolph Gysbert Malan was fascinated by guns and shooting. As a young boy he had been taught to handle and use them properly, and to respect them. As a fourteen-year-old boy he took gunnery instruction aboard the *General Botha*, where he earned high grades for his marksmanship. In 1927 he joined the Union Castle Steamship Line where he acquired his nickname. During the Second World War he occasionally lectured on gunnery when he was not actually displaying his skills in a Spitfire. He used to say, 'I like a moving target. Using a shotgun has affinities with aiming a Spitfire at a Messerschmitt. You have to learn to swing through from behind so as to get your line or direction of flight and, at the same time, pick up the relative speed of your target. That is the only way to make proper allowance for deflection.' He never forgot an experience while he was growing up on his father's farm about halfway between Wellington where he was born and Table Mountain to the south. Willie, Sailor's father, had given him a double-barrelled shotgun and a few cartridges and told him to 'Go and shoot something for the pot.' Sailor:

> I suppose he was joking. I was not more than seven or eight at the time and small for my age. But my father seemed to like thrusting responsibility onto me and he must have had a purpose in so doing. I went outside and scored a bullseye on a watering can. That got me into trouble later. Then I tried creeping up behind a turtle-dove. How I was able to get the gun to my shoulder and fire I don't know, but I did. Unfortunately, I fired off both barrels at once and the recoil knocked me flat and bruised my shoulder for days after. Then, when I reloaded the gun I got the rim of one of the cartridges jammed in the breech. I struggled very hard to break the gun open, but I hadn't the strength. In the end I took it back under my arm, and ran into the lounge to my mother, still wrestling with the triggers and pointing the barrels towards her.
>
> She was terribly angry, and snatched the gun from me. I was scolded and so was my father for letting me have the gun. I wasn't allowed to handle a shotgun for a long time after that.

* * *

Sailor couldn't recall why he had become so fixated with becoming a cadet trainee on the *General Botha*, a vessel permanently anchored off Simonstown. He was just thirteen when he announced to his parents that he wanted to be a sea cadet aboard the ship, which had been established only two or three years earlier as a training vessel for South Africans. In the Boer War, Willie Malan favoured the British side and had sustained two bullet wounds while on horseback in a clash with one of General Smuts' patrols at Twenty-four Rivers, near Porterville. It made a cripple of him and he ended up with one leg two inches shorter than the other. He endured, however, and healed himself well enough to run the farm and look after his growing family. But in the years after the First World War, there was an economic depression in farming and Willie was forced to sell the property. The depression, together with after-effects from his old wounds, caused him to have a serious breakdown and Sailor's mother, with a sick husband and five children to care for, moved the family to Wellington where she took in boarders and did dress-making to keep them going financially. With boarders occupying all of the other bedrooms, Sailor and his brother Ralph had to sleep out on the porch.

*   *   *

The *General Botha* lay at anchor just a quarter of a mile off-shore. It harboured among its cadets a gang of young toughs, senior cadets who referred to themselves as 'The Terrible Three.' These thugs were somewhat older than the majority of the sixty new cadets who, together with Sailor, entered service aboard the ship in February 1924. The gang excelled at bullying, extortion, and a 'protection' racket and at least one of them went to prison after leaving the ship. Sailor was under age, a fair-haired, blue-eyed boy, and an easy target for the bullys who took every opportunity to harass and generally make life miserable for the new boys. One of Sailor's fellow cadets recalled the gauntlet of lashing ropes that the cadets were forced to run frequently by the 'old salts', as well as the nightly beatings issued by the gunnery instructor in the middle of the night in punishment of any cadets who had upset him during the previous day. Three other instructors operated in a similar punitive fashion, freely administering the rope in official and unofficial ship's discipline. Sailor soon developed a mischievous tendency to play practical jokes on the instructors and was rewarded for his efforts on a nearly nightly basis by a few lashes.

Among the gravest offences one could commit on the ship was the violation of the 'no smoking' rule. It was strictly enforced because of the particular fire danger aboard, but there were always some who ignored the rule and paid the penalty which could be up to eight lashes. Sailor recalled:

The master-at-arms – the equivalent of a sergeant-major, had a strong arm. Six strokes from him were enough to curb anybody for a time. They used to be given in the recreation room because on the floor by the table were two ring-bolts. Through these a rope which bound you down on the table could be passed. But first you had to be certified as fit to take your medicine. This was the sick bay steward's job. Then, very obligingly, he would hang on to one end of the rope holding you down while you were being thrashed. The rule was you were only allowed to wear No. 1 duck trousers to receive this punishment. These were shorts, of course, and became very tight when you stretched over. 'Cadet So-and-so is now ready for his punishment, sir,' the NCO would report to the master-at-arms, who would then select a cane – he usually gave himself a choice of two or three – and step forward. When he stepped forward you bit harder on the squeegee, a piece of rubber you kept in your mouth to stop yourself yelling. With six cuts it was easy to draw blood. After which you couldn't sit down in comfort for a week. The first time I saw this punishment handed out was to a big chap – an Old Salt. It was quite a shock to see him break down. Later on I understood why.

In addition to the emphasis on discipline, life aboard the *Botha* in the two-year curriculum stressed mathematics, a subject in which Sailor was admittedly deficient, and science, along with seamanship, gunnery, signalling, and drill. He learned about navigation with logs, chart work, the sextant, Mercator's and plane sailings, magnetism, meteorology, latitude by meridian altitude, longitude by chronometer, and he gained a lot of experience manning skiffs and cutters that plied between the ship and shore, sailing and rowing. His favourite subject was, of course, gunnery, which included rifle and pistol firing, stripping and mounting a gun, tracing a gun circuit, sight setting, and a working knowledge of explosives. He was required to scrub the decks and wash his own clothes and dishes after meals. Fortunately for cadets who came in later years to the *Botha*, such traditions as the bullying and harassment had been ended.

In time Sailor passed out of the *Botha* cadet programme with a clean record and a First Extra certificate in seamanship. Eight months later he took up a position as a cadet aboard the *Sandown Castle*, of the Union-Castle Line, headed for New York on his first voyage.

His training ship, the *Botha*, has long since lain in twenty-five fathoms of water nine miles off the Roman Rock Lighthouse, where she sank after receiving twenty-four shells from the Scala battery above Simonstown, probably a fitting end for a vessel remembered by its cadets for so many years of harsh discipline.

Sailor would spend nine years at sea plying the lanes between the old world and the east coast ports of America, especially that of New York City. In 1921 two American women, Katherine Mayo and Moyca Newell, joined forces to reciprocate for the kind hospitality shown American soldiers in Britain during the war years of 1917–18. They reasoned: 'British merchant ships in peacetime spend more time in New York harbour than in any other port in the world, many of them carrying cadet officers in their crews, lonely young men mostly without friends in New York, with little or no knowledge of the city …' so the two women decided to create a cozy, home-like club, free of rules and always open to the British cadets aged between sixteen and twenty, to come in, make friends, play cards, meet and dance with young American girls from good homes and find an American 'mother figure' to confide in if they wished to do so. They tried to make it the sort of place that the mothers of the young men would be comfortable having their sons visit. One woman who worked in the club remembered Sailor as rather shy, though always popular and having many friends. Sailor spent much of his leave time there at the British Apprentice Club on West 23rd Street near the Chelsea Hotel. One of the hostesses recalled:

> He was very blond with a young, almost girlish face and had a shy, diffident manner. When introductions were taking place, he was usually hidden behind a group of other boys and you sometimes overlooked him altogether. So, invariably, he was the last to be introduced, but usually made the most impression, chiefly because of his shyness. He was always immaculately groomed and very fastidious – always wore the correct tie, hat, and shoes to match the suit he wore. He noticed well-dressed women too. He had a pleasing, soft, educated voice and disliked intensely loud raucous voices or crude behaviour in other people. He was very sensitive to his surroundings and associations. He worried a great deal about passing his examinations. I don't think, at that time, he was spectacular as far as intellectual pursuits were concerned – he was not interested in literature of any kind. Rarely did Adolph discuss any outstanding book because I don't think he read any. But he had keen powers of observation and was a serious thinker. He loved to take part in serious discussions and I suppose that was how he obtained most of his information. He derived great pleasure in conversing with mature people. One lady in particular was a great friend of his and she gave him a great deal of advice and understanding in his most bewildered moments, of which he had many. His first thought when he arrived in New York was usually to get in touch with her. He was sympathetic and thoughtful of others, idealistic, and somewhat introspective. He was forever trying to analyse his emotions and his actions. He lacked self-confidence. He once wrote in a letter: 'My whole life is a succession of minor indecisions and therefore I compromise by more or less drifting along and snatching at what happiness I can find along the way.' Looking back now, he probably realizes that this was just inexperienced youth, and that experience gives assurance, but whereas most young people think they know everything, he was always doubtful of his abilities.
>
> He was quite a social lion and received many invitations to parties at which he was always a great asset, as he was quite popular. He liked to have a drink occasionally for sociability, but never to excess. You could always be sure he would never make an exhibition of himself. He was always restrained in his gaiety – always perfectly controlled – in fact this was so in all matters. Whether he ever liked anything passionately I don't know. I never knew him excited over anything except over his training in the

Royal Navy, and he could talk on the subject of gunnery and give you a complete lecture on the operations.

He was most courteous and friendly to everyone, and patient; I never saw him irritable. He loved to dance and was always available; he never sat out dances while there was some girl without a partner. He was only an average dancer and stuck to his own routine which never varied. Also, he always offered to take some girl home from all dances without fuss and discrimination, provided his own friends were not present, or were otherwise taken care of. He was very reliable and seldom promised anything he could not carry out.

His biggest problem in those early years, I believe, was how his future would turn out. He knew he did not want to go to sea all his life, because, as he remarked, it was a constant round of making friends and saying good-bye. A sailor's life was too uncertain for him – he wanted a more settled existence – a home and family (six children was one of his dreams). But he couldn't decide just what he should strive for. When the Air Force was suggested to him he was positive he would not like to fly. What caused him to change his mind I do not know, as it occurred in England. He did once say that he would like to enter politics – in South Africa.

I believe he has a retentive memory. For example, the last time he was in New York as a sailor he received a torn dollar bill which he was afraid had no value. I volunteered to find out if it was usable and gave him a good one in its place. It turned out to be quite good and I immediately forgot about it. In 1941 (seven years later) when he paid the US a visit during the war he pulled out of his pocket a new dollar bill to replace the one he was quite sure had been valueless.

Then came the great depression following the 1929 crash of the New York Stock Market. Many millions in America and Europe were jobless. The Union-Castle Company, however, looked after its young officers, though it suspended its intake of apprentices. Sailor was kept on, though the best job he could get in that time was as watchman aboard small coasters on occasional trips between Southampton and Hamburg.

I'd say the sea bred in me a kind of fatalism. Long voyages get you into a certain frame of mind. You're signed on. You know your destination weeks ahead. In the meantime you jog along in a routine which seldom varies. You get, too, a feeling of not belonging anywhere in particular.

* * *

Lynda Fraser, of Ruislip, near London, was just sixteen when Sailor met her through friends there in 1930. He didn't see her again for three years but she would become his wife. She thought him very serious and largely inarticulate in that first meeting.

*   *   *

Through the lean depressed years of the early 1930s, Sailor and many of his contemporaries saw their career prospects at sea as more and more limited. Some turned their thoughts to the possibilities in the Royal Air Force. On his frequent trips to Hamburg, Sailor spent a lot of time talking with German sailors, harbour officials and civilians. He noted the aggressive spirit and industriousness in Germany and soon realized that war was inevitable. In 1935, he made his last voyage in a merchant navy uniform, as third officer aboard his old ship, the *Sandown Castle*. Back in England he sat for his First Mate's ticket and completed his Royal Navy Reserve training. It was during this time that he wrote a letter applying for a Short Service Commission in the Royal Air Force and was soon accepted. Sailor:

> I enjoyed myself in the Navy and wouldn't have missed it, but I found it starch-ridden. I didn't like the caste system. I can see its attractions and its value. Within its limits it produces, more often than not, an efficient class of officer. But it didn't suit me, either by temperament or by comparison with the life I'd known in the merchant service. The attitude of regular Naval types to RNR and RNVR, was as if we were the lowest forms of life. The biggest mistake, as I saw from an outsider's viewpoint, was the lack of human relations. The men lived, as it were, below stairs, and the officers only addressed them as underlings. The difference in relationships when I joined the RAF, was remarkable.

*   *   *

In 1935 the Filton Flying School sat in a field near the end of an ugly row of semi-detached houses immediately north of Bristol. Its neighbour was the Bristol Aeroplane Works, which was about the most that could be said for it. Sailor was billeted with a few other student pilots not far from the airfield and his initial training did little for his self confidence. He began flying training on Tiger Moths early in 1936 and was depressed by the spirited chatter of his fellow trainees as they all seemed to be making perfect turns and beautiful landings while he struggled to achieve any progress at all. Then, suddenly, he got in a few good landings and there seemed to be some hope of his being able to solo. Within a few more hours flying his instructor smiled and said 'Off you go.' He soloed safely and efficiently and was soon on his way to his first posting. But before finishing the Filton course his instructor wrote in this report on Sailor: 'This pilot is inclined to be heavy and impatient at the controls.'

* * *

On completion of his training in December, he was posted to No. 74 Squadron at Hornchurch in Essex. Hornchurch Fighter Station lay twelve miles out of London on the north side of the Thames estuary. A purpose-built pre-war facility, it offered substantial barrack blocks rather than the drafty, inhospitable Nissen huts common to later air bases in Britain; mess rooms, workshops, club rooms, lecture halls, armouries, stores, hangars, and tarred roadways. There were flower beds and ornamental shrubs and it was a comfortable station on which to practice and operate.

In 1937 the squadron was flying the Gloster Gauntlet, a relatively stable biplane with reasonable aerobatic capabilities. While visiting Ulster with the other pilots of A Flight to give an aerobatic display at Aldergrove aerodrome near Belfast, he experienced the greatest fright of his young flying career. The pair were practicing for the display and were flying north of the airfield and well out to sea. He and another pilot lost their way in closing fog. He knew he was just above sea level but could see nothing, not even the other nearby aircraft. He was nearly out of fuel and had no idea how far off the coast he was. He throttled right back to conserve what little remaining fuel he had and he began to sweat profusely as he watched the fuel gauge needle rest on empty. As he was about to give up all hope and prepare to jump from the plane when it hit the water, he had a brief glimpse of rocky coastline through a gap in the fog. He was then able to turn inland and barely clear the rocks to accomplish an immediate forced landing on a private golf course.

In 1938 Sailor's squadron was re-equipped with Spitfires and he was appointed acting Flight Commander of the squadron's 'A' Flight. He and fellow 74 Squadron pilot Paddy Treacy went down to the Supermarine factory at Southampton to take delivery of two new Spitfires. Sailor recalled:

It was like changing over from Noah's Ark to the *Queen Mary*. The Spitfire had style and was obviously a killer. We knew that from the moment when we first fired our eight guns on a ground target. Moreover, she was a perfect lady. She had no vices. She was beautifully positive. You could dive till your eyes were popping out of your head, but the wings would still be there – 'till your inside melted, and she would still answer to a touch.

The Spitfire Mk.1 that equipped No. 74 Squadron was far lighter and better handling than any of the later marks of the plane. Of course, its armament was also considerably lighter, but it still packed a punch unlike anything previously fielded by Fighter Command. It had a top speed of 362 mph at an altitude of 18,500 feet and a rate of climb in excess of 2,000 feet per minute. It was armed with eight .303 Browning machine-guns with a firepower of 9,600 rounds a minute. Sailor:

> You fix the range on the ground – 250 yards is the deadliest. The idea behind this armament is that each gun has its own little place in the heaven. By a criss-cross of fire, ranged at a selected distance, you achieve the maximum lethal pattern. A one-second burst of the eight guns was the equivalent of hurling 240 pounds a minute at a target, a firepower impact which someone likened to a five-ton motor lorry hitting a brick wall at 60 mph.'

No. 74 (Tiger) Squadron had a proud tradition dating back to the First World War, with legendary pilots like Mick Mannock and Taffy Jones who had been among the highest-achieving airmen on the Allied side in that conflict. And Jones was easily among the most outspoken of them:

> My habit of attacking Huns dangling from their parachutes led to many arguments in the mess. Some officers, of the Eton and Sandhurst type, thought it was 'unsportsmanlike' to do it. Never having been to a public school, I was unhampered by such considerations of form. I just pointed out that there was a bloody war on, and that I intended to avenge my pals.

The seventy-three-victory Mannock, for his part, had no time for what he referred to as 'bald-headed tactics'. He believed in surprise and accurate deflection shooting, and he allowed no armourer to sight his guns. He did the work himself, adjusting them so that he would have to fly in very close before firing on an enemy aircraft. Mannock:

> Good flying never yet killed a Hun. You just get on with sighting your guns and practice spotting Huns. Then shoot them down before they shoot you. A sure sign of an old hand is that he reserves his ammunition and only fires in short bursts. If he is aiming straight he knows that a burst of twenty bullets is as good as a burst of 200 and much more economical.

* * *

In September 1938, the Hornchurch station commander ordered his pilots to grab paint and paint brushes and camouflage their aircraft.

From that moment until the actual outbreak of the Second World War a year later, they were almost continuously on alert status and spent many hours in the air in exercises testing the defence systems around the Thames, Humber, Tyne, Medway and the Firth of Forth areas.

*   *   *

In an inauspicious start to Malan's combat career, A Flight was scrambled to intercept a suspected enemy bomber raid on 6 September 1939. The 'raid' turned out to be some Hurricanes of No. 56 Squadron returning from an operation. Believing the primitive radar plot of the day to be enemy aircraft, Malan ordered an attack and, tragically, two of the Hurricane fighters were shot down by 74 Squadron pilots John Freeborn and Paddy Byrne. The unfortunate 'friendly fire' incident became known as the 'Battle of Barking Creek'. In a subsequent court martial, Malan insisted that he had issued a recall order prior to the accidental downing of the planes, but in the event Byrne and Freeborn were acquitted.

*   *   *

Equipped with new Spitfires, Sailor and the pilots of No. 74 Squadron engaged aircraft of the *Luftwaffe* over Dunkirk on 21 May 1940. The scramble buzzer sounded and Sailor led the other five pilots of A Flight as they ran from the dispersal hut to their aircraft. They had been ordered to patrol above Dover at 20,000 feet and were excited as their riggers helped them to become adjusted in their cockpits. Engines were started, chocks pulled away and, as the mechanics and riggers stood back, they taxied out in the blowing grass, checking their instruments, oil pressure, air pressure, gun sight, rudder and tail trim, oxygen, propeller coarse to fine pitch, radio/telephone, and the vital radiator temperature, and they were off.

Climbing away from Hornchurch through the 800-foot cloud base, they noted the visibility limit of one and a half miles. It seemed unlikely to Sailor that they would be able to find the enemy formation they had been sent up to intercept in the broken cloud conditions they were encountering. Finally, they broke out of the cloud at 17,000 feet.

There were six of us and we came out in perfect formation. Johnny's wing was tucked right inside mine, and on the left, Bertie Aubert, who was half-American, had his wing-tip nestling close. I said through my inter-com 'Nice flying, boys,' and then I looked ahead towards France and saw something else. France was our ally then, remember. I saw black puffs about 15,000 feet over Calais. The ack-ack guns kept firing and that meant there were Jerries about. I yelled 'Tally-ho, over Calais. Let's cut some cake!'

We opened up fast. A Spit can cross the Channel about as quick as you can cross the street. There were more clouds between us and Calais. I was flying across the top of a great hummock when I nearly flew into a Heinkel 111. What happened next was done mainly by instinct. I was moving so fast that only by pulling the stick back and a quick swerve did I avoid ramming him.

Sailor was concerned that the enemy bomber would drop into cloud 100 feet below and escape, so he began shooting at the He 111 as he entered a steep turn towards the bomber. His innate feeling for deflection shooting enabled him to rip the German plane from tail to nose, causing great pieces to tear off. The bomber then slipped down into the cloud but not before Sailor saw it begin to break up in the air. He shouted over the inter-com to his mates: 'Re-form, Re-form.' 'I had tasted blood at last. The release from tension was terrific, the thrill enormous.' He had long wondered how he would react to his first aerial combat. He felt that all his work, study and training had begun to pay off. He reflected on the fact that he had not had time to feel scared. After downing the Heinkel, he encountered another enemy aircraft, a Ju 88, a much slower target which he immediately pounced on. He got onto its tail and opened fire at 500 yards and watched his bullets enter the starboard wing-root as he narrowed the distance to the German. He waited until he had closed to within 150 yards before firing again, peppering the enemy plane with shot. He received no return fire from the Ju 88, which had burst into flame and was falling away rapidly.

The next day he shared the destruction of a Ju 88 ten miles northeast of Calais, describing the experience in his combat report:

I was leading three sections off Dover at 12,000 feet when I sighted a Ju 88 steering northwest in a clearing in cloud. Formed line astern with Red Section and cut enemy aircraft off from cloud. He dived for the sea very steeply at 400 mph IAS and jettisoned four bombs. I delivered No. 1 attack at 250 yards' range. After second two-seconds burst rear gunner stopped firing from top blister. Enemy aircraft took avoiding action by skidding and turning. I saw incendiary enter port engine and all round fuselage whilst white vapour was emitted from both motors. At commencement of action IAS was 280 mph but after my fifth burst speed suddenly reduced and as my windscreen was covered in white vapour I broke off to port and observed results of action. No. 3, whose R/T had failed, then attacked from 200 yards and expended all his ammunition and broke off. No. 2 then attacked, but after his first burst enemy aircraft suddenly lost height as though both engines had stopped, and broke up. There was nothing left after two seconds, except the dinghy. Searched for crew but found none.

In an interview with correspondent Quentin Reynolds for *Colliers Weekly* magazine, Sailor talked of the scene over Dunkirk on the day the evacuation began and the Spitfires were stretched to their maximum range: 'The only way we could fly to Dunkirk and have enough juice to spend a few minutes over the battle area was by coasting and flying at sea-level up from Boulogne.' When they arrived in the area, upwards of thirty German bombers with heavy fighter cover were circling at 20,000 feet as they bombed the Dunkirk docks. 'I could not see the beginning or end of them.' Sailor led the Spitfires up to attack the enemy planes and they were fallen upon by the German fighter escorts. While climbing he closed on a Heinkel bomber and opened fire on it, his bullets striking the starboard wing. The bomber caught fire as his own Spitfire was hit. Through the arc of his turn he saw bright flashes of a Messerschmitt's guns behind him and then found that his own gunsight was inoperative. He carried a spare ring and bead sight in the aircraft and began a long, steep climb while he quickly installed the new sight.

I looked down and saw what I thought were three puffs from exploding ack-ack. Then I realized that they were three of the crew of the Heinkel I had destroyed, baling out. They were the first parachutes I'd ever seen open in the sky. It was a rough trip home. Bertie Aubert was killed. Johnny Freeborn was hit. Mungo-Park got one in the arm, and Paddy Treacy got it bad. At least his plane did. His engine was on fire, but he kept going till a bullet went through his windshield and he got a mouthful of glass. Then he baled out. On his way down a Messerschmitt kept circling and taking pot shots that peppered his chute and hastened his descent. As he got near the ground – it was just outside Dunkirk – French troops fired at him. He landed in a pigpen deep in mud. He didn't mind the mud. It helped to break his fall. He did mind the owner of the pen, a large boar which charged him and caused him to twist his ankle.

On 24 May Sailor downed an He 111 and shared in the destruction of a Do 17. His final combat over Dunkirk came on the 27 May, when he shot down a Bf 109 fighter, shared in the downing of a Do 17 and damaged two more. For these actions Sailor was awarded the Distinguished Flying Cross on 11 June. On the 18 June he downed two He 111s during a night operation. Malan: 'The first letter of congratulation that I received came from an insurance company, a firm whose correspondence used to frighten me because the only time they ever wrote to me was when I was behind with my premiums. This time they never mentioned a word about any money owing.'

In mid-June Sailor's wife, Lynda, gave birth to their first baby, a son called Jonathan, in a nursing home at Westcliff-on-Sea, near Southend. During the warm summer evenings after they brought the baby home, Sailor lay awake, unable to sleep as searchlights scanned the sky and occasional ack-ack guns blasted into action. The situation played on his nerves and one such evening he requested permission from his commanding officer to take off. The action was described by an eye-witness to David Masters who wrote about it in his book, *So Few*:

Without waiting to dress, Sailor's rigger and fitter who had already turned in, pushed their feet into gum boots, slung their rifles over their shoulders, put on their tin hats, and reported for duty in their striped pyjamas. Then they rushed out to the dispersal post.

While the mechanics worked swiftly to start up the Spitfire, Sailor methodically buckled on the harness of the parachute. By the time he had got his gear on, the engine had started, so he climbed into the cockpit and strapped himself in before opening up the throttle to warm the engine up a bit.

Meanwhile he looked up and tried to pick out a target ahead, and saw a Heinkel 111 at 6,000 feet being held by the searchlights. It was making a straight run directly across him. A second glance at the approaching bomber made him decide that discretion was the better part of valour and that the engine was quite capable of warming itself up. Leaping out of the cockpit with his parachute on, he made a dive for the little trench close at hand.

The last time he saw the trench it was only about eighteen inches deep. But unknown to him the men had continued to dig until it was about five feet deep. He dived in just as the bomber arrived slap overhead, and landed on his face in the mud at the bottom. When the Heinkel had passed over, he got in and cracked off and made straight for the same Heinkel, which was obviously blinded by the searchlights. Heading for the coast and climbing quickly, he intercepted it just as it was on a slow climb crossing the coast.

The beams of the searchlights made things very deceptive. The first thing he knew he was about fifty yards from it. One moment it looked like a moth in a candle flame, the next the wings suddenly took shape and he realized he was very close. He gave signs to the guns to stop firing when he was in position to attack and they were silent. The whole thing worked like a charm, and in he went. He pressed the button, but after a three-second burst he had to jam his stick forward to avoid collision with the enemy. In this short time his screen was covered with oil from the bomber, which spiralled out of the searchlights and soon crashed on the beach, half in and half out of the water.

As he turned to return to base, he looked back and saw another Heinkel 111 held by the searchlights. Climbing in a spiral below the enemy he signalled the guns to hold off. Then he moved in to attack at 16,000 feet. This time he was a lot more cautious and determined not to overrun the enemy, so he opened fire at 200 yards and closed to 100 yards. As he passed, the Heinkel burst into flames, and a parachute became entangled near the tail. Then the enemy aircraft went down in a steep spiral, well on fire, and crashed in a vicar's garden near Chelmsford with a terrific sheet of flame that was seen all the way from Southend.

Back at Hornchurch, Sailor rushed to a telephone to check on Lynda and the baby. They had slept through the entire enemy raid.

*   *   *

With the opening round of the Battle of Britain in July, Sailor shared in the destruction of an He 111 on the 12th, was credited with the probable destruction of a Bf 109 on the 19th, damaged another Bf 109 on the 25th and shot down a further Bf 109 and damaged a second on the 28th. One of the fitters who worked on his aircraft at the time remembered:

Having spent many hours patching up his Spitfire ready for the next trip I could well realize the marvellous escapes he must have had. Although his Spitfire came back battered each time he would not part with it in exchange for a new and more modern one. His instructions to his crew were: 'My machine has got to be service-able. There is no excuse.' His engine had to go first time, the radio-telephone just had to function even if his junior pilots' radios failed at times. And his guns weren't allowed to have stop-pages. On one occasion it was my job to work out in the open all night with a hand torch to renew his battered tail-plane. I don't know quite how I managed it, but I know it just had to be done by 4.00 am. Flight Lieutenant Malan got in his cockpit and said: 'Contact' without asking if I had finished. In fact I was struggling with the last stubborn split pin. The day came when we were shown the films of his combats, which was a tonic to us all after eight months of terrible waiting, but always ready. The greatest thrill of all was the night of the first raids when Lieutenant Malan went up alone through the intense gunfire and shot down two

German machines in what seemed less than ten minutes. In my heart I knew this was another award for our flight-commander . . .

*   *   *

The Battle of Britain got under way in July and Operation Sea Lion, the enemy invasion of Britain, was soon put in jeopardy as the Germans failed in their first two phases: destruction of Allied convoys in the Channel and south coast ports, and destruction of the Royal Air Force fighter stations defending London. These failures led to their greater failure, the concentrated bombing of London.

Malan was quickly developing into a superb tactician whose advanced, enlightened, and frequently unconventional ideas about air fighting soon drew the interest of his RAF superiors and some high-ranking government officials including Prime Minister Churchill. It was in July that he began to disregard Fighter Command's traditional formations and tactics of aerial combat. He abandoned the standard three-aircraft vic formation in favour of the four-aircraft in-line attack and the 'finger-four' formation pioneered by the fighters of the *Luftwaffe* just before the start of the war. He regularly discussed battle tactics with AVM Keith Park, AOC No. 11 Group. Sailor's efforts ultimately changed Fighter Command into an up-to-date fighting force, ridding it of the old, set-pattern attacks and tight 'display' formations of the 1930s. Believing that it was essential to get in quite close to an enemy aircraft before firing at it, he had the guns of his Spitfire realigned and harmonized to a convergence distance of 250 yards instead of the recommended 400 yards. Many fighter pilots of his squadron and others in Fighter Command, as well as in the fighter squadrons of the American Air Force, followed his lead.

Sailor was given command of 74 Squadron in August and his victories continued as the campaign raged. Throughout the Battle of Britain, the triumvirate of Malan and his lieutenants, J.C. Mungo-Park and H.M. Stephen, ran 74 Squadron with an iron discipline. Sailor's approach: 'Kick their arses once a day and I have the toughest bunch in Fighter Command.' On 11 August, three days after Sailor assumed command of the squadron, they took off at 0700 hours to intercept an enemy raid approaching Dover. It would be the first of four separate air battles they would fight that day. When the weary, sweaty pilots finally returned to base after their fourth fight of the day, they had downed an amazing total of thirty-eight enemy planes. The day was thereafter known as 'Sailor's August 11th.'

It was while 74 Squadron was in training at Kirton-in-Lindsey that Sailor developed the first draft of his famous 'Ten of My Rules for Air Fighting', which he later refined while in command of the Central

Gunnery School at RAF Sutton Bridge. They quickly became the classic tenets for the fighter pilots of the RAF and were pinned up in many fighter station crew rooms in England. Those with the sense to follow them often lived.

Generally speaking, tactics in air fighting are largely a matter of quick action and ordinary commonsense flying. The easiest way to sum it up in a few words is to state that, apart from keeping your eyes wide open and remaining fully alive and awake, it is very largely governed by the compatibilities of your own aircraft in comparison with that flown by your opponent. For example, in the case of the Spitfire versus the Me 109F, the former has superior manoeuvrability, whereas the latter has a faster rate of climb. The result is that the Spitfire can afford to 'mix it' when attacking, whereas the Me 109F, although it tends to retain the initiative because it can remain on top, cannot afford to press the attack home for long if the Spitfire goes into a turn. Obviously there are a lot of factors involved which must govern your action in combat – such as the height at which you are flying, the type of operation on which you are engaged, the size of your formation, etc.

There are however, certain golden rules which should always be observed. Some are quite obvious whereas others require amplification. Here they are:

1. Wait until you see the whites of his eyes. Fire short bursts of one to two seconds only when your sights are definitely 'ON'.
2. Whilst shooting think of nothing else, brace the whole of your body: have both hands on the stick: concentrate on your ring sight.
3. Always keep a sharp lookout. 'Keep your finger out.'
4. Height gives you the initiative.
5. Always turn and face the attack.
6. Make your decisions promptly. It is better to act quickly even though your tactics are not the best.
7. Never fly straight and level for more than thirty seconds in the combat area.
8. When diving to attack always leave a proportion of your formation above to act as a top guard.
9. INITIATIVE, AGGRESSION, AIR DISCIPLINE, and TEAM WORK are words that mean something in Air Fighting.
10. Go in quickly – Punch hard – Get out!

With the end of the Battle of Britain in late October 1940, the strategy of RAF Fighter Command became one of provocation – to 'trail the coat' and make the Germans come up and fight. In mid-October the squadron was moved to Biggin Hill, south of London, in

Kent. At Biggin they shared the field with No. 66 and No. 92 Squadrons and all frequented the *White Hart* local at nearby Brasted, which was kept by Mrs Kathleen Preston, while her husband was away serving with the Royal Navy. Neville Duke, the famed British test pilot, was a member of 92 Squadron then:

'It was a wonderful, low-ceilinged bar with roof timbers taken from old sailing ships. Kath gave the Biggin Hill squadrons the freedom of the place. She was a great friend to everyone and none of us ever forgot her. We spent many contented hours there, relaxing after strenuous ops, and a number of pilots signed their names on a blackboard that had been used for a black-out curtain.'

The signatures included those of Sailor, Mungo-Park, Al Deere and H.M. Stephen. It read like an honour roll of the greatest names in Fighter Command history.

Sailor continued to rack up enemy kills while leading the Biggin Hill Wing through August 1941, when he was posted to No. 58 Operational Training Unit at Grangemouth, near Edinburgh, as Chief Flight Instructor, before being sent to the United States to lecture US Army Air Corps pilots. By the end of the year, he was back in the UK, at Sutton Bridge in command of the Central Gunnery School, followed by ten months as Station Commander, Biggin Hill. He continued in other command roles until attending the RAF Staff College in 1945. He left the Air Force in 1946 with the rank of Group Captain, having added the French and Belgian Croix de Guerre, the French Légion d'Honneur and the Czech Military Cross to his British awards.

*   *   *

Sailor Malan returned with his family to South Africa where he became a successful sheep rancher near Kimberley. In 1948, the Nationalist Government of Dr D.F. Malan, a distant relative, came to power in South Africa with an agenda that included the removal of coloured people from the voter rolls. Sailor was outraged by the stand of the Nationalists and helped form a protest group of ex-servicemen to fight the undemocratic actions of the government. The group was called the Torch Commando and, at its height in the mid-1950s, had a membership of 250,000 that included a number of judges, public servants and military officers, with Sailor as its president. In a speech at a rally outside City Hall in Johannesburg, Sailor Malan referred to the ideals for which the Second World War had been fought: 'The strength of this gathering is evidence that the men and women who fought in the war for freedom still cherish what they fought for. We are determined not to be denied the fruits of that victory.'

The government feared and hated Sailor and soon legislated to ban anyone in public service or the military from joining the Torch Commando. His activist role in the organization began to take its toll and Sailor's health declined. He became ill with Parkinson's Disease and succumbed to pneumonia on 17 September 1963. The South African government declined to accord him a military funeral.

* * *

From *TIME* magazine, 27 September 1963:

Died. Group Captain Adolph Gysbert Malan, 52, one of World War II's top air aces, South African merchant sailor who traded his sea legs for wings, bagged 35 Nazi planes as an RAF Spitfire pilot, returned home to organize 250,000 veterans into the 'Torch Commando', which disbanded in 1953 after an unsuccessful campaign to change the racist policies of Prime Minister Daniel Malan, a distant relative; of pneumonia; in Kimberley, South Africa.

* * *

The magnificent Malan Memorial Sword, made by Wilkinson, was presented to No. 74 Squadron at Bentley Priory on the evening of 15 July 1966. The great house, the heart of Fighter Command, on the hill above Stanmore, close to the spot where many believe the great British Queen Boadicea to lie buried, was a fitting venue. It was a memorable occasion, worthy of Sailor.

Group Captain D.S. Brookes:

The presentation of the sword is made by twenty-eight former members of the Squadron of the years 1936–45 and I am deeply honoured to represent them tonight. I do so as a matter of politeness on their part, because, of those who knew him, I am the old man of the party and had the privilege of commanding the Squadron when Sailor first came to us in December 1936, almost thirty years ago.

Sailor was, I think, the outstanding fighter pilot of World War II and accounted for over thirty enemy aircraft confirmed destroyed and about another twenty probably destroyed. He joined 74 on the day he left his Flying Training School, as an Acting Pilot Officer, and served in all ranks until on 8 August 1940, at the height of the Battle of Britain, he assumed command as a Squadron Leader. He left only when promoted to Wing Commander on 9 March 1941, to become Wing Leader of the Fighter Wing in which the Squadron flew, but he continued to fly with 74. In fact, he was never in any other Squadron so it seems entirely appropriate that this presentation should be a family affair of past and present members of Tiger Squadron.

From a personal point of view, I find the most endearing thing about him was that, apart from being an exceptional shot, he was just an ordinary chap; quiet, unassuming and gentle in manner. His great gifts came from within when great gifts were called for. Tremendous courage, relentless determination and that quality of leadership which carried the whole Squadron to great deeds with him. For in those dark but glorious days the record of the Squadron in battle was, as in 1918, second to none.

The memory of Malan seemed to be a common factor; that it should be commemorated by a sword was just a blinding flash of the obvious, for what but a sword could so well symbolise that dedicated fighting spirit which was the sum of Sailor's great qualities?

*   *   *

He was a born leader and natural pilot of the first order. Complete absence of balderdash. As far as he was concerned, you either did your job properly, or you were on your way. He inspired his air crews by his dynamic and forceful personality, and by the fact that he set such a high standard in his flying.

– Pilot Officer W.M. Skinner, No. 74 Squadron

*   *   *

What I like about Sailor is his quiet, firm manner and his cold courage. He is gifted with uncanny eyesight and is a natural fighter pilot.

– Squadron Leader J.C. Mungo-Park, No. 74 Squadron

*   *   *

Sailor would never talk freely as did the others. I found him (leaning silently against the pub mantlepiece, a pint of beer in his hand which did him the whole evening) rather difficult to know, and exceedingly uncommunicative. As he had already established a reputation as a killer, and his silent stolidity was so much at variance with the extroversion of the others, I was at some pains to draw him out, and on one occasion devoted a whole evening to doing so.

'Tell me, Sailor, as a matter of technical interest, how exactly do you go about shooting down a bomber?'

After some rumination: 'I try not to now.'

'Whatever do you mean?'

'Well, I think it's a bad thing.'

'Now come, Sailor, I really want to know. Don't trifle with me.'

'I mean it. I think it's a thoroughly bad thing. You see, if you shoot them down they don't get back and no one in Germany is a wit the wiser. So I figure the right thing to do is to let them get back. With a dead rear gunner; a dead navigator, and the pilot coughing his lungs up as he lands ... I think if you do that it has a better effect on their morale ... that's what we want to aim at now. Of course, if you just mean to shoot them down, well, what I generally do is ... knock out port and starboard engines. But, honestly, Doc, the other way is best.'

– a hospital surgeon

* * *

The gratitude of every home in our island, in our Empire, and indeed throughout the world, except in the abodes of the guilty, goes out to the British airmen who, undaunted by odds, un-wearied in their constant challenge and mortal danger, are turning the tide of the world war by their prowess and their devotion. Never in the field of human conflict was so much owed by so many to so few.

– Winston Churchill, 20 August 1940

* * *

I did my flying training at Grantham in 1935 in company with my great friend, 'Sailor' Malan, who turned out to be probably one of the greatest fighter leaders of the war. It became obvious to both of us that if one was not flying accurately, it was no good pushing the firing button and hoping for the best. If you opened fire with your 'bank and turn' indicator showing a bad skid either way, your bullets would go nowhere near where you thought you were aiming as you looked through the graticule of your gunsight, just in front of your face. Hence, accurate flying was essential at the moment of opening fire.

Sailor was a very good looking, solid, square shouldered, blond chap. We had a certain kinship, both having been cadets in the Merchant Service. We were kept pretty busy, for it was nearly a year's intensive training with ground studies, meteorology, air navigation, rigging of aircraft, engines, and of course a heavy flying programme. Lots of sport – Sailor played a lot of rugger, while I was more for swimming and fencing. It was a pretty full life.

Sailor was a very experienced fighter pilot. He knew his job inside out. He was a damn good fighter leader in the air, jolly good with discipline, and yet a very pleasant personality, but strong with it. He could shoot straight, flew well and was experienced, which was what it was all about. Sailor was quieter and more thoughtful but would have as much to say as anyone else when it mattered.

– Robert Stanford Tuck

* * *

The South African 'Sailor' Malan ended the war as one of the top-scoring aces on the Allied side. He was important too, for the influence he had upon RAF tactics and formations. He was a man of burly build with an amiable smile that made the men who met him unready for the deep and clinical hatred that he had for his German opponents. He told one of his fellow officers that to badly damage enemy bombers – so that they arrived home with dead and dying aboard – was better than shooting them down; it had more effect on *Luftwaffe* morale. So that is what he tried to do.

– Len Deighton

* * *

Sunday, 28 July 1940 – Sailor Malan was leading twelve Spitfires of 74 Squadron out of Manston in Kent when they encountered four *Staffeln* of Messerschmitt Me 109s over the English Channel. As it happened, the German fighters were those of JG 51 under the command of the great ace Werner Mölders. It was Mölders' first day as commodore of the fighter group. Closing on the Me 109s, Malan selected an aircraft in the lead element of the enemy formation, fired and observed as his victim went down. Mölders then turned, got position on one of the Spitfires and quickly shot it down. It was the German commander's 129th combat mission of the war and his twenty-sixth victory. Mölders then turned on Malan and in seconds was in position to shoot at the Spitfire. Sailor reacted quickly, turning into the attack and continuing to turn more tightly until he was able to bring the German into his sights and then raked Mölders' aircraft with machine-gun bullets, wounding the pilot. Mölders was able to nurse his damaged Me 109 back to his field at Wissant, where the wounds to his leg were severe enough to hospitalize him and keep him out of action for more than a month.

* * *

On 11 August 1940, Sailor led three missions, claiming two Bf 109s destroyed and two severely damaged. Officially, the thirty-year-old Malan was too old to be a squadron commander. But lead he did. And flying line astern with him that day was Warrant Officer Ernie Mayne. Mayne was bringing up the rear and when Sailor led the force through

Tall lattice masts of the British 'Chain Home' radar system during the Battle of Britain.

Members of Britain's Observer Corps in 1940.

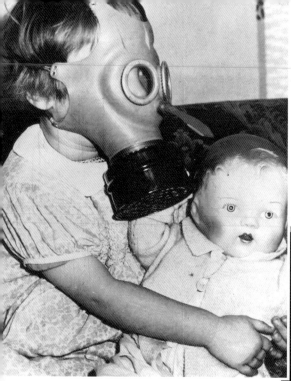

An English child wearing her 'Mickey Mouse' gas-mask during the London Blitz in September 1940.

London firemen at work during the Blitz, October 1940.

Children in Portsmouth being evacuated to the countryside during the Blitz of 1940-41.

Bomb-damaged houses in Portsmouth.

Female workers at Castle Bromwich assembling the horizontal tailplane of a Spitfire.

Generalfeldmarschall of the Luftwaffe, Hugo Sperrle, commanded German Air Fleet 3 against France in May and June, 1940. He played an important role in the Battle of Britain.

Hermann Goering was second in command of Hitler's Third Reich and commanded the German Air Force in World War II. Goering's vaunted Luftwaffe failed to gain vital air supremacy over the England in the Battle of Britain, severely damaging his reputation and influence.

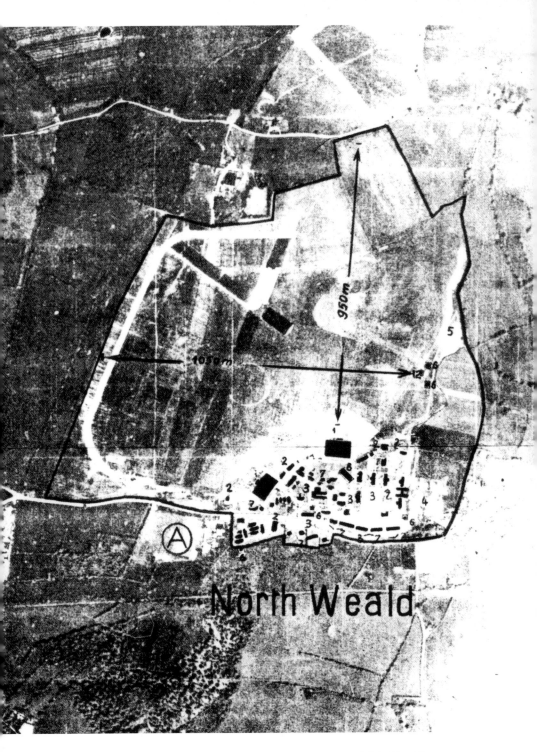

A German aerial reconnaissance photograph of R.A.F. North Weald in Essex.

The cockpit of a
Messerschmitt Bf
109 fighter.

The cockpit view from a Spitfire.

An aerial view of R.A.F. Croydon, south of London, early in World War II.

John I. Brown, a member No. 121 (Eagle) Squadron.

Bob Mannix of 71 (Eagle) Squadron.

Bob Sprague of 71 (Eagle) Squadron.

Vic Bono and Art Roscoe, both of 71 (Eagle) Squadron.

Carroll 'Red' McColpin of 133 (Eagle) Squadron.

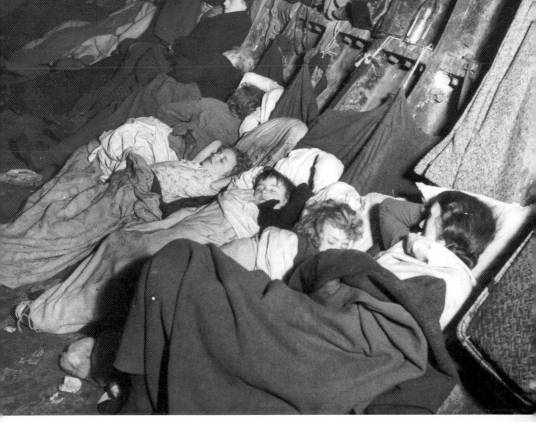

London children sleeping in the shelter of an Underground station during the Blitz of 1940-41.

Church bells rung during the Battle of Britain would have signalled a German invasion.

Fw 190 fighter pilot Oscar Boesch of IV JG 3 "Udet".

Personnel of 1/LG 2 on their airfield during the Battle of Britain.

A Royal Air Force Hawker Hurricane fighter being serviced at Exeter in 1940.

Women made up a large part of the British Air Transport Auxiliary, delivering thousands of fighter and bomber aircraft from factories to R.A.F. airfields during the Second World War.

Battle of Britain aces Robert Stanford Tuck, left, and Adolf Galland during the filming of Battle of Britain, at Duxford, Cambridgeshire, in 1968.

Group Captain Sir Douglas Bader, left, with Wing Commander Robert Stanford Tuck, in April 1980.

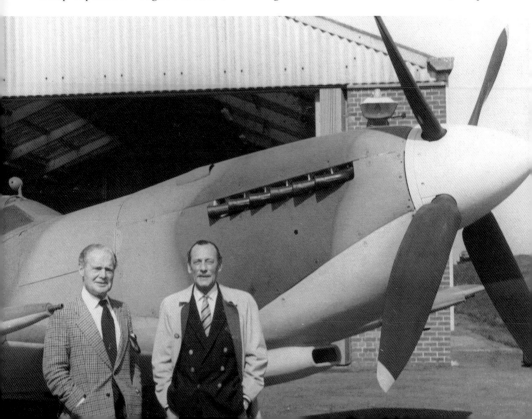

Kath Preston, who, with her husband, Teddy, hosted the Biggin Hill fighter pilots at their pub, the White Hart, in Brasted, Kent, during and after the Battle of Britain.

The Bader Arms, a pub near R.A.F. Tangmere in Sussex. It was named after the Battle of Britain fighter ace, Douglas Bader.

An R.A.F. Polish Squadron Spitfire escorting a USAAF B-17 Flying Fortress bomber of the 92nd Bomb Group (H) on a bombing attack on a German target.

a tight turn it was Mayne who had to turn tightest of all the pilots. In the manoeuvre he blacked out as the blood rushed from his brain. His Spitfire fell from the operating altitude of 24,000 feet to just 4,000 feet before Mayne recovered, saving the plane and himself from crashing into the Channel. Dazed, he spotted a distant formation of aircraft and headed for it, hoping they would lead him back to base. 'Well, of course they were Huns. I think that woke me up a bit. When I saw the crosses I had a shot at one, but then I thought this is no place for you, you'd better bugger off. So I did, and got home, but the falling hadn't done my ears any good.' WO Mayne was hospitalized as a result of falling nearly four miles in the Spitfire. He was forty years old and the only Royal Flying Corps veteran of World War I to fly in the Battle of Britain. It was his last operational sortie.

*   *   *

Oh God, how I am frightened. Now that I am alone I don't have to hide it; I don't have to hide anything any longer. I can let my face go because no one can see me; because there's 21,000 feet between me and them and because now that it's happening again I couldn't pretend any more even if I wanted to. Now I don't have to press my teeth together and tighten the muscles of my jaw as I did during lunch when the corporal brought in the message; when he handed it to Tinker and Tinker looked up at me and said, 'Charlie, it's your turn. You're next up.' As if I didn't know that. As if I didn't know that I was next up. As if I didn't know it last night when I went to bed, and at midnight when I was still awake and all through the night, at one in the morning and at two and three and four and five and six and at seven o'clock when I got up. As if I didn't know it while I was dressing and while I was having breakfast and while I was reading the magazines in the mess, play-ing shove-halfpenny in the mess, reading the notices in the mess, playing billiards in the mess. I knew it then and I knew it when we went in to lunch, while we were eating that mutton for lunch.

Each time now it gets worse. At first it begins to grow upon you slowly, coming upon you slowly, creeping up on you from behind, making no noise, so that you do not turn round and see it coming. If you saw it coming, perhaps you could stop it, but there is no warning. It creeps closer and closer, like a cat creeps closer stalking a sparrow, and then when it is right behind you, it doesn't spring like the cat would spring; it just leans forward and whispers in your ear. It touches you gently on the shoulder and whispers to you that you are young, that you have a million things to do and a million things to say, that if you are not careful you will buy it, that you are almost certain to buy it sooner or later, and that when you do you will not be anything any longer; you will just be a charred corpse. It whispers to you about how your corpse will look when it is charred, how black it will be and how it will be twisted and brittle, with the face black and the fingers black and the shoes off the feet because the shoes always come off the feet when you die like that. At first it whispers to you only at night, when you are lying awake in bed at night. Then it whispers to you at odd moments during the day, when you are doing your teeth or drinking a beer or when you are walking down the passage; and in the end it becomes so that you hear it all day and all night all the time.

The pilot was sitting upright in the cockpit. His face was nearly hidden by his goggles and by his oxygen mask. His right hand was resting lightly upon the stick, and his left hand was forward on the throttle. All the time he was looking around him into the sky. From force of habit his head never ceased to move from one side to the other, slowly, mechanically, like clockwork, so that each moment almost, he searched every part of the blue sky, above, below and all around. But it was into the light of the sun itself that he looked twice as long as he looked anywhere else; for that is the place where the enemy hides and waits before he jumps upon you. There are only two places in which you can hide yourself when you are up in the sky. One is in cloud and the other is in the light of the sun.

He flew on; and although his mind was working upon many things and although his brain was the brain of a frightened man, yet his instinct was the instinct of a pilot who is in the sky of the enemy. With a quick glance, without stopping the movement of his head, he looked down and checked his instruments. The glance took no more than a second, and like a camera can record a dozen things at once with the opening of a shutter, so he at a glance recorded with his eyes his oil pressure, his petrol, his oxygen, his rev counter, boost and his air-speed, and in the same instant almost he was looking up again into the sky. He looked at the sun, and as he looked, as he screwed up his eyes and searched into the dazzling brightness of the sun, he thought he saw something. Yes, there it was; a small black speck moving slowly across the bright surface of the sun, and to him the speck was not a speck but a life-size German pilot sitting in a Focke Wulf which had cannon in its wings.

There was no thought in his head now save for the thought of battle. He was no longer frightened or thinking of being fright-ened. All that was a dream, and as a sleeper who opens his eyes in the morning and forgets his dream, so this man had seen the enemy and had forgotten that he was frightened. It was always the same. It had happened a hundred times before, and now it was happening again. Suddenly, in an instant he had become cool and precise, and as he prepared himself, as he made ready his cockpit, he watched the German, waiting to see what he would do.

He yanked the stick hard back and over to the left, he kicked hard with the left foot upon the rudder-bar, and like a leaf which is caught up and carried away by a gust of wind, the Spitfire flipped over on to its side and changed direction. The pilot blacked out.

As his sight came back, as the blood drained away from his head and from his eyes, he looked up and saw the German fighter 'way ahead, turning with him, banking hard, trying to turn tighter in order to get back on the tail of the Spitfire. The fight was on. 'Here we go,' he said to himself. 'Here we go again,' and he smiled once, quickly, because he was confident and because he had done this so many times before and because each time he had won.

– from *Over To You*, by Roald Dahl

* * *

8 August 1940:

I was Dysoe Leader when squadron was sent off to intercept bandits approaching Dover at a reported height of 13,000 feet. I climbed on an ENE course to 20,000 feet into the sun, and then turned down-sun towards Dover and surprised eight Me 109s at 20,000 feet flying in pairs, staggered line astern towards Dover. I ordered the squadron to attack. Some of them adopted the usual German fighter evasive tactics, i.e. quick half-roll and dive. On this occasion, as the air seemed clear of German aircraft above us, I followed one down and overtook him after he had dived 2,000 feet, opening fire during the dive at 200 yards' range with deflection. He levelled out at about 12,000 feet, when I gave him two two-second bursts at 100 yards range. He was in a quick half-roll and dived towards the French coast. I closed again to 100 yards' range and gave him another two or three two-second bursts, when he suddenly burst into flames and was obscured by heavy smoke. This was at 4,000 feet, one mile NW of Cap Gris Nez. I did not watch him go in, but flew back as fast as I could. I did not see the engagements of the rest of the squadron.

N.B. – Normally I have strongly advised all pilots in the squadron not to follow 109s on the half-roll and dive because in most cases we are outnumbered, and generally at least one layer of enemy fighters is some thousands of feet above. It was found that even at high altitudes there was no difficulty in overtaking E/A on diving, apart from the physical strain imposed on the body when pulling out.

– (signed) A.G. Malan, Squadron Leader,
Commanding No. 74 Squadron

*   *   *

11 August 1940:

I was Dysoe Leader ordered to intercept enemy fighters approaching Dover. I climbed on a north-easterly course to 24,000 feet and did a sweep to the right, approaching Dover from the sea. I saw a number of small groups of Me 109s in mid-Channel at about 24,000 feet, and as we approached, most of them dived towards the French coast.

I intercepted two Me 109s and dived on their tails with Red Section. I delivered two two-second bursts at 150 yards, but as I was overshooting I went off and the remainder of the section continued the attack. I immediately climbed back towards where Blue and Green Sections were waiting above and tried to attract their attention, but owing to R/T difficulties did not manage to get them to form up on me.

I proceeded towards Dover by myself. I attacked two Me 109s at 25,000 feet about mid-Channel, delivered two two-second bursts with deflection at the rearmost one and saw my bullets entering the fuselage with about 15 degrees deflection. He immediately flicked off to the left, and I delivered two long bursts at the leading one. He poured out quite a quantity of white vapour. Eight Me 109s, who had previously escaped my attention, dived towards me, and I climbed in right-hand spiral and they made no attempt to follow. I proceeded towards Dover on the climb and saw ten Me 109s at 27,000 feet in line astern with one straggler, which I tried to pick off, but was unable to close the range without being turned on to by the leader of the formation. I circled on a wide sweep with them for about ten minutes whilst I attempted to notify the remainder of the squadron by R/T. This proved impossible owing to the heavy atmospherics, and in the end I gave up and returned to Manston.

N.B. – It seems that at 27,000 feet I had no superior speed or manoeuvrability over the Me 109. This is merely an impression, and is not necessarily a reliable statement.

– (signed) A.G. Malan, Squadron Leader,
Commanding No. 74 Squadron

*   *   *

Test pilot Neville Duke:

When I was lucky enough to be posted to 92 Squadron of the Biggin Hill Wing in April 1941, the name and reputation of the Wing Leader, Sailor Malan, was already a byword to the pupils in the Operational Training Unit – our instructors having either served with or known him during the Battle of Britain.

With a grand total of 145 flying hours and fully twenty-six hours on Spitfires, I was a very shiny new and green pilot officer aged nineteen and one of the first two wartime-trained recruits to 92 Squadron. During my time the Biggin Hill wing was led by Sailor Malan until early September 1941 when his place was taken by our CO, Jamie Rankin. It was the practice of the Wing Leader to fly with each of the squadrons (Nos 92, 74 and 609) on the fighter operations taking place over Northern France during that period – fighter sweeps, close and top cover to bomber operations, withdrawal cover, delousing sweeps and rear support.

By July I suppose I was considered a veteran of nineteen and respectable to fly No. 2 to the great man on many occasions when he led 92 Squadron. It was a daunting prospect and at all costs one was to stay with the Wingco no matter what – not only to ensure his cover but the honour of 92 was at stake! Better not to come back at all rather than lose the Wingco.

This was all right whilst he was leading the wing peacefully about our business – he was a master of the art of leading some thirty-six aircraft in such a manner that the formation could keep station without struggling. He had very sharp eyesight indeed and was constantly reporting enemy aircraft and manoeuvring the wing into a favourable attack position generally before others had picked up the target. Equally important, he led the wing in such a way that it was least vulnerable to being 'bounced' – e.g. keeping the sun in the right place to the formation as far as possible, not turning down sun and having the squadrons stepped up or down sun as appropriate.

He was a great tactician as well, and during bomber cover missions for example, would not be drawn away by the enemy but might despatch a section, flight or squadron to deal with targets of opportunity. He would always endeavour to give cover to such detached units. We normally maintained R/T silence until enemy aircraft were spotted or we were in the target area. Sailor provided almost a running commentary on the enemy aircraft situation and positions along with pretty forthright instructions to any squadron, flight or body out of position in the formation. As his No. 2 one was, of course, sticking to him like glue whilst at the same time weaving like mad and endlessly scanning above and behind.

Though Sailor flew steadily while he was leading the Wing, it was a different thing once the usual whirl of dog-fighting began. More than once I was so preoccupied with keeping on his tail and with looking around and behind for 109s that I did not know that he was on the tail of a Jerry himself. Once I suddenly found myself flying through bits of a 109 before I even realized that he had fired his guns and once he showered me with spent cartridge cases and links, which was awkward for they were known to crack hoods, pierce radiators and damage airscrews. Neither Sailor nor Don [Kingaby] flew straight and level for a second once they became separated from the main body of the squadron. They were masters in the air, and got everything out of their aircraft; with Sailor especially, it was full throttle work most of the time. From such men as these I learned to weave and to search the sky continuously, never relaxing until we had landed.

Sailor was a most aggressive fighter, hard on his aeroplane (there was then only one place for the throttle at this stage – fully forward) and both hands on the control column! He was very strong as well, with a high 'G' threshold. It was a private dog-fight for a No. 2 to stay with him – he fairly tore into the enemy and was very quick in attack. He was an incredible marksman and a 'snap' shooter, miserly with his ammunition and never firing out of range – it was really hard work staying with him but very informative.

On the ground his briefings before and debriefings after a 'show' were always meticulous. He particularly ensured lessons were driven home during debriefings in a fair but pointed manner and squadron, flight or section leaders (or individuals) seldom made the same mistake twice – it was good for us all and some lived longer for it. Those of us privileged to fly as his No. 2 of course deemed it a great honour – we learned so much so quickly and it stood us in good stead in later days. It was, I suppose, a time for learning quickly and how better?

He was a most human person with concern for his junior pilots but I seem to recall a certain ruthlessness – but little room for apparent sentiment existed in those days. He was relaxed and sociable off duty but I do not remember him as a great 'party' man – he was solid and reliable and somewhat older in relative terms. He was a family man and lived out of the mess with his wife near Biggin – I recall swimming parties at his house even though I was a very junior person and the Wingco was a formidable person in those days.

*   *   *

Malan was by far the most outstanding pilot in air gunnery in the squadron. He had a natural gift, particularly in deflection shooting; in a turn he 'knew' where his bullets would be ahead of the enemy aircraft in order for it to fly into them. He made it seem easy. Many Second World War fighter pilots were actually rather poor at aerial gunnery, but had superb flying skills which enabled them to get in so close to the enemy aircraft that they couldn't miss. Being a crack shot from virtually any reasonable distance, Sailor brought a considerable advantage into combat, but being aggressive, astute and careful, he invariably pressed his attacks in as close to his victims as he could get.

The war began in September 1939, but because so relatively little action occurred until the following May, that period was thought of as the 'Phoney War.' In May things heated up. For the fighter squadrons of the Royal Air Force, the waiting and frustration was finally at an end and the legend of Sailor Malan was about to begin. Sailor: 'I'd tasted blood at last. The release from tension was terrific, the thrill enormous. I had been wondering for so long – too long, how I'd react in my first show. Now I knew. Everything I had learnt had come right. There was hardly time to feel even scared.'

Sailor, after a three-day leave from operational flying in August 1941: 'It was queer – and salutary. I heard the birds for the first time and smelt flowers. I did a bit of rabbit shooting, looked at the scenery, heard people talking about ordinary things and suddenly I knew how really clapped-out I was.'

Al Deere: 'Anyone who said he felt no fear in action was not telling the truth. Youth and inexperience could possibly dull the senses but one quickly discovered that in war it was not all one-sided. The Germans were doing their level best to try and kill or maim you.'

*   *   *

There was a bang. Malan's Spitfire shook and a hole appeared through its right wing and he felt a jolt somewhere back in the fuselage. He had been hit by 'friendly fire' and it had severed the electrical leads near his seat and the light in the reflector gunsight went out. He pulled up and looking back he saw an Me 110 closing fast on his right and a 109 right behind him. It was no time to hang about and he pulled the Spitfire into a series of steep climbing turns into the sun and soon out-manoeuvred his two adversaries.

An early change Sailor made was the basic formation the squadron flew. Throughout his time in the RAF, the peacetime air force had flown set formations based on precedent and standing orders. In Fighter Command the basic element was a section of three aircraft, with four such sections comprising a standard twelve-man squadron in the air. The trouble with the three-man section was that the Nos 2 and

3 were kept so busy concentrating on flying formation on their leader that they could not possibly keep a watchful eye out for enemy aircraft. Unless all eyes were free to scan the entire sky for the enemy, no one in the squadron was safe. As Bob Stanford Tuck, who had discussed the matter with Sailor put it:

> I figured it out darn quick that the 109s were coming at us 'whoomph' – just like that, all in loose formations and we were flying all this jammed-in, odd numbers, which was absolutely hopeless. No freedom of action at all. You were concentrating because of the possibility of collision when you should be looking around at what was going on everywhere else. I eased them out into pairs when I took command. Copy-book formation stuff was hopeless.

While flying and fighting in Spain, the fighter pilots of the *Luftwaffe* had seen the wisdom of flying in two-man section elements and had continued to perfect such tactics in Poland and France. Sailor knew that three was wrong and two was right. He knew too, from the lessons of the First World War that the advantage of height in air combat was vitally important and by the time of the Dunkirk evacuation in May 1940 he had the Tigers of No. 74 Squadron meeting their German enemy at heights of 20,000 to 24,000 feet over and behind that part of the French coast, one reason why members of the British Army on the beach there frequently asked 'Where is the RAF?' They were there but were operating mainly so high that they could not be seen or heard by those on the beaches.

Malan influenced Stanford Tuck and Al Deere and the three of them steadily changed the RAF's accepted rules of air fighting.

* * *

As the Battle of Britain got under way in July 1940, Flight Lieutenant Piers Kelly found himself posted to No. 74 Squadron and was immediately impressed by Sailor Malan. Sailor always took a great interest in his new pilots, showing them the ropes and giving the inexperienced men all the advice he could in order to ease their transition into becoming fighter pilots. Kelly was extremely grateful for this consideration, knowing he needed all the help he could get.

He found Sailor a firm disciplinarian who kept all of 74's pilots on their toes and never let up on their training. Kelly recalled that, to get all his aircraft up above cloud while still in formation, Malan would have them practice flying up through thick cloud in sections, climbing hard, their only point of reference being the tail wheel of the Spitfire immediately ahead in the murk. It worked. Once through the cloud cover, Sailor was still leading and all twelve Spitfires were ready for action.

Malan and 74 Squadron met the first German raid of 13 August – *Adler Tag* or Eagle Day, scrambling from Hornchurch at 0555 hours. Heading out over the Thames Estuary, they ran into a force of Dornier Do 17s which was heading for the English coast. The Dorniers were unescorted. Piers Kelly remembered that the Tigers of 74 Squadron were so eager for a crack at the Germans that they were 'elbowing' each other out of the way.

August and the next phase of the Battle – the German air force attacks on the key airfields of Fighter Command and with them came the arrival of two Polish pilots to the squadron, Flight Lieutenant Stanislaw Brzezina and Flying Officer Henryk Szczesny. Their fellow pilots on 74 Squadron immediately began calling them 'Breezy' and 'Sneezy', there being little likelihood of learning the correct pronunciation of the Polish names.

Both men served the squadron with distinction and Sneezy flew as Sailor's No. 2 on many occasions. He and Sailor got along well, both of them being somewhat older than the other pilots and considerably more experienced. Sneezy, also known on the squadron as Henry the Pole:

> I was happy as a lamb to be on Spitfire I – superior to Me 109, in Tiger Squadron and, like tiger, to kill.
>
> I am very proud I was his No. 2 on many, many occasions and defending his tail, because he told me what to do and to follow blindly his orders. He was shooting down Jerries and I was very close to him, defending his tail. Order is order.
>
> Once he told me by radio to put Pipsqueak [Identification signal] on. Of course, I could not hear him; my radio was always switched off. My English was practically nil, so why bother to listen to it? So, poor Operation Room at Biggin Hill, intercepted our 74 Squadron as bandits twelve plus, with Hurricane squadron over Kent. Then Sailor show me two fingers up, so I did also show him my two fingers up. He laughed and laughed – after pancake [having landed].
>
> He introduced me to Winston Churchill, when he was passing to Chartwell, near Westerham in Kent. At Biggin Hill, at dispersal of B Flight, when we came to readiness. He [Churchill] smiled and shook hands with me and asked in his usual deep voice, 'Henry the Pole, how many today?' I replied shyly, 'Only one Me 109, Sir.' He said, 'Good. Many more to come.' Then, in my broken pidgin English, standing at attention and saluting in Polish way, two fingers closed together, said, 'Sir, please remember Poland

was, is and will forever be the bastion and the wall of Christianity of Western Europe, so make her great, free and independent.' My flight commander, Mungo-Park, translated to Mr Churchill in perfect English. Churchill smiled at me again, puffed on his long cigar, shook hands with me once more and bubbled, 'We will see on Victory day,' and showed me his V sign and drove off.

Sailor did not want me to leave, and fought like tiger to keep me in his squadron, offering me B Flight commander because my English was improving rapidly, but no luck. I had to go. Later, Sailor wrote about me, 'Henry the Pole – pilot second to none.' Motto of our Tiger Squadron was 'I Fear No Man,' but I did add 'Only God and Women.'

* * *

Roger Boulding:

Sailor was instrumental in introducing and leading during the winter of 1940 and the spring of 1941 much 'trailing our coats' over France in an endeavour to persuade the enemy to send up fighters so we would have an opportunity to knock 'em down. I flew as Sailor's No. 2 on some of the sweeps [from Manston] across the Channel to France and found that there was no going back with him until we had done all that could be done – not that he took foolish risks but he was always full of determination – his aim was to get so close behind his target that he couldn't miss. We in 74 Squadron knew him to be a tough and determined, and generally a hard man to fly with. His demeanour was quiet and very cool. He seemed to have himself very much under control and I don't remember him ever getting very excited on the ground. Whilst he would often have a few quiet beers in the evening with the rest of us I don't think he was ever a great party-goer and I don't recall him ever going on a binge in the time I knew him. We all, I think, held him in very great esteem and had great confidence in his leadership, even if we were not always too keen on his methods of stirring up trouble.

As we were his own squadron, Malan normally led his wing with 74 Squadron. He was leading us on the trip during which I was shot down. It was a clear day and we were well across the French coast. I was leading one section of four and spotted a formation of Me 109s, with the famous yellow-painted noses, climbing towards us. I radioed the sighting to Sailor who led us in a diving turn straight onto them. I followed one down in a near vertical dive but had to break off without apparently causing him major damage. At that time we had strict orders not to pursue down to low level over the other side – and Sailor was radioing us to re-form. I tagged along some little way behind him, both of us using the familiar tactic of flying towards the sun in a weaving pattern so as to present a difficult target.

I looked behind and spotted another Spitfire following me in the same fashion. Shortly afterwards Sailor began to call for someone to 'look-out behind!' and urgently to take evasive action. I looked behind, saw what I thought was the same aircraft guarding my rear and began to hunt round for the one in trouble. I had just spotted a Spitfire rocking its wings violently (probably Sailor) when my aircraft was hit from behind. The armour plate behind my seat took it and saved me. The aileron controls went and the stick just flopped from side to side without effect. My aircraft went into a spiral dive, starting from about 25,000 feet, and I had to get out fast. I pulled the canopy release without too much trouble, undid my seat straps but could not get out because of the spinning so had to get my knee up and jerk the stick forward, which effectively catapulted me out. I pulled the ripcord and parachuted down from, at a guess, somewhere above 10,000 feet. The Germans had ample time to reach me when I landed and before I could stand up there were plenty of them threatening me with an assortment of weapons.

* * *

For much of the Battle, Sailor led the Tigers from the forward airfield at Manston in Kent, known as 'Hell's Corner' where they would fly each day from Hornchurch. Being closer to the French coast and the enemy airfields, it gave them a slightly better position, but was also that much more vulnerable to strafing and bombing attacks by marauding German fighters and bombers. On one occasion when the pilots of 74 Squadron landed at Manston after having been involved in a particularly nasty fight with the enemy over the Channel, they were met by their ever-efficient riggers and fitters who quickly set to work preparing the Spitfires for their next sorties. Conspicuously absent, however, were the station armourers who were required to replenish the ammunition for the planes. Malan was uncharacteristically furious, an emotion he rarely displayed, but when it happened it was fearsome. He grabbed a belt of .303 ammunition and stormed into a nearby air raid shelter. There he hit the first armourer he found with it and yelled for them all to get out and rearm the squadron. They were holding up the war effort and he, by God, was not having it.

* * *

Flight Lieutenant R.M.B. Duke-Woolley:

I remember a misty morning at Kenley in early October 1940. A day of ground mist which would later burn off as the sun warmed up. I was temporarily in charge of 253 Squadron and we had landed the previous evening at Middle Wallop. The pilots all wanted to get back to Kenley and their razors and tooth brushes; the weather was fine in Hampshire and we could obviously return if necessary. So we set off for Kenley where visibility was reported poor.

I spotted the airfield after a bit of a search and visibility was very poor indeed laterally, and not very good vertically because of a low sun shining through the mist. However, by forming everyone into a long line astern in orbit roughly over the field, then leaving them to land myself, then immediately taking off again and going into an orbit off the runway, and finally having the long line re-form onto me, we were able to reverse the whole process by leading off downhill in orbit and landing one by one on the runway. I thought the whole performance was rather neat with everyone keeping sight of the one ahead.

Arriving at dispersal I found it all cluttered up with Spitfires, which was the mighty 74 Squadron. Sailor, who had watched us land, said nobody was going to catch him 'taking off in this stuff.' He rather nicely said that his squadron could not possibly have landed in the conditions and congratulated me on the squadron's performance.

I knew Sailor off and on for some years but never all that well. He was a very nice man, not at all the swashbuckler which one or two other aces could well be called. He was at Biggin Hill, of course, in 1940 while I was at Kenley. He was about average at Staff College, tending to be too modest to thump the table – as others might have done with his reputation. I think he was a hunter, really. Good shot, indifferent to danger and with the same killing instinct as a professional hunter.

* * *

A Fighter Pilot's Vocabulary, 1941

Sweep – General term for fighters flying an offensive mission over enemy controlled territory or sea. Could be flown in conjunction with but not in direct support of a force of bombers.

Rodeo – A fighter sweep over enemy territory without bombers.

Circus – A bomber or fighter-bomber operation heavily escorted by fighters. Designed primarily to draw enemy fighters into the air.

Ramrod – A similar operation to a Circus mission, but where the objective is the destruction of a specific target.

Rhubarb – A small scale freelance fighter operation to attack targets of opportunity, usually in bad weather.

Close escort – Surrounding and keeping with the bombers.

Escort cover – Protecting the close escort fighters.

High cover – Preventing enemy fighters from positioning themselves above the close escort and cover escort wings.

Top cover – Tied to the bomber route on Circus and Ramrod missions, but having a roving commission to sweep the sky in the immediate area of the bomber's course.

Target support – Independently routed fighters flying directly to, and then to cover, the target area.

Withdrawal cover – Fighters supporting the return journey when escorting fighters would be running short of fuel and ammunition.

Fighter diversion – A wing or wings creating a diversionary sweep to keep hostile aircraft from the main target area on Ramrod operations.

* * *

Sailor, in a radio broadcast to the people of his native South Africa, 15 September 1942:

> Not all my fellow pilots in 1940–41 have lived to see us gain supremacy in the air. As I grieve their loss I consider the legacy they have left the entire Allied air force. It is for us to remember that those who died two years ago made possible the ascendancy we now have and will hold. Because of them I have been able to talk to you in South Africa, from Britain and to wish you 'Alles van die beste' – All the best.

* * *

Johnnie Johnson, the RAF's top-scoring fighter pilot in Europe during the Second World War:

> I never served with him and my contacts were limited to attending his various lectures and meeting him socially on various occasions when he was commanding Biggin Hill. Nevertheless, in the dark days of 1940 he soon became a legendary figure in Fighter Command and was a great inspiration to all we young fighter pilots who first joined fighter squadrons at that time.

* * *

> Taking a Spitfire into the sky in September 1940 was like entering a dark room with a madman waving a knife behind your back.
> – Adolph 'Sailor' Malan

CHAPTER FOUR

Peter Townsend

The three Hawker Hurricane fighters of Blue Section, No. 43 Squadron, roared from the aerodrome at RAF Acklington on the Northumberland coast a few minutes after nine in the morning of 3 February 1940. Peter Townsend was in the lead of Tiger Folkes and Jim Hallowes. The trio had just been scrambled to intercept an intruding Heinkel He 111 bomber of *Kampfgeschwader* 26. The Heinkel was nearing the English coast at 1,000 feet just to the south of Newcastle.

Townsend led the Hurricanes south, having been vectored on his course by a young WAAF duty officer at the Danby Beacon radar station on the Yorkshire coast, 200 miles from Acklington. He had been directed towards Whitby and was proceeding there at full throttle and wave-top height, hoping to surprise the German bomber crew.

Throughout the evening of 2 February, the crew of the Heinkel drank and played cards in the mess at the desolate Westerlund base in Schleswig-Holstein, northern Germany. They were all *unteroffiziere* and got along well as a team. They worked together efficiently and reacted as they had been trained to do when, early on that bitterly cold evening, they were alerted to take off at first light to attack a southbound British convoy.

During the night 100 soldiers and a snowplough worked at clearing the nearly three feet of blowing, drifting snow that had accumulated on the Westerlund runway that day. They were assisted by the Heinkel crew, Pilot Hermann Wilms, Top Rear Gunner Karl Missy, Observer Peter Leushake, and Flight Mechanic Johann Meyer. After that exertion they reported for the mission briefing where they learned that the British convoy was off the northeast coast of England. The Westerlund bombers were to take off in pairs at three-minute intervals. It was estimated that it would take them about two and a half hours to reach the convoy.

At 0903 hours the radar observer at Danby Beacon saw a succession of blips on her cathode-ray tube and reported a number of unidentified aircraft approaching England at 1,000 feet and sixty miles out. The

plots were passed to Fighter Command and immediately relayed to
No. 13 Group and Acklington Sector station, which scrambled Blue
Section of No. 43 Squadron. With Hallowes on Townsend's left and
Folkes on his right, the pilots moved into a wide-spread formation and
scanned the low cloud base. They knew they were quite near the enemy
aircraft. Townsend was the first to spot the Heinkel of Wilms and
realized instantly that he had only a few seconds to attack before the
German bomber would slip into the protection of the cloud layer. At
that same moment, Peter Leushake saw the approaching enemy
fighters and warned his crew with '*Achtung, Jaeger.*'

Hauling his Hurricane through a ham-fisted climbing turn to the
right, Townsend positioned the fighter to fire on the Heinkel. His first
burst killed Peter Leushake and hem-stitched Johann Meyer's belly, a
wound that would prove fatal. Instantly bomber and fighters slashed
into the cloud layer, each becoming a menacing black shadow within
view of the other. In seconds they emerged with Townsend and Folkes
chasing the damaged Heinkel as it slowly turned towards the English
shore, trailing a thick plume of grey smoke.

The gunner Karl Missy continued firing at the attacking Hurricanes
even though he too had been badly wounded in his back and legs.
Wilms, meanwhile, struggled to guide the crippled bomber across the
high cliffs of Whitby and over the rooftops of the seaside houses there.

Whitby police special constable Arthur Barrett was at home in Love
Lane when the smoking Heinkel drifted over his house at less than 200
feet. He ran for his car and headed towards Sneaton Castle where he
thought the bomber was likely to crash. Karl Missy was fading in and
out of consciousness, but he was aware that the countryside below was
covered in a heavy blanket of snow just as Westerlund had been and he
wondered briefly about what fate awaited him as the plane neared the
end of its one-way trip.

Wilms' last view of Whitby was of houses and trees and a frightening
row of telegraph poles ahead of his descending aircraft which then
ripped through the wires and ramped onto the snow where it slid
towards a line of trees. Circling overhead, Townsend watched as the
Heinkel's right wing caught a tree, whipping the plane around and
stopping it short of the barn at Bannial Flat farm.

Minutes later Constable Barrett and several farm workers arrived at
the crash site of the first enemy plane brought down in England since
the war began. Looking through the Perspex, he saw Wilms on the
floor of the plane, trying to burn some papers. Before Barrett could
stop him, Wilms apparently completed his task and came out of the
bomber into the custody of the farm workers. While Barrett was trying
to bring the other crew members out of the plane, Wilms managed to
free himself from his captors and set fire to his aircraft. He then waved

his arms wildly and shouted at the small crowd of farmers and spectators, 'Boom, boom!' causing them all to back away slightly. Several fire extinguishers and shovels full of snow were then applied to douse the burning wreck. Later, British Intelligence officers managed to recover some of the valuable enemy papers that Wilms had been desperate to destroy.

In the 'tub' beneath Missy's gun position, the mortally wounded Johann Meyer lay screaming with the pain of his riddled stomach. Missy struggled to help his friend, but his own shattered legs denied him mobility. Finally he was able to lower himself with arm strength alone, partially collapsing on Meyer. Now Missy was bleeding profusely and he yelled at Wilms to come and help Meyer. Somehow he crawled from the wrecked plane and slid to the snow where he watched as his pilot brought the body of Peter Leushake from the fuselage. Wilms then returned to drag Meyer out of the front of the plane. One of Whitby's citizens later found a faint trail of blood in the snow. It had come from the Heinkel just before it crash-landed.

Meyers and Missy were carried into the nearest house where they were wrapped in warm blankets and given tea and cigarettes. Soon a local doctor came and administered morphine to the wounded German airmen. He cut the boots from Missy's legs and put splints on him. Still to come was the horrendous ambulance journey to a hospital, punctuated by the frequent moans and screams of the dying Johann Meyer.

They took Missy into the operating theatre later that night and amputated his right leg. The bullet wounds in his left leg were treated and a cast was applied. When he awoke the next morning he was still in great pain. There was an English guard at the end of his hospital bed and he was aware of the care and concern being shown him by the nurse assigned to him. He spoke no English and she no German, but, with the help of Hermann Wilms, who had been allowed to stay at the hospital for a while to help with the language problem, they were able to communicate somewhat. Later, a visitor arrived.

Peter Townsend walked into Karl Missy's hospital ward, went right over to the German and shook his hand. They could only communicate by expressions and what Townsend thought he saw in Missy's face was something akin to the look of a dying animal. 'If he had died I would have been his killer. He said nothing and only looked at me with a pitiful, frightened, and infinitely sad expression in which I thought I could recognize a glimmer of human gratitude. Indeed Missy felt no bitterness. He sank back on the pillows and I held out the bag of oranges and the tin of fifty Players I had brought for him. They seemed poor compensation. Then I left Karl Missy and went back to Acklington and the war. Peter Leushake and Johann Meyer were buried with full military honors at Catterick. A wreath was placed on their coffins. It read, 'From 43 Squadron with sympathy.'

* * *

Peter Townsend was born in Rangoon, Burma, on 22 November 1914 and was educated at Wychwood Preparatory School, Bournemouth, and Haileybury College.

When he was fourteen he was thrilled one day by the sight of three Armstrong Whitworth Siskin biplane fighters landing on the playing fields of his school. For the first time in his life he was able to get up close to an aeroplane, a glamourous one at that, and he was hooked. In that summer, Peter attended Officer Training Camp at Tidworth, Wiltshire, and was one of only three pupils allowed to fly in the camp's Bristol Fighter, a veteran of the First World War. The cold, crisp slip-stream was exhilarating and the experience of flight was so amazing that he determined that day to be a pilot.

He was among the first flight cadets to take up residence in the newly opened facilities of the Royal Air Force College, Cranwell, graduating there in July 1935.

His first attempt to gain admission to Cranwell had failed as a result of a head injury he had sustained as a scrum-half in school rugby. He had twice to sit the Cranwell written exam, interview and medical assessment before finally being admitted. There Townsend flew solo for the first time in his Avro Tutor training plane, a gentle introduction to one of history's most illustrious flying careers.

On completion of his course his initial posting was to No. 1 Squadron at Tangmere on the Sussex coast near Chichester. This was followed by a posting with No. 36 Squadron in Singapore, cut short by illness which forced a return to the UK. There followed further assignments including two additional postings to No. 43 Squadron, during which he shared in the destruction of that first enemy aircraft to be shot down over the UK in the Second World War, a course at the RAF School of Navigation at Manston, and a brief period with No. 217 Squadron of Coastal Command.

With England's declaration of war against Germany in September 1939, Townsend was promoted to a Flight Commander. Opening his account in early February with the downing of the Heinkel, his balance was increased on 22 February when he destroyed another He 111 over the Farne Islands, another on 8 April over Duncansby Head and he damaged a third on 10 April. His performance to that point earned him the award of the Distinguished Flying Cross on 30 April and on 23 May he was given command of No. 85 Squadron, then stationed at Debden, Essex. The Hurricane pilots of No. 85 Squadron had recently returned from participating in the Battle of France and Townsend would remain their boss through the crucial Battle of Britain period.

Peter came into the Royal Air Force at a time when the fifteen-year-old service had very little in the way of modern equipment or funding. It was enduring such contemptuous taunts from members of the Army and the Royal Navy as 'the Royal Ground Force' and 'the Cinderella Service.' With almost no history it could look only to the destiny it foresaw. Townsend:

> The RAF's impudent claim that priority should be given to air defence rocked the sea-dogs and the Colonel Blimps. It was unbearable that the old country should have to look for protection to pilots of the RAF, whom the old guard tended to despise as the rag-tag and bob-tail of the country's youth, beyond the fringe of respectable society, with their pub-crawling and their noisy sports cars. Insurance companies exacted an extra premium from these accident-prone young men.

* * *

In the 1931 RAF air display at Hendon, North London, 175,000 awed spectators witnessed the aerobatic performances of brave and bold pilots flying their slow but agile Hawker Fury and Bristol Bulldog fighters. One among that enthusiastic crowd was Erhard Milch who, in two years, would become State Secretary of the newly created *Reichsluftfahrtministerium*, Nazi Germany's Aviation Ministry, reporting directly to Hermann Goering. He would be instrumental in establishing the German *Luftwaffe* and, for a time, responsible for Hitler's armaments production. Milch, who was born to German Jewish parents, had his ethnicity called into question in 1935 as rumours were circulating that his father, Anton Milch, was indeed a Jew. The Gestapo investigated but that procedure was soon quelled when Goering produced an affidavit signed by Milch's mother stating that Anton was not actually the father of Erhard and his siblings. The paper named one Karl Brauer, her uncle, as his true father. Erhard was then issued a German Blood Certificate, whereupon Goering famously stated, 'I decide who is and who is not a Jew.'

Milch enjoyed his day out at Hendon, later claiming to have learned a lot at the Hendon displays, including the theory behind fuel injection for aero engines, in conversation with a member of the Bristol Aeroplane Company technical staff. 'My English then was very bad, but he explained everything so kindly that I understood. We had nothing of the kind in Germany at the time.' By 1940, however, fuel injection in the front-line fighters of the *Luftwaffe* was providing the Germans with a significant advantage in the Battle of Britain over the British, who had not followed through with development of a fuel injection system for the Merlin engines of their Spitfires and Hurricanes.

In addition to fuel injection, the Messerschmitt fighters of 1940 were equipped with a brilliant device, also invented by a British firm, the Handley Page Aircraft Company. The device, known as the wing slot, had previously been fitted to British biplanes to improve their slow-flying characteristics, but it elicited little interest among Air Ministry personnel when Handley Page wanted to put it to use on monoplanes. With no suitable British monoplane aircraft in existence at the time, the company worked with Heinkel in Germany during 1932 to try the wing slot on the He 64, with great success.

All new fighter-related development was not, however, the province of the Germans. Key air weapon work was under way at both Super-marine and Hawker, led by R.J. Mitchell and Sydney Camm respec-tively. That work would result in the Spitfire and the Hurricane – fast, well-armed, closed-cockpit fighters with retractable undercarriages and powered by the reliable Rolls-Royce Merlin engine.

It was the beginning of Peter Townsend's training on 'service type' aircraft and he was ecstatic at having been selected to be a fighter pilot, a role for which he felt well suited, having as he did the mentality and temperament of a loner. His aeroplane was to be the Bristol Bulldog, a 450 hp. single-seat open-cockpit biplane with a reputation as fairly viceless. He would soon have reason to debate that point. Townsend:

> Spinning was the most regular, if not the most frequent, of all our exercises. A spin, if it occurred too low or was not properly handled, was a sure killer.
>
> While the pilot of the Heyford bomber 'stooged' up and down, I was airborne in a dual-control Bulldog fighter at Cranwell. Flying Officer McKenna, a burly, smiling man with a rolling gait, like a sailor, was in the cockpit behind. The *dual* Bulldog was a bastard in every sense, with the single-seater's graceful upswept wings and a fuselage elongated to take a cockpit for the instruc-tor. It could also be a bastard in a spin. Spinning was forbidden under 8,000 feet, where I found myself that afternoon with McKenna. 'OK, spin her to the left off a steep turn.' Over we went and down. The Bulldog shied briskly into a spin – one turn, two, three. 'Bring her out,' McKenna called down the Gosport speak-ing tube. Stick forward, opposite rudder. No effect, save that the spin now became flat and dangerous as the aircraft refused to answer. We were sinking rapidly and I was conscious of an eerie hush, of the clatter of the engine's poppet valves and the reek of

burning castor oil, the standard lubricant for this engine, of the propeller in a slow tick-over, brushing the air, of the air rushing past my ears and through the bracing wires, making them whine, while the aircraft pitched and tossed in a sickening circular movement, totally, hopelessly out of control. We were down to 5,000 feet when McKenna yelled, now far from cheerful, 'I've got her!' and I could feel his vigorous movements, banging open the throttle lever, pumping the stick, kicking the rudder, he tried to rock the Bulldog back into flying position. Still we spun and McKenna, his voice now urgent, called, 'Get ready to bale out!' Praying I should not have to jump, I pulled the release pin of my Sutton fighting harness. With throttle, stick and rudder McKenna kept fighting the Bulldog. We were down to 2,000 feet when at last he brought her back to an even keel, with just enough height left to dive and pick up flying speed. His voice, now very quiet, came through the speaking tube: 'That was a near one. Now climb her up again and we'll do another.' I was learning to be a fighter pilot.

* * *

Townsend had been in training at RAF College, Cranwell, for two years and was one of three flight cadets under consideration for the coveted award of the Sword of Honour. Like many of the other students, however, he was impatient with the small number of hours that were devoted to flying relative to the time spent studying and his impatience was starting to distract him from his previously smooth, efficient academic performance. This led one day to his being asked to tea by the Assistant Commandant, Air Commodore Philip Babington, who told Peter that he was 'a disappointment to him and the training staff ... Your trouble is that you are a rebel. You are too much inclined to head off on your own. Still, the world needs rebels.' Townsend:

I had joined the RAF to fly. I lived only for the moment when I should settle into the cockpit of one of the little Bulldog fighters. The pilot sat in line with the trailing edge of the top wing, so that he felt the wings were his. It was supreme joy to fly away from the earth and forget its binding influences.

Early in September 1933, my instructor, Flight Lieutenant Poyntz Roberts, introduced me to the Avro Tutor, a little open-cockpit biplane powered with a 250 hp engine. My initiation in the art of flying had begun. Poyntz was a small, irascible man with a face as pink as a rose and an inexhaustible vocabulary of swear-words. The advice he gave me, laced with oaths, came straight out of the RAF Training Manual. But he left me with two dicta of his own invention: treat everybody else in the air as a bloody fool and handle your aeroplane as if she was your favourite girl.

After six hours of take-offs and landings, of diving, climbing, banking, gliding, side-slipping, spinning, rolling and looping we landed one afternoon in the middle of the vast sward of Cranwell's airfield. Poyntz climbed out of his cockpit and on to the wing below mine. 'She's all yours,' he shouted. 'Off you go'.

That day, 15 September 1933, I made my first solo. It was less than thirty years before that Orville Wright, the first man to fly, had made his – that is, the first powered, controlled, sustained flight.

I was eighteen. For the next two years I submitted, gladly for the most part, to the intensive and variegated process which was to mould me as a pilot, an officer and a gentleman. Our education, largely academic, was generously dosed with sport and parade ground drill and spiced, all too slightly for our liking, with flying. I had some difficulty in reconciling flying – to my mind all grace and zest and poetry – with its technical and military aspects. Yet I soon discovered that there did exist a nice balance between the idealistic and the material.

I did not, I admit, take easily to my bird-like view of flying being reduced to the base, technical formulae of aerodynamics and engineering terms. Yet pleasant features began to appear out of the gloomy fog of technical theory and practice. The aeroplanes we flew were 'rigged' – like a sailing ship; a 'rigger' maintained the airframe in proper trim. Our technical vocabulary included melodious names like longeron, fuselage and aileron, camber, dihedral, tailskid and undercarriage (undercart for short); joystick (which we always called the stick) was a sublime pseudonym for the control column; it evoked the essence of flying.

Airframes and wings were covered with taut fabric, and this enabled me to exercise a talent learnt in my childhood under the expert guidance of Tommy Coles, I sewed and rigged the sails of the ships he helped me to build. Now I was learning to sew the fabric of our aeroplanes, repairing a rip in wing or fuselage with a villainous curved needle, the kind that surgeons use, slapping over the seam a patch of new fabric which I daubed with red acetone dope, smelling deliciously of peardrops.

The incredible complexity of an aero-engine at first flummoxed me; but here again the terminology intrigued me to the point of enabling me to master a perplexing subject. An aero-engine is composed of a myriad of moving parts, from its fat pistons down to its miniscule contact-breakers. Within its entrails, squirming and oscillating, seething and heaving, are spigots and splines and sprockets, rockers, poppets and pushrods, camshafts and crank-shafts, big-ends and little-ends. It was the lure of these names that ultimately created an intimacy between me and my engine – plus the cold fact that my life depended on it. But when it came to choosing a subject for my mechanical thesis I selected from among fifty-odd highly technical themes one which was rarely discussed: the Flight of Birds. Never have I written about a more fascinating subject. I envisaged the use by man of a number of bird-like devices, among them the variable geometry wing. Had I possessed the genious of Sir Frank Whittle, father of the jet engine, and another flight cadet, ten years my senior, my life-pattern might have been different.

The harsh reality of flight training included more than a few fatal accidents. One of them during Peter's course at Cranwell happened when two dual Bulldogs met in a devastating mid-air collision, killing both instructors and both cadets, their dismembered remains found in trees and fields near the crash site. Townsend:

There was not one of us who did not think, 'This could happen to me,' and tried not to believe it. However, we bit by bit built up our defences against these depressing visions. We developed a peculiar sense of humour, a way of looking at things which, if macabre, suited our condition. Our jokes and rhymes and songs fortified our morale. Yes, flying was a dangerous trade. We who were learning it and accepting its risks were paid seven shillings a day. Sixpence a day was deposited to our account. We received, net, three shillings a day. It never occurred to us as being too little, for we received, on top of it, an inestimable reward. We were learning to fly.

At the end of July 1935 I said goodbye to the RAF College and to Bulldogs. At least as far as flying was concerned I had re-deemed myself in Philip Babington's eyes. He wrote in my flying logbook, 'No faults [he was overgenerous]. He needs encourage-ment.' As a pilot I was rated 'above average,' which meant little with only 150-odd hours in my logbook. Experience, as in all things – but especially in flying – was the best school.

* * *

RAF Tangmere, on the Sussex coast, was a large, grassy meadow when Peter arrived for his first Air Force posting. The buildings and hangars had been put up by German prisoners in the First World War and would, by and large, be destroyed by German bomber crews in the Second World War. Peter was happy there and thrilled to be flying the graceful, Rolls-Royce Kestrel-powered Hawker Fury fighter. It was faster and handled better than the Bulldog. The experience there left him in enthusiastic agreement with his fellow airmen that the RAF in that time was 'the best flying club in the world.'

Townsend's certificate of commission as a Pilot Officer in the RAF was signed 'George Rex *et Imperator*'. It informed him that 'we' reposed especial trust and confidence in his loyalty, courage and good conduct. It stated that he must carefully and diligently discharge his duty, exercise and well discipline the inferior officers under his command and his best endeavours to keep them in good order. Some thirty years after receiving the document, Peter's Labrador ate it, failed to digest it and became quite ill.

To Peter the Fury was like a lovely girl, slim, tender to the feel, perfect in looks and manners, tactfully and generously responsive to every demand, and never spiteful, unlike some aeroplanes and girls. With the power of a 650 hp engine she could make a bit more than 200 mph and she carried two Vickers machine-guns which safely fired through her two-bladed wooden propeller thanks to an interrupter gear. The plane was equipped with a small tool bag next to the right-hand gun. The bag contained a specific tool known as a 'Plug, Clearing, Vickers'. When a split cartridge jammed one of the guns, the pilot had to grip the control stick between his knees and fumble in the tool bag for the 'Plug, Clearing, Vickers' which he then stuck into the breech of the jammed gun and waggled it 'to-and-fro' to clear the cartridge.

Life at Tangmere was very much to Peter's liking, peaceful, bucolic; the airfield dominated by its graceful, wood-beamed 1917 hangars. The most prominent local landmarks were the spire of Chichester cathedral to the northwest, and an old windmill on the Downs to the northeast. Aerial navigation in the 1930s was still rather primitive. It would be a while before radio communication and direction finding would help. Townsend:

> Our pin-pointing exercises sent us off in search of objects as small as duck-ponds, water-troughs and odd-shaped telegraph poles. The Old Man of Cerne Abbas provided the acid test. A huge figure cut out of a chalk hill in Roman times, he was hard to spot. To prove you had done so, you had only mention a striking detail: the Old Man sported an erected phallus several yards long.'

But while radio 'homing' was available then, Townsend and his fellow Tangmere pilots were more inclined to rely on their own instincts rather than the less than reliable aid of the ground station. They instead tended to 'Bradshaw' (a reference to the railway time-table of the period); a pilot would follow railway lines, flying low enough occasionally to read the sign boards of the stations. Meanwhile, about ten miles to the southeast of Tangmere some very large, very strange lattice masts were being put up near a place called Polegate. The area was a 'no-fly' zone and the masts were never discussed. They were radar.

Taut nerves resulting from weeks of flying were relaxed once a month when the men of No. 1 Squadron were allowed to discard their uniforms in favour of overalls, and indulge in a long, beery evening of filthy songs, mess rugger, cigarettes and good cheer. Special guests ranging from air mashals, admirals, the Bishop of Chichester and the mayor, were all required to take part in a ceremony wherein the soles of their shoes were blackened and they were assisted by many willing hands to climb the walls and cross the ceiling, leaving their shoe prints as they went. Such evenings were not really Peter's idea of a good time, but as a young 'sprog' pilot, he felt compelled to participate.

Mentoring Townsend were his squadron commander, Theodore MacEvoy and another Mac, 'Rip-cord Ralph' MacDougal, a No. 43 Squadron pilot stationed at the Tangmere base. MacDougal shared his skill and knowledge of aerobatics and formation flying while stressing the precision and total concentration required of a fighter ace. MacEvoy 'taught me the serious stuff' including discipline and which sorts of risk were worth taking and which were not. Both men contributed greatly to the high-calibre pilot that Peter would become.

*   *   *

In January 1936, Townsend was posted to No. 36 Torpedo Squadron in Singapore. He arrived there four weeks later to find that he would be flying the Vickers Vildebeest, a rugged, three-seat coastal defence biplane developed as a torpedo-bomber. The aeroplane cruised at 100 mph. A notice in the cockpit read: 'This aircraft is not to be flown at a speed in excess of 140 mph'. For Peter and the airmen of No. 36 Squadron, life in Singapore, like the Vildebeest, moved at a leisurely pace. They reported for flying duties on the Seletar base each day at 7.30 am and their work day finished at 1.30 pm, after which they slept or sailed ... a seemingly idyllic existence. Townsend:

> One day the German training cruiser *Emden* dropped anchor. The Tanglin Club invited the ship's officers for golf and tennis. That evening there was a party and the band played *Deutschland ueber Alles*. Many of them thrust their arms out in the Nazi salute and we thought they looked rather funny.

Peter Davies commanded No. 36 Squadron at Seletar and was well liked and respected by his pilots. The old expression, 'We would follow him anywhere' applied to the attitudes of Townsend and the others as Davies led them on frequent patrols over the jungle and far out at sea practicing night torpedo attacks. The Vildebeests carried no radios and the pilots were unable to communicate with one another or the base. They simply followed Davies' navigation lights. His aircraft carried the only radio.

Late in 1936 Townsend flew one of twelve Vildebeests of No. 36 Torpedo Bomber Squadron to the northwest frontier of India, arriving at Risalpur exhausted after five days of cruising at 100 mph. During the lengthy flight, the pilots landed to refuel at Victoria Point, a small grass airfield in southern Burma. Using two-gallon cans, coolie labourers emptied the aviation spirit into the torpedo bomber fuel tanks. As one of them finished filling Townsend's aircraft, the man accidentally dropped the empty can, tearing a hole in the fabric of the lower wing. Peter's resourceful crewman, Flight Sergeant Spinks, produced a curved surgical needle and thread, repaired the tear and slapped a patch on it.

After a week at Risalpur and a brief stop at an Indian Army garrison in the Khyber Pass, the squadron returned to Singapore, stopping at a number of new airfields along the Burmese coast. Unfortunately for Peter, the trip resulted in a bizarre illness causing him to break out in sores and his feet to swell so much that he had to fly without shoes. In Singapore the doctor ordered him to return to England and to stop flying. It was a crushing psychological blow as he lived for flying. On arriving back in England, however, doctors there declared him cured and fully fit for flying. Even better, he was then posted back to Tangmere and No. 43 Squadron.

* * *

On 11 May 1937 a Junkers Ju 52 transport plane landed at Croydon airport south of London, bearing the German armaments chief, Hermann Goering, who had decided to visit the British capital on his own and without the authority of Chancellor Adolf Hitler, to attend the Coronation of King George VI. Scotland Yard then provided unobtrusive transportation to the German Embassy where Ambassador Joachim von Ribbontrop spent an hour trying to persuade Goering that, as one of Hitler's closest associates, he would certainly be booed if he dared show his face in London. Ribbontrop was not going to be outshone by the celebrated Goering, who returned to Berlin the next morning in a rage.

Goering would host Marshal of the Royal Air Force Lord Hugh 'Boom' Trenchard when the latter visited Berlin on 1 July. 'You are well known in Germany and I have a high regard for the air force you have created,' he told Trenchard. That evening, however, he showed a darker side to his guest at a banquet in Trenchard's honour at the Charlottenburg Palace. Dressed in a white uniform be-medalled and quickly warming to his subject, *Generaloberst* Goering told Trenchard,

'It will be a pity if our two nations ever have to fight. Your airmen are very good. It's a pity they haven't the machines we have. One day German might will make the whole world tremble.' With unconcealed anger Trenchard replied, 'You must be off your head. You said you hoped we wouldn't have to fight each other. I hope so too, for your sake. I warn you, Goering, don't underestimate the RAF.' Then, making an excuse, Trenchard left the banquet and never saw Goering again. Later, he said of the German, 'He's vulgar and coarse and brutal, but he's a great man.'

* * *

Another controversial visit between the future adversaries occurred on 17 October when German General Erhard Milch arrived at Croydon airport accompanied by Generals Stumpff and Udet. The generals were given a tour of the RAF cadet college and were impressed by the similarity of the young British fighter pilots to their German counterparts. Milch was concerned, though, by one apparent difference. 'England had the training resources of her Empire and I wondered what would happen if war came. In the *Luftwaffe* we had no experienced leaders.' Later, when he visited the fighter station at Hornchurch, Essex, and met Air Chief Marshal Dowding, who would lead RAF Fighter Command through the Battle of Britain, he looked into the cockpit of a Gloster Gladiator fighter. The biplane had been fitted with the newest optical reflector gunsight and the pilots of No. 65 Squadron gathered round the German visitors had been warned by their station commander, Group Captain 'Bunty' Frew, to say nothing should the Germans ask about the sight. When Milch did inquire about the device to future Battle of Britain ace Bob Stanford Tuck, the response was, 'I'm sorry, General, it's so new I've not yet found out how it works.'

Over drinks at a luncheon given later for the German generals, Milch surprised the British officers when he loudly asked, 'Now gentlemen, let us all be frank. How are you getting on with your experiments in the detection by radio of aircraft approaching your shores?' The question generated embarrassment, confusion and more than a bit of outrage before Milch continued, 'Come, gentlemen, there is no need to be so cagey about it. We've known for some time you were developing a system of radio location. So are we, and we think we are a jump ahead of you.' In fact, the RAF was slightly ahead in the race to develop and employ a system accurately to detect and plot 'hostile' approaching aircraft, as indicated by the results of air exercises conducted by three radar stations of the new Chain Home system, at Dover, Kent, Bawdsey, Suffolk, and Canewdon, Essex. The then incomplete system would become key in British air defences. It evolved as a Filter Room was established at Bawdsey to check and analyze the radar plots before passing them on to Fighter Command Operations. Formations of six or more aircraft were being successfully plotted at ranges up to 100 miles and altitudes of 10,000 feet and higher. Still, the system required a chain of twenty-one stations and completion was at least two years away. It would take an urgent conversation between Robert Watson-Watt, the inventor of radar, and Winston Churchill, over a cup of tea in the House of Commons to cut through the red tape and end the delays slowing completion of the chain system.

*   *   *

For Peter Townsend the next career move was, in his view, a disaster. His Singapore stint in torpedo bombers had evidently convinced some in the Air Ministry that he should be permanently assigned to Coastal Command and should be posted initially to the School of Navigation at RAF Manston, Kent on a four-month course. As one of the many RAF fighter pilots who saw the coming war with Germany as all but inevitable, he was thunderstruck by the decision and his subsequent posting. He was, he knew, a born fighter pilot and could not imagine, much less countenance, the prospect of being involuntarily converted from that natural role to the one awaiting him on the Kentish coast. He hated the course and felt shamed by the comment received with his diploma, which in no way reflected his own perspective, 'Has taken a keen interest in the work ... with experience should become a very sound navigator/observer.' His gloom was compounded when he was immediately posted to a new coastal squadron at Tangmere, under the command of a man to whom he took an immediate and intense dislike. The CO had the same attitude towards Peter and the situation was made worse each day as he unhappily watched friends in Nos 1 and 43 Squadrons continuing to enjoy flying their Fury fighters. Release finally came when a kindly RAF doctor suggested he write to the medical authorities informing them that flying as a passenger or a second pilot in a twin-engined aircraft made him ill (it really did) and, if steps were not taken to put him back in single-seaters he would resign his commission. His station commander was Keith Park, the brilliant New Zealander who would run No. 11 Group during the Battle of Britain. Park happened to be a friend of the Coastal Command Commander-in-Chief and he assisted Townsend in returning to the status of a fighter pilot. He was soon back with 43 Squadron where he felt he belonged.

*   *   *

Townsend was certainly not the only air force officer whose career was having its ups and downs in that time. His problem was as nothing when compared to that of Air Chief Marshal Dowding, C-in-C Fighter Command, whose relationship with the Air Ministry had been in serious decline for years. Communication between them had deteriorated appreciably and it was apparent to Dowding that he was frequently being ignored or snubbed in matters vital to his Command and was often deliberately excluded from policy decisions in which his view should have weighed heavily. He could be difficult and sometimes less than pleasant to deal with and, by his own admission,

> It is probably a defect in my character, but I have found that a stage can be reached where more harm than good is done by verbal discussions. It would have been easy to remain on good terms with the Air Staff if one had accepted every ruling. Since I was a child I have never accepted ideas purely because they were orthodox, and consequently I have frequently found myself in opposition to generally-accepted views. Perhaps, in retrospect, this has not been altogether a bad thing.

He was not even consulted, and only learned by chance, about plans for an emergency Fighter Command operations room. When he protested he was told that the planning was settled and could not be changed. He was, however, invited on occasion to attend Air Ministry conferences on equipment. In one such meeting he asked for bullet-proof windscreens for his Hurricane and Spitfire fighters and was appalled when the others attending laughed uproariously at his request. He responded, 'If Chicago gangsters can have bullet-proof glass in their cars I can see no reason why my pilots should not have the same.' In time the request was honoured. One of the lives saved by the new windscreens was that of Peter Townsend.

The radar chain system that would later prove invaluable to Air Chief Marshal Dowding in Fighter Command's defence of Britain slowly increased in capability, and three squadrons were now equipped with the new Hawker Hurricane fighter, all thanks largely to the unflagging efforts of this outspoken and shamefully under appreciated man.

On the morning of 5 August 1938, a letter arrived for Dowding from the Permanent Under Secretary of the Air Ministry: 'I am commanded by the Air Council to inform you that ... they will be unable to offer you any further employment in the Royal Air Force after the end of June 1939.'

*   *   *

Throughout the month of September 1938 Peter Townsend and the pilots of No. 43 Squadron at Tangmere joined the ground crews in the hangars each night preparing their aircraft for the war they were certain was coming with Germany. They belted thousands of rounds of ammunition and, to their great displeasure, painted over their sleek silver Fury fighters with what seemed to them ugly green and brown camouflage warpaint. Aesthetics aside, the camouflage cost several miles per hour from the 210 mph top speed of the aircraft, through added weight and skin friction. The harsh reality was that at around 200 mph the Fury pilots would not be able to catch much less shoot down the Germans' 250 mph-plus Heinkel He 111 and Dornier Do 17 bombers. Morale on the squadron was at a low ebb. The situation at Hornchurch where 54 Squadron was readying its 245 mph, four-gun Gloster Gladiator fighters for the coming conflict was not appreciably better. They too foresaw the imbalance and, while eager to take on the enemy, had no illusions about the match-up of equipment.

*　*　*

On 30 September British Prime Minister Neville Chamberlain returned to Heston airfield from Munich where he had conferred with Hitler. Leaving the aircraft he held up a sheet of paper bearing the signature of the German Chancellor. It included: 'We consider the agreement signed yesterday ... as [one of] the symbols of the desire of our people never to go to war again with one another.' Waving the paper, the Prime Minister said, 'I believe ... that it is peace in our time.' There was wild applause from those gathered to greet him. On that day the Royal Air Force was equipped with 750 fighter aircraft of which 90 were Hurricanes. All the rest were obsolete biplanes.

*　*　*

The outlook at Tangmere was improving in late November when No. 43 Squadron received the first two Hurricanes of sixteen that would re-equip it by mid-December. The pilots were immediately impressed with the stable gun platform the new fighter provided and the powerful eight Browning machine-gun armament it carried. They found the Hurricane to be easy to handle, highly manoeuvrable and offering good visibility from the closed cockpit. Less lovely than the faster Spitfire, it would nonetheless account for more enemy aircraft destroyed in the coming Battle of Britain than the glamourous Supermarine plane. For the pilots, though, the transition from the Fury to the larger, heavier Hurricane was not without problems. Low-speed handling at low altitudes could be deadly until experience on the type had increased, and night flying in particular brought a new set of problems, not least being reduced visibility owing to the prominent blue flame issuing from the engine exhausts. But with time and experience most of the squadron pilots came to appreciate and trust their new fighter and its marvelous Merlin engine. Most importantly, with the Hurricane, confidence in their ability to challenge and defeat the German air force returned.

* * *

In February 1939, the London *Evening Standard* announced the impending retirement of Air Marshal Dowding as C-in-C Fighter Command, his successor to be Air Vice Marshal Christopher Courtney. Within hours Dowding received a telephone call from Chief of the Air Staff Sir Cyril Newall telling him that 'No change will be made during the present year ...' It seemed that the proximity of war may have caused the Air Ministry to change its mind about early retirement for Dowding. After due consideration, however, Dowding put his thoughts down on paper:

> I have received very cavalier treatment at the hands of the Air Ministry during the past two years. I have no grievance over these decisions, except as regards the discourtesy with which they were effected. There was no need to inform me that I was next in succession as Chief of Air Staff so that I might expect to be retained up to the age of sixty [he was then fifty-six]. But the reversal of these intentions were baldly conveyed to me.
>
> I can say without fear of contradiction that since I have held my present post I have dealt with and am in the process of dealing with a number of vital matters which generations of Air Staff have neglected for the last fifteen years: putting the Observer Corps on a war footing, manning of Operations Rooms, identification of friendly aircraft, unserviceability of aerodromes, and adequate Air Raid Warning System. This work had to be carried out against the inertia of the Air Staff, a statement which I can abundantly prove if necessary. In spite ... of my intense interest in the Fighter problems of the immediate future ... there is little in my past or present treatment at the hands of the Air Ministry to encourage me to undertake a further period of service.

He later met with Air Minister Kingsley Wood to explain that he was not anxious to remain in the service, following up with a letter reiterating his position to Wood, but adding:

> If it was desired to extend my period of Command, I felt I should have a letter from you asking me to stay on and telling me that I ... should have the support of the Air Council.

After three days Dowding heard again from Chief of Air Staff Newall,

> In view of the importance of ... Fighter Command and the desire to avoid ... changes in the high appointments of the operational

commands, it has been decided to ask you to defer your retirement until the end of March, 1940. I hope this will be agreeable to you.

*   *   *

It was referred to as the 'eyes' of Fighter Command, the extensive network of Chain Home radar stations. To Dowding it was 'science thoughtfully applied to operational requirements.' While quite limited in its capability and rudimentary in its development, it did provide the most fundamental information for the process behind Britain's air defence system. The system amounted to communication beginning with the radar plots of approaching hostile or unidentified aircraft and encompassing the fighters scrambled to intercept them, gun, searchlight and barrage balloon crews and air raid sirens.

The radar stations themselves faced and searched seaward with a range of 120 miles and were capable of plotting the height, range, bearing and, a bit less accurately, the strength of a hostile raid. Added to that mix was the Observer Corps, civilian volunteers who plotted the attackers by sight and sound from positions generally more inland than the radar sites.

The product of the Chain Home sites, the radar plots, were passed directly to the Filter Room at Fighter Command, Bentley Priory at Stanmore north of London, where filter officers studied the plots to define them as either friendly or hostile and then passed them on to the adjoining Operations Room, Dowding's control centre. This sizeable room surrounded a large situation map table of southern England and the Channel. An operational duty controller sat in a balcony or a raised dais above and beyond the table. He was supported by liaison officers who stayed in contact with the Observer Corps, Anti-aircraft Command, the Admiralty, Bomber and Coastal Commands, and the Home Office (air raid warnings).

The fighter defence of England was primarily the responsibility of No. 11 Group (from Portsmouth around to the Thames Estuary) and No. 12 Group (from the Thames Estuary to Yorkshire). At the Group level, a Group Commander and a group controller monitored their own group area situation on a map table. WAAF girls sat around the table map wearing headphones and manoeuvring coloured markers around the table using croupier rakes. The markers represented aircraft positions based on the latest plots received. Watching the progress of the plots, the group controller ordered the appropriate sector to respond to the incoming raid. The sectors were limited areas within the Group geographical area with each sector home to a number of airfields. One of these fields was the Sector Station and it had its own Operations Block housing a D/F (direction finding) room and the main

Ops room. The progress of each sector's fighters was monitored in the D/F room via radio 'fixes' coming in from the small IFF (Identification Friend or Foe) automatic transmitter fitted in every aircraft.

As the positions of the fighters were passed on to the sector Ops room, two deputy controllers, assisted by two navigators, rapidly determined interception courses for the fighters and passed them to the controller whose view of the situation map table from his raised dais afforded an instant overview with the continually changing positions of the aircraft. It was the sector controller who gave the orders to the various fighter squadrons in his control area to intercept a raid. Such an order was typically like this: 'Scramble (take off); Angels fifteen (climb to 15,000 feet); Orbit (circle a given point); Vector 130 (steer a course of 130°); Buster (full throttle).' Contact with each fighter squadron required the use of a two-syllable code name such as Hornet or Lumba. Each twelve-aircraft squadron was composed of four sections of three aircraft and divided into two flights, A and B. A Flight comprised Red and Yellow sections, with three aircraft in each, and B Flight with Green and Blue sections of three aircraft each. Individual pilots within a section were identified, for example, as Blue Two.

Thus, incoming plot information about a 'hostile' came from a radar site, on by telephone first to Fighter Command, then to Group, on to Sector and from there by radio/telephone to the airborne fighter pilot leader.

* * *

Some influential officers in the *Luftwaffe* High Command were convinced that the British enemy could not be defeated through air attacks alone and that invasion was essential. A campaign plan was devised with the following objectives:

1. Gain air superiority;
2. Cripple the British war economy;
3. Blockade shipping;
4. Attack the Royal Navy fleet;
5. Attack British troop ships and transports; and
6. Carry out invasion.

* * *

The night of 24 August 1939 was the last time that Peter Townsend and the other Tangmere-based pilots would see the bright lights of south coast towns like Brighton and Portsmouth on their sector reconnaissance flights. Thereafter, the wartime blackout plunged most of Britain into total darkness for the duration.

Hitler wanted war with Britain and France and was determined to have it. All that stood in his way was Stalin and the Soviet Union, and in what he saw as a last-minute overture, the German Chancellor sent his envoy, von Ribbontrop, to Moscow to confer with Stalin about a pact that would bisect Poland following an impending Nazi invasion of Germany's neighbour, giving half to the Soviets and a free hand to the Nazis to move against the French and the British. Stalin approved the pact and, in the afternoon of 31 August, Hitler issued his Directive Number One for the conduct of the war: 'Since the situation on Germany's eastern frontier has become intolerable and all political possibilities of a peaceful settlement have been exhausted, I have decided upon a solution by force.' The next day German ground and air forces attacked Poland.

Peter Townsend, the pilots of No. 43 Squadron at Tangmere, and all of the pilots of RAF Fighter Command, were ready and waiting for the coming of the *Luftwaffe*, in the certain knowledge that they were top priority on the Germans' target list. All leave was cancelled; the Auxilliary Air Force and the Volunteer Reserve had been mobilized in the previous week and virtually everyone who could fly a Hurricane or a Spitfire was eager to have a go at Jerry. On the morning of 3 September, the British Ambassador to Germany, Sir Neville Henderson, arrived in the Wilhelmstrasse to present an ultimatum to Dr Paul Schmidt who was standing in for von Ribbontrop (who was 'unavailable'): 'I have the honour to inform you that if today, September third at eleven o'clock at the latest, satisfactory assurances have not been given … to His Majesty's Government in London, a state of war will from that hour exist between the two countries.' Before noon Townsend was in the Tangmere officers' mess with several of the other pilots when the Prime Minister, Neville Chamberlain, began his famous radio address to the nation: 'It is a sad day for all of us. All the aims I have tried so hard to attain, all the principles in which I believed … have come to nought. I hope to live long enough to see the day when, with the end of Hitlerism, a free Europe will be born.' Townsend and the others went out to their dispersals to relax in the soft grass by their Hurricanes, at readiness should they be ordered into action. It was ironic that, having just heard the news that their nation was, finally, actually at war with Germany, the day itself could hardly have been more peaceful, the sky more lovely with great puffy white clouds drifting low over the south Downs. Real war was months away. The Phoney War had begun.

Confined to the station at Tangmere, Peter and the other pilots of No. 43 were required to sleep near their Hurricanes, on a continuing alert status. Their friends and families were allowed to visit them. Occasionally the airmen would be sent off, on excursions or false alarms. The boredom and the tension increased and was only occasionally relieved when they were allowed to make the short drive over to Bosham ('bosom') and the Ship Inn, where they let off steam.

Slowly things changed. Their grass airfield was defaced with new asphalt runways. There were several flying accidents, many attributable to the disorientation that accompanied the newly established blackout. The squadrons were then ordered to new assignments. No. 1 Squadron was sent to France and No. 43 to Acklington, near Newcastle. Tangmere had been a spa, a country club compared to what the pilots discovered at Acklington. Bleak, poorly furnished and under heated, the dispersal huts were frankly disgusting. Any kind of transport was rare and they found the mobile battery starter carts frequently flat and unusable, requiring them to trudge across the field in the bitter cold and crank the starting handles with frozen hands. But their love of flying the solid, swift Hurricane and their eagerness to go up against their opposite numbers in the German air force kept their spirits up. They never doubted their ability to beat the enemy when they finally did engage him.

For the pilots of 43 Squadron the action began on 1 February when Peter's friend, Caesar Hull, found and downed a Heinkel He 111 bomber, shooting it into the sea. Townsend matched the feat two days later when he attacked and brought down the bomber piloted by Hermann Wilms at Whitby.

A few days later, Townsend shot down another Heinkel bomber. Many years after the war he told his twelve-year-old son, Pierre, about the incident. The boy asked, 'Did you really have to kill them?' He replied that he had never wanted to kill anyone, least of all young people like himself at the time, people who shared his love of flying. He explained that it was not the crew but their bomber, that enemy machine invading the English sky, that had been his target that morning long ago. 'We were not, thank God, involved in the intimate, personal killing of men which is the lot of the infantry – though we fired with the same bloody end in view. The men inside the aircraft must be killed or maimed or taken prisoner, otherwise they would return to battle. Very few of us thought of it that way, and this gave to our battle in the air the character of a terribly dangerous sport and not of a dismal, sordid slaughter.'

He had been sent out to stalk and destroy the enemy and pointed out that, while he no longer 'needed encouragement' as Philip Babington at the RAF college, Cranwell, had said of him, and he had felt remorse after destroying that first Heinkel and killing some of the crew, he admitted, 'A terrible change had come over me.'

'The killing game', as he had begun to refer to it, was soon in full flow for him when the squadron was moved further north, to Wick in

Scotland, where they were to defend the naval base at Scapa Flow. On a particular night when he had been patrolling low over Scapa, searching without success for enemy aircraft, and dodging a storm of anti-aircraft bursts, the local controller summoned him in to land. Instead, he switched off his radio and went on with the search. That was when he sighted a tiny speck at higher altitude which quickly became a German bomber. The prey was another Heinkel, and its crew fought desperately for their survival. This time, having gained the upper hand in the fight, Peter realized that he felt no emotion whatever and was completely focused on his task and the desire to destroy the bomber, which in seconds dived into the sea taking all four crewmen to their deaths. It was not until the next morning that he looked over his Hurricane, found it to be riddled with bullet strikes, and realized how close he had come to sharing their fate. He realized, too, that he had of duty and necessity now become a case-hardened fighter pilot and killer after those first few swift, violent skirmishes. The real war in the air was still a few months away. He was ready for it.

*   *   *

As the situation in France became grave and the demands on Prime Minister Churchill for more aid, especially in the form of additional Hurricane fighter squadrons sent across the Channel, the pressure on Air Chief Marshal Dowding to prevent such an action in order to protect Britain from the German menace grew. Of the 474 British aircraft already dispatched to France, 206 had been lost in action with the enemy. Churchill told his War Cabinet that French Premier Paul Reynaud was pleading for more squadrons to be thrown into the battle. The British Air Ministry had belatedly concluded that fifty-two fighter squadrons was the minimum number required for the defence of Britain, but Churchill had somehow misunderstood and believed that number to be twenty-five. He didn't realize exactly how critical the situation had become and Dowding was then alerted to prepare to send ten more fighter squadrons to France. This caused Dowding to send a note to Air Minister Archibald Sinclair asking urgently to present his case to the War Cabinet. Such a request was nearly unprecedented and Dowding was frankly surprised when it was granted.

The War Cabinet had met three times that day and the atmosphere at the table was tense and less than cordial. Dowding was not put off by the scowling Churchill, and welcomed the presence of his friend, Lord Beaverbrook – Minister of Aircraft Production. Air Chief Marshal Dowding stood and elegantly stated his case for ten minutes to what seemed a hostile group. When he finished speaking he went over to Churchill and placed a piece of paper in front of him. On it was a graph in red ink. Dowding later remarked, 'I think some people thought I was going to shoot him. I felt like it.' 'This red line,' he said to the PM, 'shows the wastage of Hurricanes in the last ten days. If the line goes on at the same rate for the next ten days there won't be a single Hurricane left, either in France or in England.' Churchill was speechless. Dowding left the room. He knew that if 'the great flood of Hurricane exports to France' was not stopped it would mean the loss of the war. He decided to put his view in writing to the Under Secretary of State for Air:

16th May 1940
Sir,
I have the honour to refer to the very serious calls which have recently been made upon the Home Defence Fighter Units in an attempt to stem the German invasion on the Continent.

1. I hope and believe that our Armies may yet be victorious in France and Belgium, but we have to face the possibility that they may be defeated.
2. In this case I presume that there is no one who will deny that England should fight on, even though the remainder of the Continent of Europe is dominated by the Germans.
3. For this purpose it is necessary to retain some minimum fighter strength in this country and I must request that the Air Council will inform me what they consider this minimum strength to be, in order that I may make my dispositions accordingly.
4. I would remind the Air Council that the last estimate which they made as to the force necessary to defend this country was fifty-two squadrons, and my strength has now been reduced to the equivalent of thirty-six squadrons.
5. Once a decision has been reached as to the limit on which the Air Council and the Cabinet are prepared to stake the existence of the country, it should be made clear to the Allied Commanders on the Continent that not a single aeroplane from Fighter Command beyond the limit will be sent across the Channel, no matter how desperate the situation may become.
6. It will, of course, be remembered that the estimate of fifty-two squadrons was based on the assumption that the attack would come from the eastwards except in so far as the defences might be outflanked in flight. We have now to face the possibility that attacks may come from Spain or even from the north coast of France. The result is that our line is very much extended at the same time as our resources are reduced.
7. I must point out that within the last few days the equivalent of ten Squadrons have been sent to France, that the Hurricane Squadrons remaining in this country are seriously depleted,

and that the more squadrons which are sent to France the higher will be the wastage and the more insistent the demand for reinforcements.

8. I must therefore request that as a matter of paramount urgency the Air Ministry will consider and decide what level of strength is to be left to the Fighter Command for the defence of this country, and will assure me that when this level has been reached, not one fighter will be sent across the Channel however urgent and insistent the appeals for help may be.

9. I believe that, if an adequate fighter force is kept in this country, if the fleet remains in being, and if Home Forces are suitably organized to resist invasion, we should be able to carry on the war single-handed for some time, if not indefinitely. But, if the Home Defence Force is drained away in desperate attempts to remedy the situation in France, defeat in France will involve the final, complete and irremediable defeat of this country.

I have the honour to be
Sir,
Your Obedient Servant,
[signed] H.C.T. Dowding
Air Chief Marshal

The impact of this letter, and possibly Dowding's little red graph, caused Churchill to rule on 19 May that henceforth no more fighter squadrons should leave the country, irrespective of events in France. In the next two days all the British fighter squadrons in France returned to the United Kingdom, except for three retained there with the Advanced Air Striking Force.

* * *

On 23 May Peter Townsend was made commander of No. 85 Squadron, which was then stationed at Debden after narrowly escaping from the calamitous Battle of France. His love of pastoral England was nourished there in the countryside and he quickly rose to the new challenge of being a fighter leader. One of his inspirations was Major Edward 'Mick' Mannock VC, DSO and two bars, MC and bar. During the First World War No. 85 Squadron was commanded for a time by Mannock, who was the leading British fighter ace of the war with seventy-three victories, forty-seven of them officially credited. He was known as both a ruthless air fighter and a great mentor to his pilots. Peter Townsend studied Mannock's period in command of No. 85 Squadron.

Major Mannock ... nursed and cherished his young pilots – and it was that that killed him. He was emotional and highly strung. At the very start of his career he had said, 'That's the way they're going to get me – flames, and finish.' He always carried a revolver in the air 'to finish myself off as soon as I see the first sign of flames.' Despite a faulty left eye, he could pick out distant objects like a hawk. A cunning tactician, one of his schemes was to act as a decoy, with Larry Callahan [two Americans, Callahan and Elliott Springs, flew with No. 85 Squadron] as his wing man. Larry admired him for many reasons. For one, 'He was not a headhunter', like Richthofen, whose score Mannock nearly equalled. 'He would always be the low man ... and I knew it because I was with him. When a bunch of Huns came along he would goad them into attacking him while the rest of the boys were in the distance, waiting ... Mannock was such a hell of a fighter and such a good shot that he could afford to get himself into the worst position and still shoot his way out.' Nobody will ever know whether Mick Mannock drew his revolver on himself. Donald Inglis, a young New Zealander, was with him at the time, low over the enemy lines, when he suddenly saw flames spurting from Mannock's machine. Then it dived headlong into the ground and was soon burnt out. It was the fate he had always dreaded. The pace was telling on everyone except, apparently, Callahan. Springs noticed, 'Nobody in the squadron can get a glass to his mouth with one hand after one of these decoy patrols except Cal, and he's got no nerves – he's made of cheese ...' As Elliott Springs wrote of himself: 'I'm all shot to pieces. I only hope I can stick it. I don't want to quit. My nerves are all gone and I can't stop. It's not the fear of death ... I'm still not afraid to die. It's this eternal flinching from it that's ... made a coward out of me. Few men live to know what real fear is.'

At Debden and its satellites of Castle Camps and Martlesham Heath, Townsend and the pilots of No. 85 Squadron experienced a welcome respite through a period of largely uneventful convoy patrolling. It was short-lived, however. The Battle of Britain had begun and, as he recalled, 'the time for killing was at hand.' An order came through for Townsend to bring his entire squadron to Martlesham, northeast of Ipswich, near the east coast. The Battle began badly for him in a short, sharp encounter.

'Yellow Section, 85 Squadron at readiness.' A thick ground mist hung in the Martlesham air that morning. Fitters were out early to start and warm the engines of the Hurricanes, first among them being VY-K, the personal aircraft of the squadron leader. It had been

Townsend's Hurricane since he had come to the squadron and he had grown comfortable with it; he felt a part of it, liked its smell and trusted it. While the fitters were doing their work, the pilots grabbed a few extra minutes of sleep and then the telephone sounded with the order, 'One aircraft only, scramble and call controller when airborne.' Moments later Peter took off through the low mist. Contacting the controller, he was vectored out to sea. While climbing he thought about how much time he had spent flying over the sea in recent months and the fact that they carried no dinghies with them; only the Mae West life jackets which would keep them afloat, but if they happened to come down in the sea too far from land to swim for it, their survival would be down to plain luck.

As he climbed through 8,000 feet, he spotted and passed a Dornier Do 17 bomber going the opposite way. He was grateful for the modern miracle of radar and its ability to guide him so unerringly to a target. He hauled the Hurricane around, straining to keep the Dornier in sight through his turn, determined that it would not get away from him. He thought the enemy crew had not seen him yet and he hoped to stalk the German bomber and hit it hard with a burst of gunfire before the crew spotted his Hurricane. He approached the bomber through heavy rain, limiting his already poor visibility. He slid the hood back to try for a better view of the Dornier.

The bomber had taken off moments before from the German-occupied airfield at Arras-St Leger, crossing the North Sea in the same filthy weather and intermittent heavy rain that was plaguing Townsend. They were going to bomb shipping in the harbour at Lowestoft and were near the English coast when gunner Werner Borner caught sight of the enemy fighter. He had enough time to grab his machine-gun and fire a burst at Townsend's aircraft. Peter tried to get closer to the bomber before firing and decided he could wait no longer. His bullets ripped into the Dornier, tearing bits from it. Blood spattered the interior as starboard rear gunner *Leutnant* Bernschein was hit in the head and *Feldwebel* Lohrer fell on top of him, wounded in the head and throat. Borner too, was wounded in the head but continued firing at the Hurricane. Townsend's most enduring image of the combat was the mesmerizing yellow-orange flashes of tracer from Borner's gun criss-crossing with the tracer and incendiary from his own guns, all standing out vividly against the bank of dark thundercloud in the background. Peter continued firing until a bright orange explosion filled his cockpit, knocking the control column with its gun button from his hands. The Hurricane fell into a dive and Peter lost sight of the Dornier in the cloud. Borner recalled: 'Bits and pieces everywhere, blood-covered faces, the smell of cordite, all windows shot up. There were hits everywhere: in the wings, in the fuselage, and in the engine. But what a surprise: no one was really seriously wounded and our good old *Gustav Marie* was still flying.'

Townsend's Hurricane, VY-K, had been hit in the engine and was powerless. It was descending in a shallow glide through the rainclouds, trailing a long, black smoke plume. Calling the ground station he said, 'Wagon Leader calling. Am hit and baling out in sea. One, two, three, four, five. Take a fix if you can.' Out of cloud now, he judged he was about twenty miles from England. He could see no ships. He banked left and then steeply right and spotted a small vessel.

With the hood all the way back and his radio/telephone and oxygen leads disconnected, he stood in the cockpit and prepared to jump out. A memory flashed through his mind then of a story he had once read about a German pilot in the First World War who had baled out, grabbing vainly for his ripcord ring and crashing to his death. Peter crossed his arms in front of him, holding the ripcord ring firmly in his right hand as he dived head first from the fighter. He was on his back with his feet towards the heavens when the broad canopy of his parachute snapped open, the harness jerking him upright. As he drifted down he watched VY-K plunge vertically into the sea well off to one side. It sank instantly.

He was wearing a light sweater, trousers and his flying boots that day, having already removed his leather flying helmet. As he splashed down he hit the harness release knob; the encumbrance came away and he sank for what seemed several seconds before he was able to surface and kick off his boots. Looking round he saw that the little ship was only a mile or so away; the crew having seen him come down had already lowered a small boat. He tried without success to inflate his yellow Mae West, which could only be accomplished by blowing into the tube. Each time he tried he swallowed large mouthfuls of sea water, so he gave up and began swimming towards the rescue boat. As his rescuers approached, one of them shouted, 'Blimey, if he ain't a fucking Hun.' 'I'm not, I'm a fucking Englishman,' Peter yelled back. The small boat came alongside and strong arms pulled him into it. A few moments later he was aboard the trawler *Cap Finisterre*, which was based at Hull. After giving Peter a set of dry clothes and a double shot of rum, the captain invited him to have breakfast with the crew.

The badly damaged Dornier bomber, *Gustav Marie*, struggled back towards her base at Arras-St Leger with the wounded crewmen crudely bandaged. They had been unable to jettison their bombs due to ruined wiring circuits following the encounter with Peter's fighter. When they managed to reach their airfield, the undercarriage could not be lowered and the pilot, *Oberleutnant* Gonzow, had to belly-land. On inspection more than 220 hits were discovered in the engines, fuel tanks, fuselage and control surfaces.

Late that same afternoon Peter Townsend was back on patrol in a new Hurricane.

* * *

As the intensity of the *Luftwaffe*'s offensive against Britain increased, Air Chief Marshal Dowding acted to improve the fighter protection of London. The Debden fighter station was transferred from the command of Air Commodore Sir Trafford Leigh-Mallory's No. 12 Group to that of No. 11 Group under Air Vice Marshal Keith Park. No. 12 Group's area of control then extended from Bournemouth on the Channel coast around to Great Yarmouth on the east coast.

* * *

On 9 August Townsend was patrolling over a convoy when he noticed a Dornier Do 17 drifting in and out of the great white clouds. He went after it and was bemused when he heard someone singing *September in the Rain* in his earphones. This was followed by a series of orders in flat German tones. The Do 17 had disappeared when the cloud gave out, but in its place were twenty Messerschmitt Me 110 twin-engine heavy fighters circling above the convoy. The singing then resumed.

Peter turned and chased one of the Me 110s, mindful that their leader, the singer?, might be lurking above them, waiting to pounce. That is exactly what happened. The leader came down towards the Hurricane, which had turned and was climbing to face the German. Again Townsend was fascinated by the ping-pong balls of tracer coming at him from the two 20 mm cannon and four machine-guns of the Messerschmitt until the two aircraft flashed past one another and the Hurricane entered the cloud. Pulling out of the cloud, Peter was being chased by another enemy fighter when a Spitfire arrived to rescue him. In the action, he had been trying to contact the ground station to order the rest of his squadron over the convoy. The other Hurricanes entered the area and promptly destroyed two of the Me 110s.

* * *

Sunday, 18 August – the pilots of No. 85 Squadron at Debden sat around impatiently at their dispersal in the late afternoon. The telephone finally rang at 5.00 pm – 'Eighty-five, patrol Canterbury, Angels twenty.' In less than five minutes they were off and climbing southeast though cloud. It was the first occasion in which Townsend was leading his entire squadron into combat. The job of the Hurricanes in that period of the war was to go after and destroy the enemy bombers. It was the Spitfires role to take on the German fighter escort. The Hurricane pilots were only to engage the enemy fighters if they barred the way to the bombers.

The 85 Squadron attack formation called for four sections of three aircraft each, with each section flying line-astern, Townsend in the lead of the centre section. With a narrow front, the squadron was relatively easy to manoeuvre and each pilot was able to scan the sky while keeping a reasonable distance from those around him. Later they would abandon this sort of formation in favour of the German-developed approach of two pairs of two-aircraft elements, each having a leader and a wingman – a safer, more efficient combat method. For that time, however, Townsend defended the British formation,

> Vectored here and there under controller's orders, our squadrons needed to keep a reasonably compact formation for mutual protection, for contact in bad visibility, and above all for con-centration in the attack. The formation we used in 85 gave us manoeuvrability, concentration, yet freedom to search. We would attack by sections, with aircraft extended in echelon for a clear field of fire. I would lead my section in first, followed by the right hand, then the left hand, and finally the stern section. We had it all worked out; it would need quick thinking, good flying, and above all blind faith in the section leaders. I knew I could count on every pilot in 85.

Townsend cautioned his men to remember at all times that their task was to seek out and destroy the enemy bombers. He told them never to follow one when they believed they had shot it down; that in doing so they might get 'bounced' on the way down. He directed them to leave it and go after another. If the Me 109 fighters interfered, the Hurricane pilots were to turn, never dive or climb. They were to weave and keep weaving. When possible they were to attack from the sun, and always to 'beware of the Hun in the sun.' Again, he told them that their aim was to destroy the enemy, not to rack up a personal score.

The controller informed Townsend that the incoming raid amounted to more than 100 aircraft. His twelve Hurricanes left the cloud over the Thames Estuary in direct line with an enormous formation of German planes, stepped up nearly a mile and a half. The top cover of Bf 109s was at 20,000 feet; the next layer down was a wave of Me 110s and beneath that Ju 88s over a layer of Dorniers covering a wave of Heinkel He 111s and lowest of all were Ju 87 Stuka dive-bombers. As the Hurricanes closed in, many of the German aircraft tightened their formations giving them a formidable concentration of gun fire. The Stukas and Heinkels veered away seaward while the Me 110s turned into a defensive circle. Townsend ordered, 'In we go'. One of the Me 110s then made the fatal error of crossing in front of Peter's fighter.

It would be the German's last mistake. In the wildly confusing seconds that followed, several of the Bf 109 fighters fell on the attacking Hurricanes. One aimed at Peter's plane, lobbing shells as it came, but Peter saw it early enough to evade it. The German skidded past in a turn trying to reposition himself for another burst at the Hurricane. Townsend easily turned inside the German, firing as he went. White vapour erupted from under the Messerschmitt and quickly became flame and thick black smoke. Then another Bf 109 tried to outturn Peter's Hurricane and failed. Bits flew from the German fighter as Townsend's bullets stitched the fuselage. The cockpit hood separated from the Bf 109, followed shortly by the body of the pilot.

Townsend continued to chase the German fighters who were determined to keep the Hurricanes from getting to their bombers. His Hurricane simply didn't have the power to catch a Bf 109 running away. In seconds Peter's ammunition was exhausted. The air battle was moving towards Margate and, as so often happened in such situations, Peter suddenly found himself in empty sky. A moment later, however, he spotted a lone Hurricane heading out to sea, trying vainly to overhaul some fleeing Bf 109s heading back to their French base. As he neared the Hurricane he saw the code on its side and realized it was VY-R, the aircraft of Dicky Lee, one of No. 85 Squadron's finest young pilots and godson of 'Boom' Trenchard, the father of the RAF. On 11 May Lee had shot down two German bombers in the morning, was hit by ground fire and crash-landed in a field near some enemy tanks. He was captured but escaped and was back in England with the squadron the next day. 'Come back, Dicky!' shouted Townsend over the radio/telephone, but Lee continued chasing the German fighters. He was never seen again and is remembered on the Runnymede RAF memorial.

For the Stuka it had been the worst day of the war. Twenty-eight of them were shot down and it marked the end of significant participation by Stukas in the Battle of Britain. In all, the Germans had lost seventy-one aircraft against twenty-seven for the British, who had also suffered the destruction of a radar station and severe damage to a key sector airfield.

That evening a congratulatory signal came in for Peter from the Chief of the Air Staff, 'Well done 85 Squadron in all your hard fighting. This is the right spirit for dealing with the enemy.' That same night the squadron was ordered to report to Croydon the next morning. They arrived and noted the fresh, lovely scent of the air at the satellite field for nearby Kenley. The Germans, in an effort to bomb Kenley three days earlier, had hit the Bourjois soap factory instead, leaving the entire area fragrant for several days. Fourteen of the eighteen pilots Townsend had led to Croydon that morning were shot down within the next two weeks; two of them twice.

* * *

Monday, 19 August – as a consequence of the bombing attacks on the vital British radar stations since 9 August, six had been badly damaged with two of them out of use. Three of the sector stations had been hit hard and Fighter Command was seriously wounded, but even with 175 aircraft lost since the 8 August, it maintained ample aircraft reserves thanks to the brilliance of Lord Beaverbrook and his ability to raise fighter production to 500 a month. Aircraft losses didn't worry Dowding; it was his losses in pilots that concerned him. In the previous ten days ninety-four fighter pilots had been killed and sixty wounded. He anguished over the tragic loss of his boys and over the broad gap it left in his ability to combat the *Luftwaffe*. Replacement pilots were keen, but lacked experience and this meant a very short life expectancy for many of them. The urgency of the problem necessitated drawing volunteers from Army Cooperation Command, light bomber squadrons, the Fleet Air Arm, and the new Czech and Polish squadrons whose eagerness for vengeance against the German enemy was unparalleled, but whose command of the English language left much to be desired during the crucial radio/telephone communication in aerial combat.

Air Vice Marshal Keith Park, in command of Eleven Group, had a force of 250 Spitfires and Hurricanes to protect southeast England and London from a potential enemy attacking force of more than 1,000. Park, too, had no worries about replacement aircraft. Each night during the Battle, Beaverbrook rang him get the latest score and the RAF losses. By the next morning he had made good the losses. Park: 'It was heartening. I was never grounded by lack of aircraft.'

It was Dowding who had established the figure of 250 fighters to protect No. 11 Group's vital area of responsibility. He firmly believed that Park's airfields and control system could cope with no more. He had ordered that the squadrons of No. 10 and No. 12 Groups be sent when requested, as reinforcements, to assist No. 11 Group when its squadrons were fully engaged. In practice though, the squadrons of No. 10 Group Commander Air Vice Marshal Quentin Brand supported No. 11 Group effectively, but those of No. 12 Group's Leigh-Mallory were less helpful, frequently failing to cooperate with the essential support.

* * *

24 August – it was Townsend's habit at Croydon to sleep out at the squadron dispersal on the western side of the airfield, to be on hand

should trouble occur. In the early hours he was rudely awakened by deafening bomb blasts. He was too exhausted from several long days and nights of combat patrols to do more than hold a pillow over his head; he was past caring. Incredibly, it seemed the German bomber had managed to hit and destroy two of the Hurricanes at the dispersal.

Later that morning, he grabbed his sponge bag, stuck his toothbrush in his breast pocket and headed for the bathroom. He remembered that the Duke of Kent, brother of the King, was due to visit the squadron at 10.00 am. On his way to the bathroom the alarm sounded. 'Eighty-five Squadron, scramble!' With Peter in the lead the Hurricanes leapt from the grass at Croydon on their way to intercept the enemy aircraft heading for Dover. They were too late, however, and the German aircraft were already on their way back to France when the British fighters arrived in the Dover area.

When they landed back at Croydon, the Duke had already arrived on the station and wanted to meet the pilots. As he escorted their guest down the line of his men, Peter noticed with irritation that one of them seemed to be nearly unable to contain a laugh as he was introduced to the Duke. At that moment, Peter happened to glance down at his own tunic and saw the toothbrush sticking up from his pocket by his wings and Distinguished Flying Cross ribbon.

* * *

On the rare days when they were not ordered into the air, the pilots of No. 85 Squadron exchanged trivialities frequently laced with the macabre humour they had cultivated since the start of the Battle. Townsend:

> Some of us would die within the next few days. That was inevitable. But you did not believe it would be you. Death was always present, and we knew it for what it was. If we had to die we would be alone, smashed to pieces, burnt alive, or drowned. Some strange protecting veil kept the nightmare thought from our minds, as it did the loss of our friends. Their disappearance struck us as less a solid blow than a dark shadow which chilled our hearts and passed on. We seemed already to be living in another world, separate and exalted, where the gulf between life and death had closed and was no longer forbidding.

* * *

Within No. 85 Squadron and the other squadrons defending the southeast, the fatigue factor was intense and unremitting. On 28 August Townsend led the squadron up from Croydon four times. Late in the day they were patrolling at 18,000 feet over Dungeness when he spotted twelve Bf 109s below and slightly to the right of his course. The enemy fighters were just above a broken cloud layer, and were irresistible to Peter. As usual, they had been ordered to attack the bombers and ignore the fighters, but this was an opportunity too good to pass up. 'Come in Red and Yellow sections. Down we go! Pick your own.'

Immediately one of the Messerschmitts rolled across Peter's gunsight and received his attentions. It erupted in white smoke having taken hits in the cooling system. Chasing a second 109 proved fruitless for him when the German dived away and even with full boost on, Townsend was unable to catch the enemy fighter. Still pursuing the Bf 109, he neglected to keep checking behind him and a bullet slammed into the cockpit of the Hurricane. Fortunately, he was able to evade the German on his tail. In the action, six enemy aircraft had been brought down by the pilots of No. 85 Squadron in the encounter.

For the Germans, it was almost a matter of pride to be shot down by a Spitfire, the more glamourous of the two principal Royal Air Force fighter planes. On many occasions German pilots claimed (incorrectly) to have been downed by a Spitfire when the opponent was actually a Hurricane. Such claims began during the Battle of France when no Spitfires were involved. In the Battle of Britain the majority of German aircraft downed were accounted for by Hurricanes in a ratio of three to two. More Hurricanes were involved in the Battle than Spitfires and, in terms of serviceable aircraft available each morning, on average 63 per cent were Hurricanes and 37 per cent Spitfires.

*   *   *

Possibly the most disproportionate engagement faced by No. 85 Squadron occurred in the mid-afternoon of 29 August when the twelve pilots were ordered up from Croydon against more than 200 enemy aircraft approaching the south coast near Eastbourne. Still climbing, the Hurricane pilots sighted eighteen Heinkel bombers several thousand feet above them, crossing over Beachy Head. Far above the German bombers were more than 200 Messerschmitt escort fighters ready to pounce on the approaching Hurricanes. The British pilots saw no other RAF aircraft in the area as they continued towards the Heinkels, suddenly aware of a dozen Me 110s trying to divert them from the German bombers. Then came the inevitable assault by the German fighter escort. A cloud of Bf 109s fell on the Hurricanes, leaving them no choice but to fight. Nearing Hastings, Townsend watched one of the German fighters fill his windscreen as it crossed. Taking advantage of the Hurricane's greater turning ability, he aligned on the German aircraft and shot a large piece off it. Enveloped in white smoke, it appeared to stall and began falling off as the pilot left his cockpit. The Messerschmitt plummeted into the ground close to the seaside town.

Back to Croydon, desperately tired, but the action of the day wasn't over yet. Townsend:

> Quick rearm and refuel. Men on the wings. Men with spanners, with bands of belted ammunition. Cowlings are 'unpinned,' the 'bowser's' nozzle rammed into the tank, right wing, fuselage, left wing – three tanks full up. Oil checked. Radio checked, retuned. Oxygen bottle changed. Windscreen cleaned. Five minutes, and the Hurricane is ready to go again. A close bond linked us with the ground crews – skilled, loyal, enthusiastic youngsters working under the eagle eyes of their NCOs (themselves seasoned by experience, dry of humour). Between them they held our lives in their hands. The public encouraged from the stands, but our brave and loyal 'ground troops' cheered right from the touch line. Solitary individualists as we were in our tiny cockpits, they gave us heart to go back again and again into the battle.

* * *

30 August – remembered by Peter Townsend as the beginning of the fiercest forty-eight hours of the whole battle. It underscored the desperation of both sides by that point to overcome the other.

A thick layer of cloud at 7,000 feet over southeast England was hampering the efforts of the Observer Corps as No. 85 Squadron orbited over Dungeness at 18,000 feet. At that height they watched as a swarm of enemy aircraft assembled across the Channel over Cap Gris Nez. Townsend was then able to fill the Observer Corps gap, providing the course, altitude and numbers of the German planes to the ground controller. Twenty Heinkel bombers were being shepherded by scores of Bf 109s and Me 110s toward the English coast. As the Hurricanes approached the Heinkels head-on, the bomber pilots seemed to panic and began to scatter. But many more German aircraft came in their wake.

Keith Park's challenge that day was to prevent the destruction of his two critically important sector stations near London, Biggin Hill and Kenley. Park managed to get fifteen additional squadrons involved in the effort, but once again his request for assistance from Leigh-Mallory's No. 12 Group to guard Biggin produced no results and Biggin was badly bombed. The damaged airfield was still operational, however, when the Germans returned in a second strike. This time Park saw to its defence, employing eight squadrons to guard it, including No. 85 Squadron.

In the evening haze the job that the *Luftwaffe* had failed to accomplish that day was done when all the southeast radar stations were put out of action as an electrical mains failure occurred, 'blinding' Fighter Command. Several Dornier Do 17 'Flying Pencil' bombers were then able to dash up the Thames Estuary, turn south and attack Biggin Hill, taking the base completely by surprise. The hangars and technical buildings were smashed, the main telephone cable was cut and sixty-five personnel were killed, several of them WAAFs. With the entire base now inoperative, Biggin's squadrons were transferred to Hornchurch in Essex. Fighter Command lost twenty-five aircraft in over 1,000 sorties that day. The *Luftwaffe* lost thirty-six. By noon the next day, after a night in which a brave and resourceful repair crew struggled at the bottom of a huge muddy bomb crater to fix the seventy-four pairs of severed mains cable wires, the airfield at Biggin Hill was operating again almost as normal. In France two more formations of Dorniers had just taken off to strike at Hornchurch and again at Biggin.

At Croydon Peter Townsend and his pilots had just sat down to lunch when the Kenley controller telephoned him to say, 'Please be on your toes. We may need you in a hurry.' It would be the last time he would lead the squadron into daylight battle. Bombs were already falling on the Croydon aerodrome as the Hurricanes raced to take off. A nearby explosion rocked Peter's fighter as it lifted from the surface; his engine cutting out briefly when the blast hammered the Hurricane as he raised the undercarriage. Behind him the other Hurricanes struggled to climb through the dust, debris and acrid smoke as Peter directed them towards the Me 110s above.

Climbing away from Croydon, Townsend and the pilots of No. 85 Squadron noticed a massive black mushroom cloud over Biggin Hill to the south. This new raid on Biggin had destroyed the Ops Room and undone much of the frantic repairs performed during the previous night.

No. 85 Squadron caught up with the Me 110s as the Germans went into the familiar defensive circle. An angry Townsend pushed his hood back for better visibility and roared into their midst. Then the sky seemed to rain Bf 109s and the area immediately surrounding his Hurricane filled with tracer going in many directions. One of the enemy fighters slipped in front of him. Two seconds later it rolled over, consumed in black and white smoke and fell from view. Another Bf 109 met the same fate under his guns. While manoeuvring for a shot at yet another Bf 109 his Hurricane shuddered as a barrage of shot tore into it. The control column was knocked from his hand while aviation spirit gushed into the cockpit where the fuel tank in front of him had been holed. He then realized that his left foot had been kicked off the rudder bar. He was distracted for an instant by the sight of another Hurricane plunging vertically ahead of a long black smoke plume, before he realized that he too was diving. He recovered from the dive, unable to understand why his aircraft had not burst into flames.

His windscreen was starred with bullet strikes eliminating forward visibility. The Hurricane was not going to get him back to base or, it seemed, anywhere else where he might safely put it down. With no other option he baled out and, as he slowly descended, watched his Hurricane fall into the trees and explode.

Luckily he landed among some soft young fir trees, released his parachute harness and stared blankly at the large, bloody hole in his left shoe. Like a scene in a comic opera, a man with a rifle appeared, levelling the weapon at Peter's head. He was followed immediately by a policeman who produced a small notebook and asked, 'Name and address, please.'

*   *   *

In the frenzied fighting of 30/31 August, the savage attacks by the *Luftwaffe* on the sector airfields protecting London had been carried out with nearly 2,800 sorties and were opposed by 2,020 Fighter Command sorties. A total of sixty-five RAF fighters were downed; 115 pilots killed and wounded. For the British the situation was becoming desperate. The massive damage to the airfields of No. 11 Group caused Keith Park to report that,

> ... it greatly reduced the defensive power of our fighter squadrons. The destruction of numerous telephone lines ... using emergency sector Ops Rooms ... and an almost disorganization of the defence system made the control of our fighter squadrons extremely difficult ... had the enemy continued his heavy attacks against Biggin Hill and the adjacent sectors ... the fighter defences of London would have been in a perilous state.'

Later he added bitterly, 'By persistently declining to give fighter cover to my sector aerodromes ... in late August and early September, No. 12 Group jeopardized our victory in this critical battle.'

*   *   *

At Hawkhurst Cottage Hospital, a doctor looked at Peter's wounded foot and said, 'I could sew it up, but there might be something in it.' Peter knew there was something in it and it was beginning to hurt ... badly. Reassured that his was merely a superficial wound, Peter was soon loaded into a truck with another downed and wounded pilot, Bill Millington, to be transported to Croydon. They lay there on the bed of the Bedford, wrapped in their parachutes and shivering as waves of pain washed over them and the driver tried for their sake to avoid the worst of the bumps and holes.

Late that night Peter lay on an operating table in Croydon General Hospital while a surgeon gravely offered, 'We'll try to save the toe.' For Townsend it was the end of the Battle. For two weeks he lay in that hospital unable to walk and, with London and the outlying areas then being subjected to frequent bombing raids, he discovered some of the effects of the Blitz at first hand. Enemy bombers appeared overhead every night and the explosives they dropped shattered the window glass sending shards flying into the ward. Nurses moved the patients' beds well away from the windows but the experience was still terrifying.

Nagging at him was the recurring thought that, with him wounded and away from the base, with both of his flight commanders recently killed and several pilots dead or wounded, the squadron had just been withdrawn from front-line service and sent north to Church Fenton, in Yorkshire. If he wasn't able to rejoin them and resume command within three weeks, he would be replaced. At the end of two weeks of convalescing he left the hospital and went directly to Church Fenton. On arriving there he went straight to the hangars and was helped up and into a Hurricane, took off and reacquainted himself with the aeroplane. He later reported to the station doctor who said to him, 'It will be some time before you can fly again.' 'But I've just been flying', Townsend replied.

*　　*　　*

In early October, increasingly frustrated by his *Luftwaffe*'s inability to knock out the RAF fighter force, blind its radar capability, smash its key fighter airfields and achieve air supremacy over southeastern England, Hermann Goering ordered his bombers to complete the annihilation of London. The night-bombing Blitz had begun a month earlier and as he raised the tempo of his campaign, the night-fighter capability of the RAF was strengthened. More squadrons were assigned to the night-fighting role, including No. 85 Squadron which, at that time, had only six pilots who were qualified as 'night operational.' Peter had one month to get the other pilots qualified.

At RAF Kirton-in-Lindsey, Lincolnshire, they were exposed to the basic elements of the task. The squadron was then relocated to Gravesend, a station as dreary as the name, east of London. There they waited each night, wearing dark glasses to keep their night vision in a state of readiness, for the call to take off.

The Hurricane was not well-suited to all-weather night-fighting operations, lacking radar, de-icing equipment, and cockpit heating. The crude navigational and landing aids of the time handicapped the night pilots further. Without radar, they could not hope to be terribly effective against the enemy aircraft setting great fires around London each evening. Ironically though, the red-orange glow of those fires served to help some of the Hurricane pilots spot the silhouetted German bombers below them.

From Gravesend No. 85 Squadron was moved back to Debden where their interception and navigational problems continued, as they had to rely entirely on radio directions transmitted from the controller. On one occasion when the weather was particularly filthy, Townsend's Hurricane suffered generator failure. Radio reception faded and then ended followed shortly by the failure of his cockpit lights and signalling lamp. Then, by mere chance, in the darkness below he spotted what appeared to be an aircraft navigation light. He dived to investigate and came upon several aircraft circling and landing. He slipped in behind one and followed it in to land after it. When he taxied to a stop on the apron a man climbed onto his wing. Peter shouted to him, 'I'm the commanding officer of 85 Squadron', to which the man replied, 'We'll see about that!' and pointed a revolver at him until Peter proved his identity.

The onset of winter brought a series of bitterly cold nights with the Merlin engines faltering through ice blocking the air-intakes. On one such night Peter was flying above a low cloud layer, unable to locate the airfield. He radioed the field asking that another pilot, James Wheeler, come to the control tower. When Wheeler contacted him, Peter asked him to start firing rockets and to have the searchlights trained horizontally. As the rockets began appearing through the cloud layer he spotted a break in the cloud, dived through it and followed the illumination of the bluish-white searchlights to a safe landing.

In six months of nocturnal hunting, only one enemy aircraft was caught and shot down by an No. 85 Squadron pilot. It was Townsend and it happened when a Dornier bomber strayed into the beams of the Debden searchlights and was coned by them. Peter flew close to the bomber, identified it by the black crosses marking it and began shooting at it. The enemy aircraft plunged into the ground.

After twenty months of nearly continous day and night operational flying, Townsend was, by his own admission,

'. . . a nerve-racked, sleep-starved wreck. I was flying more like a tired chicken than an avenging angel. In my last night combat, a Junkers 88 riddled my aircraft and continued blithely on its way. The fight had gone out of me. I had flown myself to a standstill. The doctors grounded me and put me on barbiturates. In June 1941, I was sent to a staff job with the title 'Wing Commander-Night Operations' – one that provoked smiles, for it was at this time that I married.'

CHAPTER FIVE

Brian Kingcome

He referred to it as 'the strange double life' – moments, 'each one curiously detached from the other. One moment high above the earth, watching a sunrise not yet visible below, killing and avoiding being killed; and the next chatting with the locals over a pint of beer in a cosy country pub.' At times the civilian shared an opinion of the air battle he witnessed that day, like recounting the play of his favourite team. 'This sort of thing could only happen to a fighter pilot.'

The days seemed endless to the pilots of Royal Air Force Fighter Command during the Battle of Britain, stretching from half an hour before dawn to half an hour after dusk. Precious sleep was never enough and was reduced by the need to get off the base and let off steam. For Brian Kingcome and the pilots of No. 92 Squadron stationed at Biggin Hill, Kent, that usually meant one of two possibilities: a short, quick drive to the warm and welcoming White Hart, a pub run by Kath and Teddy Preston at nearby Brasted (more on the White Hart later). The other frequent destination was Shepherd's Market in London's West End, a much longer but most rewarding trip. At Shepherd's The Bag O'Nails or, if they could afford it, the Four Hundred, they would blow the bulk of their fourteen-shilling day's pay on whatever alcoholic sedation was on offer.

Shepherd's was 'the unofficial headquarters of RAF Fighter Command,' and, according to Geoffrey Page, a Hurricane pilot of No. 56 Squadron at North Weald and an old friend of Brian's, 'Oscar, the Swiss manager, seemed to know where every fighter pilot was ... who was dead and who was alive and who was shacked up and everything like that.'

* * *

Brian Kingcome was born in India where his father was stationed, and was looked after by a good and caring *ayah*, an Indian nannie, until at the age of two and a half he was brought to England eventually to begin his education at a boarding school in Launceston, Cornwall, together with his elder sister, Pat. He changed schools several times, often after his mother happened to hear about something substandard at his current school. One school he greatly enjoyed was Allhallows, located in a lovely valley near Honiton in Devon. There he enthusiastically sang in the choir until a day when the choirmaster was away and the substitute discovered that Brian couldn't actually carry a tune. He was sacked.

Brian was introduced to flying while attending yet another school, Paxton Park, in Huntingdonshire. There was a park, an attractive Georgian manor which housed the school, and an adjoining home farm. The school was owned by Mr and Mrs Boardman, a pleasant couple who ran a successful operation. Brian got on well with the Boardmans, especially so after a visit to the school by a friend of his sister, Pat. Philip Gordon-Marshall had also attended Allhallows but was four years older than Brian. He evidently fancied Pat, and yearned for a career as a pilot in the Royal Air Force, but when he applied he failed the medical examination. Civil aviation was to be his route to flying.

One day during Brian's first term at Paxton Park, all the students rushed outside as the relatively rare sound of an aircraft engine filled the air. The aeroplane flew low, circling the buildings of the institution and, finally, throttling back, it landed in the park and stopped near the house. The pilot was Gordon-Marshall in leather helmet and silk scarf looking like he had just appeared in *Dawn Patrol* and asking if there was a Brian Kingcome here? Brian became the instant envy of all the pupils and Mr Boardman then ran out of the house and was introduced by Brian to Gordon-Marshall who asked permission to take Brian for a short flight. The flight transformed Brian who immediately shared Gordon-Marshall's love of flying.

*   *   *

Years later, Kingcome happened to see an advertisement in *The Times*. It stated that applications for permanent commissions in the army and the General Duties branch of the Royal Air Force must be received by such and such a date in time for entry to the relevant cadet colleges by September, the start of the academic year. Candidates had to be between the ages of seventeen and a half and nineteen and a half, were required to sit a written examination, attend an interview and be found medically fit. Failure to pass either the interview or the medical would not only nullify a candidate's current application, but would disqualify him from applying again at any time in the future. Only the top twenty-five qualifiers would be eligible for the Royal Air Force Cadet

College at Cranwell; the first sixty for Woolwich, where candidates for specialist branches of the army, such as gunners and engineers, were trained; and the first 200 for Sandhurst, where officers of the army's fighting branches were trained. Brian was intrigued by the challenge.

Further research informed him that General Duties was the executive branch of the RAF and the pathway for ultimate promotion to the highest command positions; a prerequisite being the successful completion of pilot training. General Duties officers would be trained in a two-year course at Cranwell.

The air force also required a pool of pilots of junior commissioned rank who would be available to serve in an emergency. With minimal education requirements, these young men were to be selected mainly on the results of their interview and medical examination. Most of the successful candidates were offered a five-year 'short-service commission'. Following their commissioned service the officers became part of the reserve pool.

As Brian neared his eighteenth birthday, he was intrigued by the possibility of an air force career, but had reluctantly promised his mother that he would not pursue it. He wanted to fly, however, and the RAF was offering him the opportunity. As he saw it, the air force provided an exciting, rewarding career with the chance actually to be paid to fly the best aeroplanes in the world; the coming war was clearly inevitable and his age group would be the first to be called up so why wait for that to happen and end up as a cook or an infantry soldier when he could act immediately and get in on the ground floor?

He became convinced that the only way to get his mother to change her mind about a flying career for him was through it being a permanent career, meaning Cranwell. There were only eight weeks to prepare for the examination. Brian had no aptitude for mathematics, one of the six required subjects on which he would be tested, and knew that no amount of study would make a mathematician of him. He attended classes in the various subjects and studied as hard as he had ever done, and then he sat the exam. In London he cruised through both the interview and the medical. He would have to wait until mid-August when the main exam results were to be published in *The Times*. The day finally came. He dreaded the possibility of failure as he bought a copy of the paper and found the page with the results. He had passed, twenty-first out of twenty-five and a mere one point above failure in mathematics, but he had made it.

Brian then had to face the ordeal of telling his mother about his plans. If anything, he dreaded that more than reading the exam results. He anticipated an unpleasant scene in which she would be greatly upset and probably reproachful. But she made it easy telling him that, if he was that serious about a career in the air force, he must pursue it. His father, too, sent his approval from Calcutta.

* * *

A night of thick fog in 1936 contributed to a devastating car accident in which Brian and a friend found themselves inverted in his open two-seater Clyno, a £5 investment (nearly a month's pay for a cadet at Cranwell). They had been running in and out of heavy fog patches along one of the straight Roman roads of Lincolnshire when they encountered an unexpected turn and a telegraph pole. Spinning the steering wheel he managed to clear the pole by inches, but as the car drifted out of a slide the rear wheels clipped a grass verge and, still moving at a considerable speed, its momentum flipped the car over and through three complete rolls before coming to rest on its back in a field.

The friend had been thrown clear and was unhurt, though in some danger of drowning in the muddy, water-filled ditch where he had landed. Luckily for him, Brian had not lost consciousness and was able to rescue his friend. Brian, however, was not as lucky.

There was almost no traffic on the stretch of road that night as they walked slowly towards Cranwell, but after what seemed a long time a car approached and, with some reluctance, the driver gave the dishevelled pair a lift to the sick quarters of the college. Before the duty medical officer arrived, Brian decided to eat one of the oranges from a bowl in the waiting room and found that he could not open his lower jaw. It seemed to have become detached. The doctor examined and released Brian's friend but found that most of the bones in Brian's nose, cheek and jaw had been crushed or broken and would require extensive surgery.

Brian had definite doubts about the calibre of surgeons then practicing in the military services and agreed with a prevailing view that they were mainly medics who were unable to make a living in the civilian world. After reassembling his face they confined him to the sick-bay for six weeks with his jaw wired together. He was unable to eat for all that time and could only suck soup and other liquids from a tube that was passed through a gap created where two of his teeth had been knocked out in the crash.

His visitors during that month and a half included his mother, who thought she had entered the wrong room when she saw her son's ruined face. Other cadets dropped by, usually after having enjoyed a sumptuous meal which they never failed to describe to the patient. Kingcome:

As my six-week sentence drew to an end, my imagination began to work overtime as I mentally drew up and discarded menu after menu for the first solid meal with which to celebrate the end of . . . fasting. Gastronomic delights followed one another in slow procession through my imagination: hors d'oeuvre of fresh young English asparagus served cold with a subtle, quite gentle *sauce vinaigrette*, smoked salmon with Beluga caviar, sharpened slightly with fresh lime juice and finely chopped shallots; a succulent steak, done charcoal crisp on the outside, rare in the middle, sitting on a bed of fried bread and *foie gras a la Tornedo Rossini* with really young, tiny broad beans fresh off the plant and Cornish new potatoes; fresh raspberries smothered in heavy Devonshire clotted cream; strong black coffee; and a savoury to give bite to a glass or two of vintage port. It was nothing but daydreaming, but it passed the time and, whatever the menu might be, I awaited the unlocking of my jaws and my first solid meal with the excitement of a school-boy taken out for a binge.

Eating turned out to be the least of my worries, however. True to their reputation, the superannuated surgeons of the air force had more or less put my face together back to front. The sinuses were rendered useless, the nose was flattened and inoperative. Worst of all, my left eye had floated half-way down my face, leading to double vision. Unless this fault could be corrected, it was enough on its own to mean the end of my flying days, and hence of my RAF career, quite apart from any frightening effect I was liable to have on small children and dogs.

It was then that Brian's mother stepped in, taking him to see Harold Gillies, the plastic surgery pioneer who had learned many of his techniques dealing with facial injuries in the First World War. He agreed to operate on Brian and would be assisted by a young Archie McIndoe, later to become world-famous as a great plastic surgeon and founder of the Guinea Pig Club at the Queen Victoria Cottage Hospital, East Grinstead, in Wiltshire. During and after the Battle of Britain, McIndoe worked tirelessly to repair and rebuild the burnt, battered faces and bodies of scores of pilots.

Gillies and McIndoe worked their minor miracle on the Kingcome face. In the end, his left cheek-bone was still wired together; the left eye was still slightly lower than the right; and his nose was no longer quite as straight as it had been before the accident. The double vision, however, was gone and that had concerned Brian most, relative to his flying career. All the rest was vanity, which, in the 1930s was not something for men to entertain. 'However unhappy I may have been privately over a loss of looks, publicly I had to appear indifferent.'

It was six months since the accident and Kingcome worried that the air force may have by then become disillusioned with him and be about to fire him from the cadet programme. So he declared himself recuperated and returned to Cranwell where he had to resume studies in the term below his own.

*   *   *

What mattered most to Brian about his time at Cranwell was the relatively small number of hours each month devoted to flying training. The cadets began that training on the Avro Tutor, 'a completely vice-free biplane that stood up to the cruelest abuse with a happy smile.' They progressed to the Hawker Hart, followed by the Hawker Fury, both of them easy, forgiving and pleasant to fly, and then on to the Bristol Bulldog, a small, single-seat fighter with a mixed reputation, that was then being withdrawn from front-line service.

Brian shared Peter Townsend's jaundiced view of the Bulldog and its behaviour when in a spin, one of the most fundamental and essential exercises that a trainee aviator must master. 'One of [the Bulldog's] least endearing habits was every so often to decline to recover from a spin', and, as Townsend had noted, it could be utterly unforgiving.

At Cranwell too, Brian learned to drink and smoke and adjusted to the new and stringent demands of Royal Air Force academia.

> Parades were followed by classes, including an hour or so a day of flying instruction. Wednesday and Saturday afternoons were set aside for sport. We dined formally in mess each night from Monday to Friday. From Monday to Thursday we wore mess kit consisting of leg-hugging mess overalls strapped under half-Wellingtons, with black tie, blue waistcoat, stiff shirt and butterfly collar. Refining my technique, I found I could leave the squash court eight minutes before dinner, shower, change and still arrive in mess on time. Friday nights were guest nights, when black tie and blue waistcoat were replaced with white. Dining in mess at weekends was optional, but if you did you wore a suit on a Saturday, tweed jacket and slacks on a Sunday.

As the end of his final term at Cranwell approached, Kingcome and the other graduating cadets were asked for their preference in a service posting. The choices were Bomber Command, Fighter Command, Coastal Command, and the Army Co-operation squadrons. With few vacancies available in any of the options, there was only a slim chance of being assigned to one's preferred choice.

Brian felt that bombers were too vulnerable, sitting ducks with the odds stacked heavily against them. He saw no attraction there. Likewise, he found no appeal in the area of Army Co-operation flying, a job employing light, slow, unarmed aircraft, which evolved into roles such as the delivery and extraction of Allied agents in tiny European clearings beyond the enemy lines, mainly at night. Coastal Command, on the other hand, presented an entirely different image in those pre-war days,

> Equipped with Sunderlands, those giant four-engined long-range flying boats, each with a crew of nine and furnished with mess, cooking galley and bunks, they were self-contained airborne hotels. With their enormous range, they roamed the vast island and coastal possessions of the British Empire, landing in crystal-clear lagoons that flanked untouched, story-book islands, where the white man was still a curiosity. There their happy crews could swim, fish, laze a few days before moving on to the next island in the sun.

For Brian it had to be fighters. 'If shooting there was to be, then I was determined that I would be among the shooters, not [merely] one of the shot at.' There were two reasons behind his choice: the first being a frankly romantic comparison he made between the jousting of medieval knights and the aerial duelling of his Great War heroes in the Royal Flying Corps. Second, and of at least as much importance, the primary role of Fighter Command was the air defence of the United Kingdom and its vital concentrations of people, government and industry, in particular, London. With so many fighter squadrons stationed around the perimeter of the capital city and all that it offered, a posting to one of them seemed ideal and he made Fighter Command his first choice, with Coastal Command his second option. When the posting lists came out he was ecstatic to learn that he was going to No. 65 Squadron at Hornchurch, a front-line fighter station east of London.

In his early days at Hornchurch, Kingcome learned about the structure, organization and lifestyle on fighter stations in the RAF and found the latter much to his liking. Sixteen aircraft and roughly twelve pilots comprised the typical fighter squadron which normally fielded twelve aircraft operationally, divided into two flights, A and B. The commanding officer was a Squadron Leader by rank and his two deputies were Flight Lieutenants commanding the Flights. The rest of the pilots in the squadron were generally Flying Officers and Pilot Officers, the lowest of the low. In addition to these commissioned officers, there were a few non-commissioned pilots, a Flight Sergeant, one or two sergeant pilots and possibly a Warrant Officer. Promotion was mostly slow in coming, although in wartime that changed.

RAF policy and procedure was based then on a number of assumptions, many of which turned out to be of questionable foundation. The operational task of Fighter Command, as defined in the 1930s, for example, was to be a purely defensive one in which its pilots were required to defend Britain against attack from the air. Factors that would only emerge in later years as changes in aerial warfare came in would force a new and different approach, aggressive and offensive.

In the years before the start of the Second World War, British fighter planners assumed that enemy air attacks would be delivered by long-range heavy bombers; they would be made in daylight as night-bombing required a level of technology still to be perfected, and the bombers carrying out the raids would not be accompanied by fighter escort as no known fighter aircraft of the time had sufficient range to reach England from Germany and return. Apparently, it never occurred to anyone that France might fall to the Germans, providing them with airfields much nearer England. The planners further assumed that the enemy attackers would come over in massed formations and rely on their own guns for self-defence. Thus, the Fighter Command brain trust developed its game plan of basic attack formations, a half dozen or so approaches to meeting and dealing with the enemy in the air. These included echelons port and starboard, line abreast, and line astern. In actual combat, they proved to be of little use and were quickly replaced by cleverer methods already being employed by the Germans, based in part on their learning experience in the recent Spanish Civil War.

In his first months with the squadron, Brian's flight time was largely devoted to aerobatics, air gunnery, fighter tactics, formation flying and cross-country practice. While there were a number of fundamental rules for the survival and success of a fighter pilot in a combat situation, and he had to know how to handle expertly his aircraft in every conceivable attitude and speed, he also had to know its limitations, strengths and weaknesses, and any nasty characteristics. Something else that in practice may not have been stressed either in training or on the squadron usually came to light with early combat experience. The best and most successful fighter pilot had to be capable of throwing away the textbook when the situation demanded, and flying his aeroplane with ham-fisted abandon if necessary to get the edge on his opponent or to save himself in the more dangerous and challenging encounters. That meant developing unusually high confidence in himself and his aircraft that enabled him to act with split-second spontaneity, with total trust in his skill and decisions. That state only came with practice, experimentation and determination ... assuming the pilot had the consummate skills, fitness, intelligence and common sense required. He needed luck as well.

*   *   *

How the pilot coped with the forces of gravity, or 'G' forces, in aerial combat was vital to his performance and survival. When the stick is pulled hard, centrifugal force presses him down into the bottom of the seat. The more he pulls, the tighter his horizontal or vertical turn and the heavier the forces on him until he is no longer able to move and his arms and legs are too heavy to lift. Meanwhile, his blood is being forced down from behind his optic nerves, bringing a loss of vision ('blacking out'). Individuals are affected differently by G forces. Most pilots are feeling the effects at about four G when 'greying out' begins. Kingcome:

> This may sound like a frustrating handicap in a fighting situation, but it can also be a useful defensive ploy when you have an enemy on your tail who is difficult to dislodge. If you pull the stick hard enough to black yourself out, then whoever you have on your tail is going to need to pull his back even harder. To allow for deflection, he can only turn within your trajectory, and thus will attract more G than you do. If you are blacked out the chances are that your opponent, unless he is Superman, will be blacked out as well, which will prevent him being in the position to get a clear shot at you. Blacking out is a controllable condition which does not affect thinking. This means you can ease it off now and then to snatch a quick look round, or else you can hold it for as long as you need to think up a new ploy.

Normally, a small number of the pilots in a fighter squadron were responsible for most of the enemy aircraft destroyed by the squadron. They were the few who combined the other necessary qualities with an innate understanding of how to shoot and hit a target moving in three dimensions. All fighter pilots were required to fly their aircraft, operate their radio and navigate as well as locate, and shoot their opponent's aircraft. The aeroplane designers had these things in mind when planning the positioning of the controls, switches and instruments of the fighter cockpit. For efficiency, the gun-button was located on the handle of the control column or stick, enabling the pilot easily to fly the plane and fire his guns simultaneously. Unlike in bombers, with their movable gun turrets, the machine-guns and cannon of a fighter were fixed rigidly in the wings or fuselage of the aircraft and fired on the line of flight of the aircraft. The machine-guns were usually 'harmonised' either to converge at a point between 150 and 300 yards ahead of the fighter (depending on the pilot's preference), or as a spread pattern.

Fighter pilots in that time practiced by firing live ammunition at long, airborne windsocks called drogues which were towed at a considerable distance behind tug aircraft. It was a useful exercise but in no way did it replicate the preparation, sighting and shooting problems faced by the pilot in actual combat where the fast-moving enemy aircraft was constantly changing direction, climbing, diving and skidding.

The situation was further complicated by our pilot's aeroplane (his gun platform) also moving wildly through three dimensions as he pursued his prey. Finally, he had to develop and refine an understanding of deflection in air gunnery. With his bullets taking a few seconds to reach the target, he had to be good at calculating where that enemy aircraft would be when the bullets arrived, instead of simply aiming directly at the target. He was helped a bit by a reflector gunsight which was mounted at eye level between him and the windscreen. The sight provided an illuminated orange dot on a glass plate and he could aim the dot at his target, but it was little more than a guide and provided no information about required deflection.

One further discipline required of the successful fighter pilot was safe and efficient formation flying. As Kingcome recalled,

Even when you were flying blind in the thickest cloud, there was always enough visibility to see the aircraft immediately next to you, if little else. Each aircraft had its place in the formation and each pilot had to concentrate 100 per cent on his immediate neighbour. You also needed to have implicit faith in your leader. As the only one among you who was flying on instruments, he held the fate of the formation in his hands.

*   *   *

In the pre-war days at Hornchurch, Brian and the other pilots enjoyed the freedom to fly wherever they wanted in their free time, whether to meet friends somewhere for lunch, on air force business, or for purely personal reasons. Such *ad hoc* flying was actually encouraged as it added to the sum total of a pilot's flying experience and was thus looked upon as beneficial to the service by improving his skills, knowledge and self-confidence and exposing him to new situations and unfamiliar conditions. For such flights he was not required to get permission from anyone other than his flight commander. No flight plan had to be filed and only the specific flying altitude was mandatory for the trip. He could navigate by map reading and, while on the ground having lunch at his destination, his aircraft was refuelled and made ready for his return flight.

The hazards involved in such flights related mainly to weather. Without the sort of radar systems that came into use in later years, the fighter pilot had to rely largely on map-reading and visual contact with the ground. When weather or cloud cover interfered, he could easily drift off course and, when emerging from the conditions, be miles from where he expected to be. Danger often lay in a situation where he had to rely on his altimeter which had been set to the height of the airfield where he took off. Letting down through cloud cover in preparation to land could be tricky, as Kingcome noted:

> ... if the weather clamped down and there were hills between you
> and your destination, you needed to hold your breath as you
> began to let down, and pray you had not picked a spot where the
> clouds were shrouding the hills – 'clouds with hard centres', as
> they were known with ominous wit. And once you were safely
> down through the cloud, you were likely to find yourself in un-
> familiar territory amid poor visibility. The usual trick then was to
> try to spot a railway line and grope your way along it until you
> came to a station, when you could read its name.

*   *   *

No. 65 Squadron at Hornchurch re-equipped from Gloster Gladiator
biplane fighters to Spitfires beginning nine months before the outbreak
of the Second World War. The pilots of No. 65 Squadron gained a
considerable advantage, having had several months experience with
Spitfires prior to Dunkirk, the first important action with the enemy
for the Spit. For the first time, the fighter pilots of the Royal Air Force
were given an aeroplane capable of reaching 400 mph in level flight and
armed with eight machine-guns. The friendly rivalry between Spitfire
and Hurricane pilots over which was superior in this way or that
continued, but in Brian Kingcome's view, the Spitfire won hands
down:

> Even if I had been a Hurricane pilot, I would still have had to
> award the supreme accolade to the Spitfire in any final judgement.
> The Hurricane was a solid, reliable, uncomplaining workhorse,
> but the Spitfire personified symmetry and grace. She was a thing
> apart, defying comparison. She was as relaxed, as elegant, as
> obviously and effortless at home in her natural environment as a
> swallow; and equally poetic in motion. To compare the two
> models would be as invidious as comparing a champion ice skater
> with the skill of Morris dancers: each is brilliant in his or her own
> way, but each displays a widely different talent and technique.
> There is an old truism that, if a car or an aeroplane looks good,
> then it almost invariably is good. And nothing looked better than
> the Spitfire.
>
> Not that the Hurricane failed to possess one or two advantages
> over the Spitfire. It was more robust and could take more punish-
> ment; it had a more concentrated fire pattern, its guns being
> grouped more closely together. It was also marginally more
> manoeuvrable, and was far more stable on the ground – the result
> of its undercarriage being wider and positioned farther forward, a
> characteristic which often proved useful on the rough terrain of

temporary landing strips. The Spitfire, on the other hand, was faster and could out-dive and out-climb the Hurricane; and since it could also out-turn the German front-line fighter, the Me 109, it had all the manoeuvrability it needed. Yet in the end these are only details of performance, and it was in the respective operational life of the two aircraft that the truly huge difference between them became crystal clear.

The Hurricane was already more or less at the peak of its operational and design potential when it first came into service. As time passed, it was given bigger and better engines, heavier and more powerful armament, and was tried out in various ground-attack roles. Nevertheless its future was strictly limited by its rugged, uncouth airframe. In other words, it had virtually no development potential. The Spitfire, by contrast, possessed a unique capacity for development. On one occasion Jeffrey Quill, the legendary test pilot who nursed the Spitfire from cradle to grave, gave me his definition of the range of its development throughout its life as a fighting machine. The difference in capability between the first Spitfire off the drawing board and the last to be built was to be measured, he said, by the fact that the latter could carry an extra load equivalent to an additional thirty-six airline passengers, each with his or her regulation 40 kilos of luggage.

Brian recalled his first flight in a Spitfire and the fact that, being a single-seater fighter, it was a voyage of discovery,

With no possibility of dual instruction, one had to find his way around it on his own. The solo flight offered no problems and the aeroplane responded in the air to any demands he made on it. He found its main weaknesses to be evident when it contacted the ground. When taxiing, the long nose eliminated any forward vision for the pilot, requiring him to weave from side to side to see where he was going, and one had to use the brakes delicately to keep from tipping the aircraft on to its nose.

*   *   *

The year-long 'Phoney War' gave way to the real thing for Brian and the pilots of No. 65 Squadron at Hornchurch in May 1940 as the soldiers of the British Expeditionary Force trudged onto the beaches at Dunkirk and awaited evacuation to England. A strange fleet of barges, coasters, ferries, lighters and small private vessels was assembled by the Royal Navy's Admiral Sir Bertram Ramsay for Operation Dynamo, the rescue of more than 338,000 British and French troops. The British Admiralty had required all private owners of self-propelled pleasure craft of between 30 and 100 feet to register them. In the actual evacuation, many of the owners of these craft were allowed to skipper them and become a part of history.

The cloud conditions did not favour the Spitfire pilots of No. 65, who had been ordered into the Dunkirk area at an altitude of 30,000 feet, well above several layers of intermittent cloud, and 15,000 feet above the operating level of the Hurricanes that first day of the evacuation. It would, however, bring Kingcome his initial opportunity to fire his guns in anger.

There were other British aircraft in the skies over Dunkirk that day, notably a squadron of Boulton Paul Defiants, a single-engined aircraft that resembled the Hurricane but was operated by a crew of two and mounted an unusual four-gun turret behind the pilot. It had no forward-firing guns and could not defend itself against head-on attacks. As the evacuation began the Defiants were bounced by a squadron of Messerschmitt Me 109s. The German pilots mistook the Defiants for Hurricanes and attacked them from above and behind. Many of the German fighters were shot out of the sky and the *Luftwaffe* quickly learned how to attack the Defiant. Later that day more Messerschmitts rose to engage the Defiants and this time things were different. The enemy fighters attacked from below and behind. In the action, the Defiants were defenceless and their entire squadron was wiped out. By August the Boulton Paul machines had been withdrawn from operational duty.

*   *   *

The stark reality of air fighting was made clear to the inexperienced Hugh Dundas on 28 May 1940 high over those same Dunkirk beaches. Flying a Spitfire with No. 616 Squadron from Rochford, near Southend, Essex, he witnessed a pair of Fleet Air Arm Blackburn Skua fighter/dive-bombers under savage attack by Messerschmitt Me 109s. The Skua is an all but forgotten type, distinguished for having been the first Fleet Air Arm aircraft to shoot down a German plane (a Dornier Do flying boat on 26 September 1939). It later became the first FAA aircraft type to sink a German warship in wartime when Skuas attacked the cruiser *Königsberg* in Bergen harbour (Norway, on 10 April 1940).

Dundas watched for five seconds as the little party of friendly and enemy aircraft fell away and behind him. The scene was instantly erased as his own section leader suddenly broke into a hard, climbing turn in the midst of garbled and confusing voices over the radio. Rushing into Dundas' view was a yellow-nosed Me 109 curving toward him. It occurred to him that he was about to be shot at for the first time. Someone he didn't know and who didn't know him was about to try to kill him. Following his leader, he was fascinated by the sight of the rapidly closing enemy fighter:

> ... I saw the ripples of grey smoke breaking away from it and the lights were winking and flashing from the propeller hub and engine cowling. Red blobs arced lazily through the air between us, accelerating dramatically as they approached and streaked close by, across my wing. With sudden, sickening, stupid fear I realized that I was being fired on and I pulled my Spitfire round hard, so that the blood was forced down from my head. The thick curtain of blackout blinded me for a moment and I felt the aircraft juddering on the brink of a stall. Straightening out, the curtain lifted and I saw a confusion of planes, diving and twisting. My eyes focused on two more Messerschmitts, flying in quite close formation, curving down towards me. Again I saw the ripple of smoke and the wink of lights; again I went into a blackout turn and again the bullets streaked harmlessly by.
>
> At some stage in the next few seconds the silhouette of a Messerschmitt passed across my windscreen and I fired my guns in battle for the first time – a full deflection shot which, I believe, was quite ineffectual.
>
> I was close to panic in the bewilderment and hot fear of that first dog-fight. Fortunately instinct drove me to keep turning, twisting my neck all the time to look for the enemy behind. Certainly the consideration which was uppermost in my mind was the desire to stay alive.
>
> ... there was no thought of right or wrong, courage or cowardice, in my mind as I sweated and swore my way through that first fight over Dunkirk. When, at last, I felt it safe to straighten out I was amazed to find that the sky which only a few moments before had been full of whirling, firing fighters was now quite empty. It was my first experience of this curious phenomenon, which continually amazed all fighter pilots. At one moment it was all you could do to avoid collision; the sky around you was streaked with tracer and the thin grey smoke-trails of firing machine-guns and cannons. The next moment you were on your own. The mêlée had broken up as if by magic. The sky was empty except for a few distant specks. It was then that panic took hold of me for the second time that day. Finding myself alone over the sea, a few miles north of Dunkirk, my training as well as my nerve deserted me. Instead of calmly thinking out the course which I should fly to reach the Thames estuary, I blindly set out in what I conceived to be roughly the right direction. After several minutes I could see nothing at all but the empty wastes of the North Sea –

not a ship, nor a boat. At last I saw two destroyers steaming at full speed in line ahead, and beyond them in the haze I could see the flat coastline of France. The sight of the two ships restored me to some measure of sanity and self-control. I forced myself to work out the simple problem of navigation which sheer panic had prevented me from facing. After a couple of orbits I set course to the west and soon the cliffs of North Foreland came up to meet me.

Soaked in sweat, I flew low across the estuary towards Southend pier. By the time I came in to land at Rochford, the little grass field behind Southend where the squadron had arrived the night before to take part in the Dunkirk evacuation, a sense of jubilation had replaced the cravenness of a few minutes earlier. I was transformed, Walter Mitty-like: now a debonair young fighter pilot, rising twenty, proud and delighted that he had fired his guns in a real dog-fight, even though he had not hit anything, sat in the cockpit which had so recently been occupied by a frightened child and taxied in to the dispersal point, where excited ground crew waited to hear the news of the battle.

*   *   *

Following the Dunkirk evacuation, Brian Kingcome was invited to join No. 92 Squadron which then moved to Llanelli in South Wales, to defend the industrial towns and harbours along the Bristol Channel. During the Dunkirk action, the squadron had been commanded by Roger Bushell, who was shot down over the beaches and became a prisoner of war confined in the notorious *Stalag Luft* III, Silesia. In that camp Bushell was known as 'Big X', the head of the committee which planned and executed the 'Great Escape.' As one of the apprehended escapers, Bushell was among the fifty who were murdered by the Nazis in direct contravention of the Geneva accords for prisoners of war. He was replaced as commanding officer of No. 92 Squadron by Bob Stanford Tuck of No. 65 Squadron. Tuck had been promoted to Squadron Leader and when posted to No. 92 Squadron, asked Kingcome to join him there.

From the moment he arrived on the squadron, Brian sensed that certain chemistry that made the group unique and special, in spirit and performance. These were people who enjoyed life, living it to the fullest, on the job and off, while never taking it or themselves too seriously. He remembered Neville Duke and Trevor 'Wimpy' Wade, exceptional pilots who both survived the war and went on to become famous test pilots, Don Kingaby and Ralph 'Titch' Havercroft, both of whom were highly decorated non-commissioned officer pilots who ended up as Wing Commanders, the bright, able and determined Allen Wright, and Tony Bartley, the handsome and brilliant pilot who later married the movie actress, Deborah Kerr. There was Bob Holland, revered by the rest of the squadron for his ability on the piano. Holland survived the war only tragically to be killed while instructing at the Fighter Leader's School, when a student got onto a collision course with him and both men died. It was Tuck, however, who left the most indelible impression on Kingcome:

> ... extravert and flamboyant, tall and very slim. His jet-black hair was oiled and brushed back close to his head, and he had a pencil-slim moustache (contrary to regulations). He also sported a scar down one cheek, though it was not a duelling scar, as he used to delight in conning strangers. It had been caused far more glamorously, to my mind, by a broken flying wire when he baled out of a Gloucester Gauntlet after an aerial collision when practicing tied-together formation acrobatics.
>
> Bob's striking good looks and illicit Clark Gable moustache brought him a lot of good-natured ribbing, to which he responded happily with a nonchalant smile. He could afford to be non-chalant. In the air he was a total professional, and none was more highly respected. He was a superb pilot and a first-class shot, and most importantly he had the uncanny hunter's instinct for arriving precisely where the enemy was; then, as lesser mortals turned for home believing the skies vacated, he would find a few stragglers still within firing distance.

*   *   *

In the midsummer of 1940 the squadron chafed at the relative inactivity in Wales, both in the air and socially. The pubs, in Brian's opinion, lacked the sort of ambiance that appealled to young fighter pilots, and the Germans rarely appeared in No. 92 Squadron's area of responsibility. In late August, to their immense relief, they were transferred to Biggin Hill, south of London, in Kent. With the move, Bob Tuck left the squadron, posted to a Hurricane outfit in East Anglia.

*   *   *

As Brian remembered it, the White Hart pub at Brasted a few miles from his base at Biggin Hill, was his squadron's spiritual home,

> It is with enormous gratitude and affection that I recall Teddy and Kath Preston, the warm hearted and generous couple who made their pub our haven. No. 92 Squadron was the most successful fighter squadron in the Battle of Britain and was longest in the firing line, and I know beyond question that the 'Preston Factor' played a significant part of the strange, schizophrenic existence we led ... Other squadrons retired to the Mess, to early nights and

talk of shop. We retired to the White Hart to talk of blondes and booze and where would we go at closing time. And always there, always encouraging, always creating peaceful, informal atmosphere where stress and tension daren't intrude, were the Prestons.

Their influence was magical: Teddy, the archetypal 'mine host', the reassuring, avuncular, jovial *bon viveur* with a welcome that engulfed us all in warmth; and hovering ubiquitously, always where she was needed, invisibly oiling the wheels, smoothing every hiccup, his beautiful consort Kath. And somehow, at a time when rationing was exerting its tedious stranglehold on food and drink, the White Hart seemed to rise disdainfully above such problems. And always that lovely, gentle, hypnotic ambience that restored our spirits and refreshed our souls.

*   *   *

One day late in the Battle of Britain, a day when the *Luftwaffe* was not very active over southern England, No. 92 Squadron was finally scrambled in the mid-morning with Kingcome in the lead. Vectored to intercept enemy raiders over Maidstone in Kent, the British pilots located the German formation, broke it up and sent them packing for their French base. It had been a typical operation for Brian, a brief encounter which had been successful. With his ammunition used up, he headed back towards Biggin, having found himself in that strange yet familiar empty-sky phenomenon, except for three Spitfires in the far distance, seconds after the air fight. Now it was midday and the weather was glorious; the sky cloudless. He had missed breakfast and was hungry:

> I put my nose down to head straight for home and lunch, but then thought I might as well kill two birds with one brick and decided to throttle back and practice a 'dead stick' forced landing; one with simulated engine failure.
>
> It was breathtakingly stupid behaviour. The skies of Kent were at all times a hostile environment, whatever the illusion of emptiness, yet here was I, as operationally experienced as anyone, casually putting at risk my aircraft and my life – a vital, valuable piece of equipment and a trained pilot, each disproportionately crucial, with supplies of both dwindling fast. I can only put the action down to an over-confidence fostered by constant exposure to the dawn-to-dusk rotation of 'take off, climb, engage, land, refuel, rearm, take off, climb, engage ...' two, three or sometimes four times a day, familiarity reducing what had begun as exciting, adrenaline-pumping action to mere routine. I had grown blasé. Perhaps I needed to be shot up to reawaken me to reality.

And here I was, oblivious to danger, admiring the view, enjoying the sensation of speed as I pushed the nose down towards distant Biggin Hill, forgetting the fighter pilot's golden rule to watch his tail however safe he thought he might be – always to watch his tail. I was sailing in a dream when my reveries were rudely shattered by an almighty thump to the back of the right leg. It came as a bit of a shock to one who believed himself alone with 20,000 clear feet between himself and other human company. Worse was to follow: a rattling clatter as if someone were violently shaking a giant bucket full of pebbles close to my ear. Still it took me a further moment or two to realize that this sound was the jarring impact of bullets striking in and around my cockpit. Glancing down at my leg, I saw blood welling out of the top of my flying boot, and knew that what had felt like a thump from a blunt instrument had also been a bullet. I felt no pain. With bullet wounds the pain comes later.

I jerked myself around, but could see no sign of anything except the three Spitfires I had noticed before. Now they drew alongside, peered at me briefly, then peeled away. Whether they had mistaken me for a German, or whether they were white knights who had shot someone else off my tail, was something I was never to know. I was left with blood flowing out of the top of my flying-boot and my ailerons gone suddenly sluggish.

Here was just the sort of situation I had often mentally rehearsed, behaving with dignity, competence and calm, emulating those phlegmatic First World War movie heroes of *The Dawn Patrol* and *Hell's Angels* sitting imperturbably in smoke-filled cockpits, nonchalantly saluting their opponents as, engulfed in flames, they began a long spiral to a fiery death. I regret to say I failed dismally to match the image of the Errol Flynn prototype. I was panic-stricken, gripped in a blind, paralyzing terror. This could not be happening to me. This only happened to the other Chap! For what felt like a century, though it could only have been a few moments, I sat rigid and disbelieving, my stomach churning. Here was the real thing. This was what it felt like. All at once I had become the other chap for whom I had always felt sorry, though I had never lost any sleep about it.

The effect was devastating: one minute relaxed and carefree, in total control with nothing more dramatic in mind than a simulated forced landing and the day's lunch menu; the next, inhabiting a doomed aircraft at 20,000 feet, losing blood at a rate that suggested consciousness might slip away at any moment with death following within minutes. Death: so far I had managed to keep him discreetly imprisoned in the back of my mind, vague and ill-defined, a subject fit for black humour, not to be taken too seriously. Now he became a terrifying reality so close I could smell him. Or was this simply the smell of my own fear, unlocking feelings I thought I had defused and put safely aside?

Then, almost miraculously, Brian's panic was gone; he was calm with rational thoughts. The fear, however, was still present, but now it was working for him. His adrenaline was pumping and his brain working efficiently again. He quickly evaluated the situation and realized he had two options: either stay with the aeroplane in the hope that he could bring it back to Biggin without the control cables parting at the last minute when he was too low to jump, or simply bail out hopefully to save himself. The success of this latter choice depended on his opening his parachute before passing out from loss of blood, and then not bleeding to death on the way down. His imagination kicked in at that point with visions of jumping into freezing, hostile space ... but, all things considered, baling out seemed to him his best option. Still, the Spitfire was not on fire and was reasonably stable and he still felt secure in the cockpit. It was only the blood loss that motivated him to leave that formerly cozy environment.

Now he had quickly to assess the possible ways of baling out. Going over the side was probably not the best choice due to the risk of being blown back onto the tailplane and maybe cut in half, which had been the fate of at least one fighter pilot. A better way, supposedly, was to roll the aeroplane onto its back, jettison the canopy, undo the straps and leads, and allow gravity to take over. But with aileron problems, Brian was not keen to trust the rolling manoeuvre. He decided instead to dump the canopy, undo the straps etc and shove the control column hard forward, which he hoped would catapult him out of the cockpit. He got as far as undoing his straps when he was sucked from the aeroplane and thrust like a rag doll into space, tumbling uncontrollably. The forces acting on him were brutal and literally bruising. He later estimated that he had left the Spitfire at between 350 and 400 mph, but soon slowed to the terminal velocity of the human body falling through space, about 120 mph. He felt relaxed and the lack of oxygen and his blood loss was shielding him from fear. There was no sense of falling or wind. In a semi-conscious state he plunged earthward, with no real sense of how long he had been free-falling or how far he had fallen. He was somehow reminded that he had lost a lot of blood and had to get down fast. Then he recalled that the flight had climbed through a layer of cumulous cloud at about 4,000 feet and thus knew that he could fall about 15,000 feet before he had to open his parachute. He seemed to recall too, that his own parachute had been away for routine inspection that morning and he had grabbed the nearest available one as he left for the dispersal. One of the parachute packers had warned him that that one too was due for inspection and he ought to take another one, but he couldn't be bothered, believing, as most pilots seemed to do, that they were invulnerable.

The moment came to open the 'chute and when he pulled the ripcord it worked just as it had been designed to do. 'There was only a split second in which to wonder whether I had made a bad choice of parachute before, with a satisfying crack, it snapped open and braked my downward rush with a bone-cracking jerk' and he began slowly descending towards the lush patchwork countryside of Kent. His senses cleared somewhat and he noticed that he had instinctively pulled the ripcord just hard enough to release the canopy while retaining the cord itself. The natural reaction when baling out was to pull the ripcord as hard as one could and then toss it away as it came off in your hand. It had been drummed into him though, to keep the thing or be charged ten shillings, nearly a day's pay, if you failed to bring it back. Ten shillings was the equivalent of a night out in London or four nights in the local pubs.

He had been well trained. He recalled the descent as he approached the ground from several hundred feet above it,

I dangled in the harness, swaying gently, studying the ground beneath me. What astonished me was not what I could see – I was used to that – but what I could hear: the sounds that rose up to me from the ground. I was accustomed to a noisy cockpit and earphones that cut out all other sound, but now, as I drifted down the last thousand feet or so, the silence was broken by car horns, by cattle lowing, even by human voices, which came up to me with startling clarity. As I floated down over open farmland I could see below me a small group of agricultural workers armed with pitchforks and other businesslike farm implements heading across to the field towards which I was drifting. For the first time since parting company with my aircraft I began to feel a definite alarm. There had been stories of parachuting Allied airmen being beaten up and, on one occasion, even killed by incensed locals, working on the patriotic assumption that if they had been shot down then they must be the enemy. To complicate matters, I was wearing a German Mae West [that] I had commandeered from the body of the crew member of the Ju 88 [that I had shot down previously]. Apprehensively I gazed down at the group who gazed up at me, gripping the formidable tools of their trade.

Brian landed hard, permanently damaging a disc in his back and knocking the breath out of him, but he managed to sit up quickly and pull the German life-jacket off to show the farm workers his RAF uniform. Fortunately, they smiled and seemed friendly, having seen his Spitfire crash nearby. One of them offered, 'We'd better get you to a hospital before you bleed to death' staring at Brian's blood-soaked trouser leg. Once again he was to suffer excessively and needlessly at the hands of a less than competent surgeon who, in probing along the track of the bullet wound, cut through a blood vessel. The act caused the two ends of the vessel to spring apart, whereupon he lost them. He then complicated the situation further by cutting down the leg in search of the missing items. Failing to locate them he elected to simply stuff the wound with dressing, sew it up and cover the leg in plaster. When Brian regained consciousness and learned from a concerned nurse what had been done to him, he got word to the station adjutant at Biggin Hill and got himself transferred to a hospital near the base where a more skilful surgeon located the bullet by X-ray and removed it through a small incision. After a six-week recovery Kingcome was back with his squadron.

While Brian waited to become fit enough to be operational again, No. 92 Squadron received a new commander, Johnny Kent, a well-known and accomplished Canadian who had recently commanded one of the Polish fighter squadrons. Early in spring 1941, the squadron was detached to RAF Manston on the Kentish coast to protect that hot little corner of England.

* * *

The pilots of RAF Fighter Command had gone on the offensive and were flying regular sweep attacks on targets in German-occupied France. The British fighter force was growing in strength while the *Luftwaffe* was weaker in the west, having had to transfer many units to the Soviet front, leaving the Channel front with less German protection. Looking to capitalize on an opportunity to gain air supremacy in the Channel area, the Royal Air Force was poised to take advantage of any such openings.

* * *

Since June 1941, the two powerful and modern German pocket-battleships, *Scharnhorst* and *Gneisenau*, and the battle cruiser *Prinz Eugen*, had been sheltering in the French port of Brest. They had been bottled up there and under frequent attack by RAF Bomber Command aircraft, while the harbour was blockaded by continuous Royal Navy submarine patrols. The British were protecting their convoy traffic in the Channel from attack by these German warships and, though the bombing raids on the warships were largely ineffectual, they did serve to keep the threat of these menacing enemy vessels contained for the time being.

Concerned that the Allies were planning to open a new war front in Scandinavia, Hitler ordered that the three German warships be moved from Brest to Norway via Germany. If they were routed around Scotland they faced the possibility of a battle with units of the British Home Fleet, then stationed at Scapa Flow, in the Orkneys. If, on the other hand, they were sent through the English Channel, they would be exposed to the attentions of the RAF, to British warships and coastal gun batteries.

They chose the latter option, believing that, with the support and protection of the *Luftwaffe* fighter force, their battleships and battle cruiser could make a successful 'Channel Dash', which they called Operation Thunderbolt.

It was Group Captain Victor Beamish, then commander of RAF Kenley, west of Biggin Hill, who, on 12 February 1942, was flying an impromptu sweep into France with another Kenley Spitfire pilot, when he happened to spot and report a little flotilla of E-boats and destroyers escorting the three German warships off the coast near Le Touquet.

Bob Tuck, then wing commander at Biggin Hill, had asked Brian Kingcome to take command of No. 72 Squadron which, at that point, was on temporary detachment at Gravesend, one of Biggin's satellite airfields where the squadron that day was on 'thirty minutes' availability status. Ensconced in their quarters at Cobham Hall, home of the Earl of Darnley, the officers of No. 72 Squadron read newspapers and tried to catch up on some sleep that morning, until noon when the telephone rang bringing them to readiness. Moments later they were at the dispersal and ordered to 'cockpit standby.'

Confusion reigned throughout Fighter Command over the next half hour as to what was actually happening in the Channel. Over that period, Kingcome was given four different sets of instructions, before finally being ordered to take off immediately and head for Manston at full throttle, where he would meet four more Spitfire squadrons in the air over the base. The other squadrons would form up behind No. 72 Squadron, all of which Kingcome would command. When they rendezvoused, six Fleet Air Arm Swordfish torpedo-bombers would be scrambled from Manston, to be escorted by the wing of Spitfires to the Straits of Dover where some enemy naval activity was evidently under way. Several British motor-torpedo boats were known to be engaging a German E-boat flotilla there. Kingcome considered all of this on the way to Manston and thought about the Fairey Swordfish biplane, which, in his view, was 'a testimony to the navy's attachment to the prehistoric: antediluvian aeroplanes with fixed undercarriages and three crew members crammed into two open cockpits. They had been designed to function as torpedo carriers and this was a task they could just about manage, thought the weight of a torpedo left them with a top speed of between 85 and 90 knots – about or below the stalling speed for most other aircraft of their generation.'

He knew too, that there was no shortage of guts, heroism and dedication among the crews of the Fleet Air Arm and that, to some extent at least, counterbalanced the obvious deficiencies of their air-craft. This was shown in a naval action of May 1940 when the great German battleship *Bismarck*, easily superior in most respects to the capital ships of the Royal Navy, out-ran and out-shot the British warships that were trying to sink her. It took a torpedo attack by the obsolescent Swordfish from the carrier HMS *Ark Royal*, with an admittedly lucky strike when one of the weapons hit *Bismarck* in her rudder, seriously damaging her steering gear, to pave the way for the British warships *Rodney*, *Dorsetshire* and *King George V* finally to send her to the bottom.

As Kingcome, in the lead of nine other Spitfires, arrived over Manston, he was surprised to find the six Swordfish biplanes already airborne and orbiting the airfield. He was more surprised to discover that none of the other Spitfire squadrons scheduled for the operation had appeared. As soon as they spotted the Spitfires, the Swordfish pilots straightened and headed off without waiting for any more Spitfires to show up. Brian was then surprised yet again when the Swordfish flight set course due east rather than south towards Dover, as he had expected. The torpedo-bombers were heading out over the North Sea at wave-top height; the sea was rough and immediately overhead lay thick, intermittent cloud cover, which made the visibility only 200 yards at best. As the top speed of the Swordfish was only equal to the stalling speed of the Spitfire, the only way the small Spit-fire force could maintain visual contact with the Swordfish, without spinning into the sea, was to weave behind the torpedo planes in large figure-eights. Had the other Spitfire squadrons arrived as planned, the coordination of their movements might have proven disastrous.

A few moments away from the English coast, the Spitfires were attacked by enemy fighters but the British pilots quickly repelled them without sustaining any casualties. Shortly after the encounter, Brian sighted 'the most magisterial warship you could have imagined. Its sinister beauty and overpowering menace were palpable. Mentally I began to ... congratulate the Royal Navy. At last, it seemed they had made a dramatic move up-market and got themselves a real ship of battle for the present and future.' Then it seemed that every gun in the mighty warship opened up in Brian's direction. The Royal Navy did have a reputation among airmen for shooting first and asking questions afterwards. But the six Swordfish bore in on the great vessel without the slightest hesitation. Their intent was clear. The Spitfire pilots were uncertain; some thought they might be about to witness a torpedo attack on a capital ship of the British fleet.

At that point the big ship lowered her guns and began firing shells and salvoes into the sea ahead of the approaching Swordfish. Huge towers of white spray erupted in front of the plodding torpedo planes which, somehow, were able to dodge the worst of the gunfire. Brian thought that one of the Swordfish had been hit, but he wasn't sure about it. The small troup of Swordfish never faltered. They drove on until reaching torpedo range. There was nothing the frustrated Spitfire pilots could do to help. And then Kingcome and the British fighter pilots were bounced by a swarm of Bf 109s.

The fourth surprise of the day for Brian was the appearance of a new German fighter in the midst of the Bf 109s; it was his first contact with the Focke-Wulf Fw 190, an impressive, radial-engined single-seater about which the pilots of No. 72 Squadron had not yet been briefed. He later learned that the German commander in the air was General of the Fighter Arm Adolf Galland, probably the *Luftwaffe*'s most celebrated fighter leader and one of its greatest fighter pilots.

Of the six Swordfish, none survived the attack. Of the eighteen Swordfish aircrew, five were later rescued from the water. After dealing with the audacious torpedo planes, the mighty battle cruiser *Prinz Eugen* rejoined the *Scharnhorst* and *Gneisenau* and the three of them, together with their protective flotilla, moved on to vanish in the North Sea gloom.

The Spitfires had been airborne for just over an hour when they landed back at Gravesend, some of them shot up from the encounter with the enemy fighters. The operation had been an utter disaster for the British, whose intelligence facility had been entirely out-foxed by the enemy, as evidenced by the decision to employ the six Swordfish in a hopeless cause on a suicidal mission against three such formidable warships, wasting the lives of all but five of the air crewmen. The British military planners had been fooled too, after the RAF's last bombing attack on the German battleships in Brest harbour appeared to have damaged the vessels sufficiently for the British to call off their surveillance and blockade of the harbour. The Germans had pulled off a magnificent ruse by cosmetically dressing the decks of the warships with debris to make them look from the air as though they had suffered severe damage. British photo interpreters took the bait and the planners did just as the Germans thought they would. After clearing the decks, the enemy warships were able to steal out of Brest on their Channel Dash. Of the Swordfish crews, the navigation officer of *Scharnhorst* later stated, 'Their bravery was devoted and incredible.

They knowingly and ungrudgingly gave their all to their country and went to their doom without hesitation.'

* * *

In the summer of 1942, Brian Kingcome was posted to Kenley to take over as Wing Commander Flying. His Command was known as the 'Canadian Wing' and was made up of Nos 401, 402, 412 and 416 Squadrons and, at last, he felt he had landed in a virtually perfect situation. The Station Commander at Kenley then was Group Captain Richard Atcherley, a man Brian liked and respected, and he had charge of four fine Spitfire squadrons.

The job of the Kenley Wing was two-fold: fighter sweeps penetrating as far over France as they could go, attempting to lure German fighters into combat; the other to provide fighter escort protection for the heavy bombers of the US Army Air Force in their daylight bombing missions at a point in the war when the Americans could muster relatively few planes and crews to face a powerful *Luftwaffe* on the defensive. Due to the still quite limited range of the Spitfires available at the time, Kingcome's pilots could only shepherd the bombers during the first, and least vulnerable portion of their missions, or rendezvous with them for that same part of the return trip. For the rest of the journey, the bomber crews were largely on their own, reliant on their own gunners and their clever 'box' formations for protection through maximum cross-fire.

At about this time some RAF fighter squadrons were beginning to be equipped with a significantly improved Spitfire, the Mk.IX. It featured a new engine, the Merlin 61, with a two-stage, two-speed supercharger which overcame one of the Spitfire's few weaknesses. Previously, the aeroplane simply began to run short of power as it climbed through about 15,000 feet and the thinning air robbed the earlier Merlin of energy. The engine produced a whole new power regime for higher altitudes as the new supercharger kicked in around the limits of the old engine, enabling the plane to operate efficiently at far higher altitudes. In August, Kingcome's 402 Squadron was the first in his wing to be equipped with the Mk.IXs and, as Wing Commander, he immediately commandeered one for his personal aircraft and had it marked with his initials as part of the fuselage code,

The first time I flew the Mark IX I could hardly believe the experience. The effect was magical. I had expected an increase in power, but nothing to match the reality. To enhance the dramatic effect, the second stage cut in automatically without warning. One minute I was, relaxed and peaceful, as I climbed at a leisurely pace towards 15,000 feet, anticipating a small surge of extra power as I hit the magic number. The next minute it was as though a giant hand had grabbed hold of me, cradled me in its palm like a shot-putter his weight and given me the most terrific shove forwards and upwards. The shock was so great that I almost baled out. It literally took my breath away. It was exhilarating, a feeling I could never forget. I yearned at once for a chance to demonstrate this astonishing new tool to the Germans.

Another organization then receiving the new Mk.IX Spitfires was the American Eagle Squadron, actually comprised of three squadrons (No. 71 Squadron stationed at Debden in Essex, No. 121 at North Weald in Essex and No. 133 at Biggin Hill). The Eagles had been formed of American volunteer fliers in the days before the US had entered the war. They were squadrons of RAF Fighter Command and their pilots wore the RAF uniform and flew its aircraft. After the Japanese attack on Pearl Harbor in December 1941, the US declared war on Japan and Germany, and with the presence of the US Army Air Force in Britain, the Eagles would soon transfer to the USAAF and become the No. 4 Fighter Group, based at Debden, an outfit that would finish the war as the highest scoring American fighter group in the European Theatre of Operations. For most, but not all, of the Eagles, the transfer was not mandatory; they could if they wished remain with the RAF, and some did so despite the better pay of pilots in the USAAF. One of these was Carroll 'Red' McColpin, the commander of No. 133 Squadron,

I knew that a big mission to Morlaix was coming up, but I'd been ordered to transfer to the USAAF. *Ordered*. I kept delaying it week after week.

We were down at Biggin Hill, but 133 was being moved up to Great Sampford, near Debden. The mission was being laid on ... then off ... then on again. I decided I wouldn't go and leave the outfit until the mission was over with. I was gonna lead that mission. Then General 'Monk' Hunter called up from Fighter Command Headquarters of the Eighth Air Force and said, 'I understand you haven't transferred,' and I said, 'Yes sir.' He just said, 'Well you get your butt in there and transfer, right now!' To which I came back, 'Sir, I'm waiting for this Morlaix mission and I'm trying to keep enough boys in here to run it 'cause it's a big one.' 'To heck with that ... you get in there and transfer,' Hunter replied. 'Well, sir,' I said, 'You understand that I'm in the Royal Air Force, sir, and I have an ops instruction which says we are going to Morlaix when they lay it on. I'm the CO here, and I've got my squadron on the line.' With that he snorted and hung up. About an hour later I got a call from an air marshal in the group.

'McColpin, do you take orders from me?' I said, 'I certainly do, sir. Yes, sir.' 'That's how I came to transfer over.

When the Morlaix raid was finally laid on it was a disaster and a tragic way for the Eagles to bow out of the RAF. British pilot Gordon Brettell was made commander of 133 Squadron and led the Morlaix mission in place of McColpin.

The mission called for the Eagles, along with other Fighter Command Spitfire squadrons, including Brian Kingcome's, to escort American bombers in an attack on a Brest peninsula target. They were to cross the widest part of the English Channel and fly over a heavily defended area. At Great Sampford, 133 Squadron awaited transfer into the American Air Force, but they would still fly the Morlaix mission before the transfer came about. They, along with the other Spitfire squadrons, were sent down to Bolt Head, a blustery and desolate forward airfield on cliffs between Dartmouth and Plymouth, Devon. At Bolt Head they were to be refuelled and briefed for the mission, and join up with the other squadrons. On the flight from Great Sampford down to Devon the weather was deteriorating and began to threaten the impending mission.

Crucially, without the leadership and discipline of Red McColpin that day, the pilots of No. 133 Squadron were overly nonchalant and cavalier. Most of them didn't even attend the briefing for the raid. Gordon Brettell and one other pilot were the only ones briefed. In the briefing, they were told, incorrectly, that there would be a 35 knot headwind at their cruising altitude of 28,000 feet. Incredibly, the exact take-off time of the bombers, and the time for their rendezvous with the fighters were unknown and not provided in the briefing. McColpin had a reputation among the Eagle commanders as a brilliant planner with exceptional attention to detail. Those qualities were blatantly missing on the day of the Morlaix raid. Even the take-off of the fighter mass was chaotic, with a number of near-collisions; pilots received incorrect instructions about radio frequencies and some neglected to bring their maps and escape kits.

Thirty-six Spitfires were airborne from Bolt Head, fitted with auxiliary fuel tanks and en route to meet the bombers. Kingcome:

We had been flying for hardly more than five or ten minutes before a layer of cloud began to gather below us. It was thick and mountainous and the sea was entirely concealed by the time we were half-way across the Channel. For about twenty-five minutes we continued climbing steadily until we had reached to around 20,000 feet and were, by our calculations, directly above the French coast. We then went into a gentle orbit as we began to scan about us for the Flying Fortresses. The sky seemed empty, but then I spotted them a long way to the south, little more than dots on the horizon and evidently forced up by the towering clouds to about the same altitude as ours. I thought it odd that they were so far from the target area. Then, as we watched, they turned north-east and headed for home. The heavy cloud cover must have made them abort the raid. We then turned for home ourselves.

After flying due north for roughly a half hour, Brian and the other Spitfire pilots thought they must be nearing the English coast, but the massive cumulus clouds were stretching ahead and below, seemingly without a break. On the outbound flight the sky over England had been clear. They had been climbing slowly to 20,000 feet and now, they had been flying straight and level at that altitude and should certainly be at or inbound of the coast and the sky should have been clear. He knew that in the hour or so that they had been airborne, the weather could not possibly have changed that dramatically. The other thing that worried Brian was his inability to get a response from ground control each time he tried. He knew ground control would be listening for a call from him and was puzzled by their failure to respond.

Contrary to the met officer's briefing prediction of a 35 knot head-wind on the course of the fighters to Morlaix, both the bombers and the fighters had been shoved along by a 100 knot tailwind. Far ahead of the fighters, above the solid cloud cover, the bombers had un-knowingly flown across the Bay of Biscay and continued on to the Pyrenees mountains where they realized their predicament and dumped their bombloads. They then turned for home and spotted their Spitfire escort. By that time, all the bombers and fighters had ceased to register on English radar plots and any communications between their bases in England and the fighters and bombers was impossible.

The Spitfires had been in the air for more than two hours and, convinced that they had to be near their bases, began to let down through a gap they found in the cloud cover ... except for Kingcome and his squadron,

I was sorely pressed to follow, but ... found myself hesitating. Perhaps I was being too clever by half. The time element, along-side the fact that the coast was south-facing, surely confirmed that this could be nowhere else than Devon. There could not be another south coast within 100 miles. Nevertheless the incon-sistent weather pattern and ground control's sphinx-like silence continued to feed my profound unease. I decided that 401 Squadron ought to press on.

The flying range of the Spitfires was between two and quarter and two and a half hours. There was still no response from ground control.

Moments later the cloud began to thin, to Brian's intense relief. But when it cleared he found that the squadron was over an endless expanse of ocean. Now he definitely doubted his earlier reasoning and began to think that they must be out over the Irish Sea. He had visions of losing the entire squadron as, one by one, they ran out of fuel and were forced to bale out. The situation had become desperate.

The Spitfire pilots of the Eagle Squadron, meanwhile, had followed a different course and, in the belief that they were near their base, began letting down through the murky cloud cover. As the visibility cleared they sighted a coastline and assumed it was England. It was France and they soon crossed over the harbour at Brest through a terrifying flak barrage. In only a few moments ten Spitfires were lost, shot down or forced down through lack of fuel, with four of the pilots killed and six captured, among them the leader, Gordon Brettell. Another Eagle Spitfire had had to abort after taking off, due to mechanical trouble. Their twelfth Spit crash-landed in France, but the pilot evaded capture and made it safely back to England. Brettell became a prisoner of war in *Stalag Luft* III and was one of those involved in the 'Great Escape'. Recaptured, he too was one of the fifty prisoners later murdered by the Nazis for his part in the escape attempt.

The situation now seemed hopeless to Brian. Logic seemed of no value and he chose simply to rely on instinct. They would press on.

Shortly after that decision he heard an all but inaudible crackle in his earphones which then became, 'Hello, Brian. Hello, Brian. This is ground control. Are you receiving me? Over.' The voice told him that he was still about eighty miles south of base, to fly due north and to watch his fuel carefully. With plenty of altitude, he throttled back to minimum revs and set up for a long, shallow descent towards Bolt Head. They made it with only one pilot running out of fuel and having to bale out short of the coast.

Many years later, the true cause of the Morlaix disaster was discovered: the odd phenomenon we know today as the 'jet stream', strange bands of air moving at high speed at altitudes above 20,000 feet, which can sometimes create unpredicted tailwinds that can propel an aircraft along at 100 mph (or more) faster than its top speed.

The Morlaix mission had produced tragic consequences for the Eagle Squadron pilots and was a sad and inglorious final action on which to depart from the RAF. For Brian Kingcome and his pilots, it so nearly brought an equally disastrous end.

Bibliography

Bekker, Cajus, *The Luftwaffe War Diaries*, Doubleday & Co., 1968.

Brown, Eric, *Wings of the Luftwaffe*, Airlife Publishing, 1993.

Bishop, Edward, *The Battle of Britain*, George Allen and Unwin, 1960.

Bishop, Edward, *The Guinea Pig Club*, New English Library, 1963

Brickhill, Paul, *Reach For The Sky*, Collins, 1954.

Collier, Basil, *Leader of the Few*, Jarrolds, 1957.

Collier, Richard, *Eagle Day*, Pan Books, 1968.

Crook, D.M., *Spitfire Pilot*, Faber & Faber.

Deere, Alan C., *Nine Lives*, Coronet Books, 1959.

Deighton, Len, *Fighter*, Ballantine Books, 1977.

Dundas, Hugh, *Flying Start*, St Martin's Press, 1989.

Forrester, Larry, *Fly For Your Life*, Bantam Books, 1977.

Franks, Norman, *Sky Tiger*, Crecy Books, 1980.

Freeman, Roger, *Mighty Eighth War Diary*, Jane's, 1981.

Galland, Adolf, *The First and the Last*, Ballantine Books, 1954.

Gallico, Paul, *The Hurricane Story*, Four Square Books, 1967.

Gelb, Norman, *Scramble*, Michael Joseph, 1986.

Gurney, Gene, *Five Down and Glory*, Ballantine Books, 1958.

Hall, Roger, *Clouds of Fear*, Coronet Books, 1975.

Hillary, *The Last Enemy*, Pan Books, 1942.

Kaplan, Philip, *Fighter Pilot*, Aurum Press, 1999.

Kaplan, Philip and Collier, Richard, *The Few*, Blandford Press, 1989.

Kaplan, Philip and Saunders, Andy, *Little Friends*, Random House, 1991.

Kent, J.A., *One of the Few*, Corgi, 1975.

Kingcome, Brian, *A Willingness to Die*, Tempus, 1999.

Lee, Asher, *Goering: Air Leader*, Hippocrene Books, 1972.

Lloyd, Ian, *Rolls-Royce The Merlin At War*, Macmillan Press, 1978.

Lyall, Gavin, *The War in the Air*, Ballantine Books, 1968.

Mason, F.K., *Battle Over Britain*, McWhirter Twins, 1969.

Masters, David, *'So Few'*, Eyre & Spottiswoode, 1942.

Middleton, Drew, *The Sky Suspended*, Longmans, Green & Co., 1960.

Mosley, Leonard, *Battle of Britain*, Ballantine Books, 1969.

Orde, Cuthbert, *Pilots of Fighter Command*, George G. Harrap, 1942.

Page, Geoffrey, *Tale of a Guinea Pig*, Pelham Books Ltd, 1981.

Quill, Jeffrey, *Spitfire*, Arrow Books, 1985.

Smith, Richard, *Al Deere*, Grub Street, 2003.

Tidy, Douglas, *I Fear No Man*, Macdonald and Co., 1972.

Townsend, Peter, *Duel of Eagles*, Simon and Schuster, 1970.

Townsend, Peter, *The Odds Against Us*, William Morrow and Co., 1987.

Townsend, Peter, *Time and Chance*, Methuen, 1978.

Walker, Oliver, *Sailor Malan*, Cassell & Co., 1953.

Williams, Peter and Harrison, Ted, *McIndoe's Army*, Pelham Books, 1979.

Willis, John, *Churchill's Few*, Michael Joseph, 1985.

Wood, Derek & Dempster, Derek, *The Narrow Margin*, McGraw-Hill, 1961.

Index

197